T0203226

The Art of War in the Network Age

Intellectual Technologies Set

coordinated by
Jean-Max Noyer and Maryse Carmes

Volume 1

The Art of War in the Network Age

Back to the Future

Joseph Henrotin

WILEY

First published 2016 in Great Britain and the United States by ISTE Ltd and John Wiley & Sons, Inc.

ISTE Ltd
27-37 St George's Road
London SW19 4EU
UK

www.iste.co.uk

John Wiley & Sons, Inc.
111 River Street
Hoboken, NJ 07030
USA

www.wiley.com

Library of Congress Control Number: 2016946873

British Library Cataloguing-in-Publication Data
A CIP record for this book is available from the British Library
ISBN 978-1-84821-912-0

Contents

Introduction

> Since no plan survives actual combat, and the art of forecasting is imperfect, efforts to predict with certainty the future of today's revolution in military affairs (RMA) must inevitably fail.

Stephen J. Blank[1]

Military systems naturally reflect social, cultural and technical evolutions. In light of this, the study of strategic literature in recent years shows that much attention has been given to the evolutions implied by the implementation of computer networks, not only from a technical but also, and mostly, from a strategic viewpoint. The application of the Revolution in Military Affairs (RMA), which appeared in 1992, and then of the *Transformation*[2], 10 years later, are tightly linked to the spread of information technologies, but also to the actions and practices they imply [GOL 05]. Yet, if the art of war theory still represents "the art of dialectics of opposing wills using force in the resolution of conflict"[3], it also seems to represent the poor relation of technological developments. This is partly caused by its likelihood to become a real techno-military ideology, profoundly defined by technology [HEN 13b]. RMA and *Transformation* are both driven by strategic cultures full of techniques. Involvements in Afghanistan (2001–2014) and Iraq (2003–2008) seem to have overshadowed RMA and *Transformation*, the rational aspects of which seemed too remote

---

1 [BLA 97b, p. 61].
2 This word appears in italics given its politico-military use.
3 [BEA 85, p. 16].

from the imperatives of the counter-irregular struggle. This led Desportes [DES 06] to state that "transformation as the only way of evolution is now dead"[4].

These figures have shaped the practices and understanding of strategic actors and thus prepared their return at the heart of strategic debates. Works on the *AirSea Battle, Anti-Access/Area Denial* (A2/AD) and those focusing on regular operations in general now see a resurgence of themes linked to "technological war" and, along with it, to networks. However, quoting the debate of the 1990s, it is also about the "RMA after-next" implementation throughout technical artefacts – robots and autonomous weapons systems, nanotechnologies, networks, precision weapons, "augmented" soldiers or tandem "aviation, special forces". In certain aspects, if we considered the debate on RMA as being a historical episode, a "moment of technological optimism" in the evolution of the understanding of Americans and Europeans, the exact opposite could appear to be true. From this viewpoint, we have not yet given much thought to the strategic consequences of RMA's permanency – or of its resilience to the reality of conflicts. For the strategist, the risk is that RMA, among other issues, turns strategy into "tactics" – reducing strategy to pure technical execution, and taking away any political aspect it might hold. This would force us to reconsider the structuring between effectiveness and efficiency, with the risk of leading to "new old-regime armies", very advanced in terms of techniques, but inept in terms of strategy.

In the area of the conduct of warfare – so no longer on a theoretical level – these evolutions could suggest a "revolution", meaning an abrupt occurrence followed by a paradigm shift. This would represent a new phase in the historical evolution of the *character* of war and the way it is waged – considering that for many authors from the 1990s to today, it represented a change in *nature*. This statement is highly questionable since it is not so much a matter of a breakdown in the very notion of opposing wills than in the way this concept will be carried out. In reality, the disruptive character of evolutions since the 1990s can be debated from factual as well as conceptual viewpoints. It has already been the subject of many publications, which have somehow been forgotten:

– first, through the recurrence of the figure of the RMA as a *revolution* in the debate of the past few years, when dealing with the transformation of the

---

4 [DES 06, p. 39].

debate taking place in military history around the military revolution of the 15th and 17th Centuries. This debate showed that if the concept can be expressed as a hypothesis and be thoroughly discussed, the conditions of achievement of this "revolution" are as specific as they are broad, and affect society as a whole;

– second, a study of the works carried out during the 1950s and the 1960s on technologies likely to be used in future conflicts shows that many contemporary artefacts come from there, such as for example the rationality of their use. This is particularly true for the network figure, whether it be in aviation (with the SAGE detection and tracking system, see *infra*) or in the naval sphere, with the appearance of data links, or also in the implementation of data centralization artefacts such as the "central operation" of ships under its modern form, as imagined by Admiral J.C. Wylie [WYL 14]. These evolutions show a willingness towards centralization coming from diverse sensors not only as means of representation of reality, but also as an attempt to master and reduce uncertainty. In this way, there is a *strategic desire*, which cannot be entirely fulfilled but through constant reification;

– finally, we can make the assertion that this strategic desire has been recurrent since the Cold War and, even more peculiarly, since the Vietnam War. This war triggered the process of RMA/*Transformation*, partly because it confronted rationalities linked to a high-technology regular combat with counter-irregular operations.

In this way, the purpose of this work is quite unique. Many studies have analysed the contributions of network theory and of information warfare, as understood in the broader sense of warfare. Yet, another angle of approach seems more important in order to understand the significance of information revolution and of RMA/*Transformation*: their impact on strategic theory. The purpose here is to critically analyze the contributions or the problems that the spread of information technologies in its broad sense can bring, in relation to categories of classic strategic theory. The purpose here will be to analyse the consequences of what we will call "informationalization" on all strategic levels, but with a broader view than the sole art of regular warfare. If we only focus on the art of regular warfare, we would only reassess the confirmations which can be found in the works of the 1990s – often linked to their treatment by American researchers. Consequently, it seems necessary for us to include the irregular aspects of the art of war and their hybrid extensions right away.

In the first two chapters, we will revisit the epistemology of revolution in military affairs: first and foremost, it is necessary to understand its composition as well as its legitimation process (including throughout history). It is also necessary to understand its spreading in the strategic debate since it is the frame within which informationalization will develop. The goal will then be to re-examine the terminology of the aforesaid revolution, and also its relation with temporality, which we can question depending on the different time periods we are focusing on. The third chapter will focus on the disruptive nature of RMA/*Transformation*. Does it reflect a paradigm shift? We will analyse the political bases of strategic action – what will enable us to determine the real extent of the "revolution" – before incorporating the strategy of means analysis, which is a focal point when it comes to technology questions. We will then focus on operational strategy.

In this way, the next two chapters will focus on the historical construction of the process of getting to know your opponents in combat zones. We will refer to the question of intelligence, be it tactical or strategic, and also to the classical Clausewitzian referents such as "fog of war", "coup d'oeil" and "friction". We will thus study the theory of fluid and solid spaces suggested by Laurent Henninger, based on the works of G. Deleuze [HEN 13a, HEN 12a, BIH 14c]. The purpose here will be to show that our way of considering information collection as an action first derives from rationalities, which are linked to naval and air strategies (Chapter 4), before its attempt to be adapted to ground strategies (Chapter 5). Here, we can especially see the catalytic role of the Vietnam War, but we can also hypothesize that RMA/*Transformation*'s sole intent is to "render solid spaces more fluid".

Chapter 6 will get back to the process of "informationalization" in the doctrinal meta-referrer of armed forces, especially in Western countries[5]. The goal will be to focus on operations' kinematic nature, but also on the way of conducting a network-centric warfare. On this subject, our hypothesis is the following: RMA/*Transformation* is not finished, because the tools it enabled to create experience a dissemination and adoption process by

---

5 Also assimilated and understood as allies to the United States (Japan, South Korea, etc.). The processes linked to RMA also have an impact on other armies, such as the Chinese or the Russian army, for example. See the different contributions within [COL 15] or [LOO 08], [NEW 10] and [ADA 10].

irregular actors. As a consequence, we can witness the emergence of techno-guerrillas, embedded in a hybrid warfare mode, and which are the "answer" – a logical one, since warfare is a dialectic – to a quest of superiority from Western countries. Finally, Chapter 7 will seek to specify the attempt of Western countries to counter-adapt by studying the rationalities linked to the strike from a technical viewpoint, but mostly when considering its socio-strategic outcomes. These outcomes appear to be highly paradoxical, specifically due to the fact that, if it represents a "strategic attractor", technology seems to be an "impossible way out" of the invariants of strategy and, as such, of politics.

Approaching Military Revolutions

The notion of military revolution appeared in the vocabulary of strategists, historians and political scientists during the 20th Century. However, before further examination, it is important to try and understand it, and to tackle three preliminary points. First, questions concerning military revolution appeared in two distinct realms. From one side, in the historical realm, in Roberts' work [ROB 56], who, in his research supported by tactical reforms of the Dutch army, tried to show a radical break with the recent past. Even though Parker [PAR 88, PAR 76] and Black [BLA 91a] criticized this thesis, it remains the most quoted study of the emergence of the debate on American RMA[1]. From the other side, in the realm of political and strategic science, the nuclear question was quickly perceived as a revolution in itself, since the goal of the armies was no longer to make war but to avoid it[2]. In both cases, these "revolutions" were techno-centered, and were respectively supported by the power of fire (artillery, individual weapons), maritime navigation techniques or the process of popular mobilization (through a slow process of state constitution [FIN 75, FOR 09]), and the scheme of the nuclear weapons and its vectors. In some ways, they already imply information flows.

---

1 In the field of history, this debate remains very much alive and burning. We can also refer to [CON 72] and [DOW 92].

2 We owe the first observation on the subject to Bernard Brodie who, it is said, after the explosion of the Hiroshima bomb, told his wife that he wanted to give up his research on classic strategy. Yet, from a practical viewpoint, the revolutionary outreach of political consequences of nuclear weapons will be widely questioned.

We can thus consider that the definition of RMA in the debate of a possible "revolution" in the 1990s quickly embraced the ideas that had been previously developed. In a first approach, RMA and its current state in the debate could be based upon the use of computers and network technology in operations conduct. Consequently, it could also be based on the importance given to information as a means of knowledge (of the tactical situation, whether it be operational or political) as well as a means of efficient forces activation. It might also find its basis in the importance given to forms of information prohibition (stealth technology, information warfare, psychological warfare and influence operations), in the positioning of precision-guided munitions fired from a stand-off distance, regardless of climate and operational conditions. Moreover, it might be based on the positioning of armed forces, which have a more gathered organization, but with a capacity to be placed more quickly on farther theaters of operations[3]. In a broader sense, we will base our study on a definition of the concept of military revolution as "a fundamental breakthrough in technology, doctrine and organization, which renders the existing methods of warfare conduct obsolete"[4].

Second, if the relevance of the definition "RMA" as a revolution can be questioned, we can reasonably assess that the notion of "military revolution" is historically relevant. Even historians who are reluctant to consider the concept of RMA as true revolution do not deny the relevance of the concept of military revolution. Third and finally, there are some keys and concepts that are necessary in order to fully understand the concepts of military revolution and RMA, and they will provide a framework for this chapter. The first is about the lexical varieties present under the notion of military revolution, which can be found in the American debate on RMA, especially when speaking about its political implications. The second refers to the categorizations of RMA done in the 1990s and of its analysts.

---

3 The focus here is only on the major categories of connotations assigned to RMA, which we find in its literature. We will come back to what it can cover more thoroughly [SLO 02].

4 Considered as being the first academic contribution on American RMA, this definition is sufficiently operating for now, even if the subjectivity implied in defining an innovation as a "fundamental breakthrough" remains problematic. More specifically, it does not include what we could call "military revolutions ontology" and what these military revolutions are or are not [MAZ 93, p. 16].

1.1. Lexical varieties

Three lexical categories of the conceptual object of "RMA" coexist in the field of strategic studies. They were the subject of a debate, between 1992 (when the first studies appeared on this subject) and 1998. Its goal, *in fine*, was to try and determine the magnitude of the phenomenon of accelerated technicization (meaning the introduction of new military technologies) of American forces. In view of its contemporary understanding, the concept goes back to observations made by the Soviet marshal Ogarkov in the beginning of the 1980s, of a *Military Technical Revolution* (MTR), and the observations of the American *AirLand battle* [FIT 87][5]. The latter was itself the result of a specific technological effort concerning DARPA[6], the second *Offset strategy*[7] and of the deep questioning – the *reform movement* – of the American forces' methods of action. The Soviet marshal, as he noticed the occurrence of this MTR in the United States, meant to adapt the Soviet forces to it [PAR 95].

It is supposed that this MTR may have solved the qualitative deficit of conventional Soviet forces by "synthesizing new technologies, evolving military systems, operational innovation, and organizational adaptation into a whole that was more powerful than the parts"[8]. And this regardless of whether it was based on a conceptual "system implementation" or on information and communication technologies as such, due to their interactions and their reticulation. Direct energy weapons, stealth technology, "strike-reconnaissance complexes" and reorganizations may then have given the USSR a straight comparative advantage over the United States[9]. In truth, the concept of MTR is the evidence that the Soviets considered the United States to be clearly

---

5 On the Russian perception of Ogarkov's considerations before the "application" of MTR before the Gulf War, see [FIT 91].

6 *Defense Advanced Research Project Agency*, in charge of the works linked to research and technologies in the United States.

7 See Chapter 5. The first offset strategy dealt with technologies linked to nuclear energy and to ballistic weapons.

8 [DAV 96, p. 15].

9 Ogarkov's plans, which were then passed on to Akhromeev at the head of general staff, were almost never implemented. For some, it would be due to a lack of political interest [SLO 02], whereas others consider that the USSR, by following the same path as the United States' strategic defense initiative, engaged in the MTR race. We must note that in the 1990s and 2000s, the different reorganization plans of the Russian army show many elements which call back to MTR as it was imagined by Ogarkov.

behind[10]. However, the concept was soon to be criticized as being too techno-centered (whereas only a few technologies were supposedly used). The concept may not show the doctrinal or organizational adaptation of the forces that implement it. In the same way, technology may have been conceptualized in a much too static way and may have failed to highlight the evolutions it could experience or even to report its own contributions [WAT 95]. In the end, MTR would supposedly be restricted to tactical and operational levels.

1.1.1. *MTR versus RMA*

At that time, in the United States, a second lexical field appears, and which attempts, in its varieties, to show the impact of said revolution on other scopes than the strictly technological and military ones. By re-examining Ogarkov's work, Andrew Marshall – who will play a major part in the debates over RMA[11] – favored the phrase "Revolution in Military Affairs", in order to better report the implications of political, doctrinal and organizational processes in the military institution by technology. All the most, in this sense, RMA implies an organization of technologies, which will be introduced in a given military system, and it also implies what their interactions will be [LAN 99]. With this mind, RMA becomes the "*process*

---

10 Actually, when studying the Soviet debates on the subject, Andrew Marshall will draw the conclusion that American efforts should be accelerated, so that Washington definitely ensures a technological superiority [TOM 07, ADA 08].

11 Andrew Marshall was the Head of the *Office of Net Assessment* (ONA) from its creation in 1973 until 2014. In charge of detecting the emerging threats against the United States, he answered directly to the Secretary of Defense and has had a major, yet discrete, role in the research institutions network. S.P. Rosen admitted that ONA "*was the first to develop the idea that the American military can be transformed by the revolution in information technology*" (quoted by [SCH 97]). He is said to be the first who foresaw the fall of the USSR, in 1977, based on its loss of economic steam. He also supposedly declared in 1980 that AIDS was a threat to national security. Said by a Chinese General to be the "*intellectual engine of American strategy*" (quoted by [WIN 99, p. 45]), ONA and Marshall are one and the same entity in most publications. From an economic educational background, Marshall was a research member at the RAND (1949). As he was always renewed by all administrations, his influence remains major ("the Church of St. Andrew") thanks to the schooling he brought to academics who also praised an RMA and who worked with him, such as A. Krepinevitch or T. Manhken, or also thanks to his close relation with a *think tank* such as the *Center for Security Policy* [KRE 15]. See also [ROS 10].

of socio technical transformation (which) *should be supported by a network of cultural and economic forces which takes a concrete shape during a time interval which is hard to define, yet easy to influence*"[12]. From the start, information plays a decisive role.

In practice, Martin Libicki will show the coextension, rather than the opposition, of the notions of MTR and RMA by telling that *"the most fundamental strategic challenge (...) is the conversion of a military-technical revolution into a revolution in military affairs"*[13]. Yet, this lexicon, which is the basis for all works on American RMA, will also be called into question. R.J. Bunker thus suggested the concept of *Revolution in Political and Military Affairs* (RPMA). According to him, the notion of RMA *"ignored the massive political ramifications that the development of future warfare will have over our society and government"*[14]. However, when put into practice, this concept only rarely appears in the literature and was mentioned rather than studied in-depth in the article. Also pertaining to this situation could be the American tendency to favor a relation based on the break from Jomini's concept rather than on the Clausewitzian continuity between the political and the military scopes as highlighted by Colson and Desportes Following this, the concept of *Revolution in Strategic Affairs*, suggested by Freedman, also takes us back to an attempt to broaden RMA to a political level [FRE 98].

With the same intention of broadening the field of RMA, Andrew Bacevitch stated at the United States, which benefited from revolutionary changes in their armies, were less subject to RMA than to a "revolution in security affairs" [BAC 96]. Like Bunker, the author's goal was to bring to light the impacts of the evolutions of the military institution on the international community – a combination of the social and political field – these impacts being seen as insufficiently highlighted. Retrospectively, we can consider that this influence does not go from the military to the socio-political, but that it proceeds from an interaction – particularly in view of information technologies, which come, for a great part, from the civilian world. This lexical quest will also find other ramifications. As he studied the concept of RMA in the scope of geopolitics, Richard Ek unveiled the concept of

---

12 [BAL 03, p. 19].
13 [LIB 94, p. 1].
14 [BUN 96, p. 9].

"revolution in military geopolitics"[15], based on the political and sociological consequences of the arrival of computers and new military technologies[16].

1.1.2. *Military revolutions versus RMAs*

In a third category of lexical fields, the attention paid to RMA as it was just starting to be conceptualized and to receive intellectual credit led several authors to study past revolutions from a strategic viewpoint and to take some distance in order to try and grasp differentiated magnitudes. To this end, an author such as Krepinevitch could consider, over time, the succession of several RMAs, based on four elements: technological change, systems development, operational innovation and organizational adaptation. These RMAs include the revolution of infantry (14th Century), of artillery (15th Century), of fortifications (16th Century), of navy rudders (16th Century), the military revolution of the 17th Century (with the linear order), the Napoleonic revolution, the revolution in land warfare (with the Civil War, the use of railway and of breech loading rifles), naval revolution (from the use of steam and the use of belt armor), revolutions of the interwar years (mechanization, aviation, information) and, finally, nuclear revolution [KRE 94]. Yet, very quickly, the author encountered the problem that some revolutions seemed to hold disproportionate impacts on military as well as political practices. Retrospectively, we can also argue that such a rigid classification ends in discrediting the interdependencies of what he defines as revolutions: indeed, phenomena of this magnitude do not appear *in abstracto.*

This led Murray and Knox [KNO 01] to differentiate the notions of "revolution in military affairs" and "military revolutions," thus converging with the debates of the historians in the 1950s. The first revolutions are then conducted by the military institution, which welcomes and incorporates technological innovations. Yet, they could also be based on deep political and social evolutions within society. By nature, an army, and the way it

---

15 However, the goal will be less to question the concept of RMA than to study its implications for the theory of geopolitics, particularly the postmodern theory of geopolitics [EK 00].

16 We could argue that "military geopolitics" more specifically take us back to a type of geostrategy, which almost always took into account the evolution of weapon systems. Mackinder himself thought that technology as such held a strong relation to geopolitics, since the first helped to put the second "into action", railways being the keys to mastering the *Heartland,* according to him [LON 99].

develops, is first and foremost the result of its socio-political environment [MUR 01a]. On the other hand, military revolutions would be the result of great social, political and cultural evolutions, and they would also have direct impacts on the organization of societies as well as on the distribution of powers. The military sphere would then interact directly with the political one, as they would shape one another in turns, in the same space–time[17]. The number of military revolutions is supposedly incomparably lower than that of RMA [MUR 01b, MOL 02]. In this way, they reckon that five waves of military revolutions succeeded one another (Table 1.1):

Period	Founding element of the revolution	RMA
17th Century	Modern state and modern military institutions	1) Dutch and Swedish tactical reforms; French organizational and tactical reform; naval revolution; fiscal revolution 2) French military reforms (after the 7 Years' War)
End of 18th Century	French revolution	National political and economic mobilization Napoleonic Wars
19th Century	Industrial revolution	1) Financial and economic strength based on industrialization 2) Technological revolution in land warfare 3) Naval revolution
Beginning of 20th Century	World War I	Tactics and joint operations, *blitzkrieg*, strategic bombing, submarine and naval air warfare, radar and electronic intelligence
Mid-20th Century	World War II	1) Nuclear dissuasion war 2) Conventional deterrence, precision strikes, lethality radicalization

Table 1.1. *Past military revolutions, according to Murray and Knox [MOL 02]*

In a similar view, Rogers considered that introducing a group of innovations could give rise to RMA; yet its transformation into a proper military revolution depends on much more complex factors [ROG 00, ROG 93]. According to him, the switch from one form to the other is determined by specific political and social conditions. In this regard, the military revolution induced by artillery in the 15th Century does not find its cause in the cannons themselves, but in their political use. By enabling the

---

17 A typical example would be the Napoleonic war. The 1789 revolution and its political project led to the emergence and the legitimization of a masses rising model. In return, Napoleon's conquests will have direct international impacts.

rapid destruction of its fortifications, its operators were able to quickly conquer new territories, thus initiating an international redistribution of forces when the state adopted modern instruments of power[18]. It will also be the case for the French mass movement in Napoleonic Wars. Therefore, even what can be seen as a revolution on a scientific scale has low chances of resulting in a true military revolution if no political conditions are conducive to enable its achievement. Following this logic, the *blitzkrieg* thus seems to be more of a RMA than a military revolution. According to a similar viewpoint, Metz thinks that this dichotomy reflects a distinction between "tactical and operational revolutions", referring to RMAs and founded on the contributions of technologies, and between "strategic revolutions" being the *stricto sensu* equivalent to military revolutions [MET 00].

If most of the authors agree on the observation of the non-linear succession of several revolutions, the relevance of the resort to the concept of military revolution itself still needs to be questioned. The process of technological transformation (technicization), and in regard to integration of new technologies, but also technical processes in the armies, is constant throughout history. Heilbroner indicates that what makes the true noteworthy revolutions is not so much their frequency rather than their rarity on a historic scale. Following this, David Jablonsky considered that the word "revolution" is more often misused than properly used [JAB 94b]. In truth, bureaucratic institutions can be so heavy that even the smallest innovation can generate the perception of a revolutionary change. Thus, by deconstructing the military revolution induced by the appearance of firearms, Hall shows that the technological artefact does not represent the origins of a revolution. He will see Renaissance as an evolutionary period – rather than a revolutionary one – opening the way to a process of transformation of the armies while interpreting, sometimes well, sometimes wrongly, the contributions of new technologies [HAL 97].

Combining military history and the history of technology, Hall underlines the importance of the cultural melting pot within which transformation will fall, following a methodology which can be compared to one followed by Azar Gat [GAT 91]. He thus shows how the force of siege warfare during the Middle Ages came to weaken due to the technological combinations,

---

18 Consequently, by adopting the most offensive strategy, the State would actually strengthen its positions. Indeed, the conquest of new territories was the prerequisite to the implementation of administrative and fiscal order, the profits of which would directly benefit the conquering army. Finer called this the "extraction–coercion cycle" [FIN 75].

which were implemented, introducing tire arms little by little and not violently, firearms. In this way, *"basic technological changes stimulated the offensive and defensive capacities in a spiral towards both technical refinement and increasing costs"*[19]. According to Hall, the emergence of a consensus on techniques among manufacturers and then of another on the tactical use of weapons in the middle of the 17th Century shows a subtle evolution in military organizations, tactics and strategy[20]. A similar reasoning can be applied to artillery cannons[21], seriously questioning the revolutionary nature of technology diffusion. The highlight of the "time" factor will thus become significant in the definition of "revolution"[22].

It is important to note that the combination of political, technological, organizational, doctrinal and tactical factors seems to form the base of military evolution at the end of the Middle Ages [MOL 02], and then induces a *combinatorial thematic* which will become recurrent in RMA literature. The effects of feedback and mutual constitution between these different elements will remain constant. In this way, we need to moderate in an "evolutionary way" the "revolutionary" theory according to which the use of cannons will enable feudal walls to be brought down (opening the way to a nation-state able to develop its military capabilities in return, throughout taxes and scientific development [DUP 84, GAT 91]). Even in doing so, we must not deny its relevance. To this end, Hall calls into question the notion of revolution. According to him, it is not neutral in its methodological understanding, because it underlies a legitimation of American strategic rhetoric.

1.1.3. *Reassessing the notion of military revolution*

Still, the notion of military revolution in itself can be called into question, and even denied. E.A. Cohen indicates that an entire school of authors on RMA reject the concept of military revolution in itself [COH 97]. According

---

19 [HAL 97, p. 18].

20 This could be supported by the diversity of technical options chosen in weapon manufacture. The production and development of firearms has thus shown a constant interaction with their environment of use and a technical refinement until today [BRU 99].

21 However, if it introduces an artillery technical innovation, the use of shells instead of cannonballs is not a strategic revolution in itself.

22 Besides, it only is in the sole field of military history, political science and strategic studies. In the history of economics, Cochet and Henry asked themselves why it took more than 150 years for the first "industrial revolution" to spread [COC 95].

to them, change occurs throughout an evolution, which is technological and conceptual, iterative and progressive, and not a disruptive one. In this regard, for example, the *blitzkrieg* would be an exploitation of infiltration tactics from World War I, but this time by means of tanks, pairing them up with aviation and also with radio, which will be used more broadly during the Great War. Precision guided weapons, which are of major importance in the pro-RMA rhetoric, arose during the same period. However, the majority of authors consider this the radical position in relation to military revolution. Indeed, in a theory which would consider the political and strategic innovation from the sole viewpoint of evolution and which would exclude the possibility of a revolution, the following points would fail to be presented:

– differentials in the understanding/using of innovative combinations (France making a better use of artillery than Burgundy, or the United States having a better use of information and command systems than Iraq);

– major technological and doctrinal breaks, which, when properly used from a political and strategic viewpoint, give results which are seen as surprising (Germany's use of *blitzkrieg* whereas the French, even if they have better tanks, do not embrace such a position, or the use of nuclear weapons in 1945, which will result in an international order which will almost entirely be regulated by the nuclear weapon);

– kinematics, which are differentiated in the spread of military innovation. If more than a century passed before European armies enter the "artillery revolution", it will take less than 2 years for American and Soviet armies to see tanks as the heart of their ground forces; 4 years for USSR to adopt nuclear weapons after the United States[23], and a few months before European armies took note that the United States' success in 1991 was due to their mastering of a number of technologies, including the ones linked to networks.

We can consider that, for the most sceptical authors, RMA referred more to the social discovery of the political and military effects of new technologies than to a proper revolution. Indeed, the study of the reactions of politics and the media during the 1991 Gulf War meets this reasoning. In fact, the war was nothing more than the application of doctrinal and strategic

---

23 This will somehow complete the "nuclear revolution", showing that the Soviet Union did not intend to stay away from a path leading to power. The same kind of reasoning can be applied to France, Great Britain or China.

concepts, which were more than 10 years old, and which were supported by weaponry manufactured for the most part in the 1970s [TOM 07]. The idea of a "bright" victory, which was, in reality, very much predictable, came out from the lack of knowledge in the state of the art in this area. This approach enabled Henry and Peartree to state; "New technologies emerge to either exploit or compensate for weaknesses in existing technologies. Inventing a theory of information warfare risks falling victim to the kinds of fallacies that Douhet encountered. Unable to see the future, he imagined one based on linear projections of extant technologies" [HEN 98].

For them, as a transposition of the past evolutions, the current RMA would be nothing more than an expensive delusion, in terms of financial but also intellectual investment. Yet for many authors, beyond the validity of the concept of military revolution, the concept of RMA in itself, when applied to the United States and their allies, is the result of a lack of clarification, which could seriously weaken its outreach as well as its relevance. Thus, for Tertrais, at the end of the 1990s, RMA is a "*nebulous concept (...) flexible, practical, but in reality a catch-all*"[24]. Thérèse Delpech stated that "*the key technological evolutions, those impacting the art of warfare, have been few through centuries*"[25]. However, let us stress the fact that RMA has been discredited from the viewpoint of France, which was strategically attentive, but conceptually in a "wait-and-see" policy at the time of American questionings[26]. Yet, France still embraced the rhetoric and logic of *Transformation* when the concept was approved after a NATO summit in Prague in 2002 – and when Paris was reinstated in the integrated military structure in 2008. Yet, several American authors are also sceptical concerning the outreach of RMA, which could not mean anything more than a slogan.

1.1.4. *An incomplete RMA? From revolution to transformation*

According to the pessimistic counterpart of the sceptical approach, the concepts of RMA and military revolution could be relevant, yet they would be burdened in their realization. In this sense, Murray indicates that RMA could not become the melting pot of a major evolution of the American forces

---

24 [TER 98, p. 612].

25 [DEL 98, p. 27].

26 As it was going through important dissents within its civil institutes, France did not really produce any innovative concept outside of its military research centers [COU 01].

because hierarchical structures, bureaucratic barriers or competitiveness among services (US Army, US Air Force, Marines, US Navy) are such that any type of modernization would become a relatively slow evolution rather than a proper revolution [MUR 01a]. Basing himself on the works of Heilbroner, Jablonsky speaks of a "viscosity" of history, which would most likely destroy the promises of RMA as they were too techno-optimistic in a unilateral way [HEI 60, JAB 94a]. However, this viewpoint is – partly – called into question by the development of American forces.

Indeed, we must point out that with *Transformation*, which was promoted in the *Quadriennal Defense Review* (QDR) of 1997, 2001, 2006, 2010 and 2014[27], the political level intends to implement some of the lessons and recommendations produced by the debate on RMA. This evolution towards *Transformation* thus foreshadows a fourth lexical form of "revolution", but this time with much more praxeological orientations[28]. If the term *Transformation* was reused many times – and it was structurally institutionalized by NATO throughout the *Allied Command Transformation* (ACT)[29] – it still holds various connotations. These connotations go from the least critical admiration to the most open scepticism. In particular, this *Transformation* supposedly remains linked to ideas from the Cold War, which are unfit for the contemporary international community, and supposedly did not give way to a radical process – a properly revolutionary one – particularly in the design of weapon systems [GON 00, BER 16].

Transformation could then be nothing more than a deceptive process that would highlight a punctual adaptation of structure and forces' equipment, but which would extend America's – and NATO's – preference for high-intensity regular operations. The goal would then be to reproduce, behind the

---

27 QDRs were established after the *Government Performance and Results Act* (1993) and must isolate the means and views of the department of defense in the short term.

28 Inasmuch as the process would enable the incremental transformation of forces. As a result, the US Army experiences a "split" between *Legacy Force* (deriving from divisionary structures and from the disposal of equipment dating back from the Cold War) and *Interim Force* (represented by *Interim Brigade Combat Teams* – IBCT – equipped with *Stryker* vehicles). The final goal is to result in the *Objective force.*

29 The ACT is one of NATO's two major commandments and is in charge of assisting the *Transformation* of the forces of the member countries. Settled in Norfolk, it is located near the *Office of Force Transformation* (OFT) which was created in 2001 in order to initiate and to guide American *Transformation,* and then dissolved in 2006.

veil of change, the preferences of strategic cultures. According to a more optimistic viewpoint, *Transformation* might be partly limited by the lack of financial resources and by military interventions after 9/11. It would then progressively augment RMA's benefits, keeping its initial dynamic. At this stage, we can distinguish the different opinions, from the possibility of "permanent revolutions" – usually seen as techno-centered (and then based on biotechnologies or nanotechnologies) – to a more classically evolutionary model[30]. Let us note that, once more, these opinions and viewpoints are in themselves progressive[31].

1.2. Types of RMA

To this point, a lexical classification of RMA does not necessarily render the diversity of positions towards the subject, nor the diversity of acceptations RMA can cover, being examined by a group of authors.

1.2.1. *An example of techno-centric classification*

According to Timothy Andrews, we can distinguish three types of RMA based on the nature and the speed of changes they imply in the strategic behavior of actors [AND 98]. The first type affects the whole scope of military operations quickly, and also the conduct of politics. In order to support his thesis, he refers to the appearance of nuclear war, which takes us back to the notion of military revolution as Murray, Knox and Rogers understand it. In this regard, this revolution would affect the conduct of warfare as much as its nature. The second type of revolution is characterized by technological and/or organizational changes, introduced quite quickly in military systems, and which can disturb the classical balance of power on a national and/or regional scale. For the author, and for other proponents following him, this is typically true of the "armed nation", or of the introduction of submarines or aircraft carriers [MUR 95, GAL 95]. With its way of changing the character of wars but not their nature, this type of

---

30 We will come back to these different opinions *infra*.
31 Many authors saw an evolution in their thinking throughout debates not only on RMA but also on the process of *Transformation*. This is particularly true since operations carried out in Afghanistan and Iraq.

revolution can have direct political consequences, and can thus be put closer to RTM[32].

Finally, the "third type" of RMA is related to "capacitating technologies", which still need to be integrated to weapons systems. The author defines as such the introduction of steel or steam propulsion in naval construction, of jet engine in aviation or, closer to us, computers and information technologies. According to Andrews, revolution stands more in the speed with which technologies are adopted than in their implementation. At the same time, he thinks this type of revolution rarely affects the balance or the distribution of powers, as long as it is was not converted to any of the two previous types mentioned. For the author, a technological evolution considered minor in its outreach can play an active role in a real revolution thanks to the combination of technological and strategic dynamisms. If he remains unclear on the modalities of conversion of these types of revolutions, he does state that, logically, they can produce effects on the international system. For him, the United States, in order to keep their leading position, must make use of their technological and strategic capacities [AND 98].

With this reasoning, the author meets the rationality already developed by Possony *et al.* [POS 97], and according to which technology becomes a factor that will make Washington's capacity of influence on the international system durable. This view of "capacitating technology" also fails to take into account the proper "enriching" dynamic of technologies such as information technologies. The applications on the subject by default went through a great evolution: if the computer management of armies' logistical stocks was, for example, seen as revolutionary in the 1980s, the contributions of information technology then went through a considerable transformation. Through their widespread growth in the 1990s, network communications and data links paved the way for contemporary concepts of aviation and urban combat networks (see *infra*), without even mentioning the convergences between networks and robotics. We can also criticize the fact that, if the outreach of these conceptions is operational, it does not necessarily report the intersecting factors between technologies and international relations.

---

32 One example among many is that of the purchase of six stealth frigates and as many submarines by Singapore, added to a fast modernization of its air and land forces. This had a radical impact on the balance of forces in the region. Consequently, the freedom of strategic maneuvre of the city-state increased significantly [COU 05].

1.2.2. *Unlikely revolutions*

Noticing that the variety of conceptions for RMA leads to different meanings and connotations for the word "revolution", Galdi offers a ternary categorization of RMA [GAL 95]. First, he states that the notion of RMA exceeds technological change. Basing his argument on the erosion of the nation-state in the international system, on the evolution of military institutions (with its evolving relation to violence) and on the spread of technologies at the hands of sub-estate groups, the author notes that conflicts could multiply in the future. Consequently, the state should try to adapt to the international environment through the evolution of its armed forces towards RMA. This weakening of the state would not lead to an over-technicization of its forces, and would mostly highlight its constabulary missions. This view coincides with Moskos' perceptions on postmodern war [MOS 94] and, in some regards, the French conception of a "strategic break" following the fall of USSR and the re-organization of the distribution of powers it triggered[33].

The second connotation to the notion of RMA is supposedly the most widespread, stressing the evolution of weapon systems and their integration in the arsenals of the most advanced states. Implicitly, such a viewpoint would reify a nation-state born from the Westphalian system, and which would seek to reproduce over time throughout the modernization of its forces. A variation of this thinking implies a continuous succession of technological revolutions in different areas (stealth technologies, information warfare, network-centric warfare, biotechnologies, direct energy weapons, etc.), which would be taken over by military institution. The third connotation denies the "revolutionary" value of RMA. In this regard, a continuous succession of technological evolutions in the whole spectrum of military missions is constantly integrated to armed forces. Supposedly, there would be no RMA per se, since the art of warfare would integrate a continuous succession of evolutions, but not necessarily a linear succession[34]. This is also the case for Colin Gray, who positions himself on the level of strategic theory, which is not necessarily revolutionized by the technological factor, so that *"the future is the past – with GPS"* [GRA 02].

---

33 The political factor then overcomes the technological one, yet this does not mean that the latter is ousted. See [TOM 07] and [COU 97].
34 Previously quoted by [MUR 98a, p. 50].

Coming back to Galdi, his approach does not seem satisfactory. First, because the erosion of the nation-state is stressed in the majority of studies and works on RMA, and because this criterion is not specific to the RMA school of thinking. In the same way, this erosion did not lead to erasure: if it had been mentioned since the end of the 1980s, the state remains indeed the main actor of international relations – moreover, sub-state actors most often aim at becoming states. Second, Galdi fails to underline the variety of sceptical thinking on the occurrence of an RMA – and which actually shaped the majority of works about it. Thirdly, the states are not the only ones looking to adapt to the new international environment: sub-state groups also seek the support of new technologies. RMAs are thus inducing a techno-strategic emulation [BRU 05], which partly translates into the rise of actors using hybrid strategies (see *infra*).

1.2.3. *Cohen and the "revolutionary types"*

In this framework, a third classification of RMA forms comes from Eliot A. Cohen [COH 97]. It is taxonomic and enables us to classify its intellectual operators. It also appears to be the most operating. In order to define it, Cohen asks four questions: Is a revolution occurring? What is the dynamic leading to RMA? In virtue of these questions, what main political challenges await American planners? What is the main external threat impacting the security of the United States? Ideal-typical, the classification gives rise to four main groups:

1) "Owens' disciple", named after the Admiral who first coined the "system of systems" concept, combining the ensemble of the American means of command, control, communications, computers, intelligence, surveillance and reconnaissance (C4ISR)[35]. Advocates of this view consider that RMA does not lie in technologies themselves, but in the structuring and networking of means already available and which, in virtue of technological dynamism, experience a natural and constant evolution[36]. In this regard, naturally, the United States must focus on the knowledge of their own

---

35 Owens was vice-president to the Committee of Military Chief of staff during the Clinton administration [OWE 95, OWE 00].

36 "If the United States could integrate sub-systems (already available, or developing) in a system of systems, they would be able to reach a dominant knowledge of the battle space, to teach this knowledge to American forces, and to react to the battle space with speed, precision and with devastating effects. A successful integration could propel the United States to a new qualitative order of military strength" [BLA 97a, p. 29].

technologies – which Owens believes is insufficient[37] – but also on their full development. "Owens' disciple" is generally closer to the decision-making groups taking part in the process of *Transformation*[38]. This is particularly true of the very influential Admiral Cebrowski[39].

2) The "uncertain revolutionary" considers that he is certain that revolutions will occur but that the kinematic of implementation of this change is less clear. Proponents of this category then tend to focus on the maturation of technologies and on a search for experimentation. Rosen [ROS 91], just like the proponents of the first category, focuses less on technology than on the doctrinal, conceptual and organizational translation in armed forces. Yet, in practice, whereas "Owens' disciple" solves this question through organizational measures, the "uncertain revolutionary" tends to stress the conceptual factor, because he does not think that a fit organization can give rise to the certainties which "system of systems" promises. Authors like Petraeus, in charge of operations in Iraq since 2007, or Bassford, meet this reasoning[40].

3) The "Gulf War veteran" also believes in the possibility of RMA, but thinks that it dates back to the 1980s, when the technologies which were used during *Desert Storm* were designed and integrated to military institution. In this regard, the quality of soldiers' recruitment and training as well as their marital ethos took a clear priority over new technologies. Authors supporting this reasoning do not reject the contributions of technology but fear that we forget the elementary military constraints or that we underestimate the vulnerabilities induced by technology and politico-military decision-makers [FRE 02, SPA 02, KIP 01, BOL 04]. Even though

---

37 Owens used to present a diagram with many acronyms representing weapon systems, communication and intelligence systems which nobody in the room – including himself – was able to define.

38 Let us note that Owens' superior was General Shalikashvili (former Chief of Staff of the US Army, then Joint Chief of Staff and "father" of the very "RMA-shaping" Future Combat System), who "protected" him against the attacks that targeted him.

39 A.K. Cebrowski, former Head of the Office of Force Transformation, is also the author of the concept of *Network-Centric Warfare* (NCW). Following Owens, he considers that the interaction of systems C4ISR to combat systems should enable a radical optimization of the US forces' effectiveness. They would then have access, in close to real-time, to any kind of useful information [CEB 98, DE 04b, DE 06, DE 07b].

40 On top of being General and Director of the CIA, Petraeus also took an important part in developing the last version of the American doctrine on counter-insurgency. Specialized in Clausewitz, Bassford will also take part in the writing of the new document.

this category of opinion seemed to disappear at the turn of the 2000s, it experienced a resurgance after American operations in Iraq in 2004.

4) The "sceptical" is the most critical toward RMA. It can be completely called into question, thus highlighting the natural evolution of tactics and technologies, so that authors adopting this thinking are those who most often get closer to the ideal aspect of the debate between the preeminence of strategy and that of technology. They tend to adopt an "incrementalist" opinion as they see, little by little, the integration of innovations – which they surely do not deny – in strategic systems. A majority of military historians (among them Rogers or Murray) and some "pure strategists" like Colin Gray meet this reasoning.

Later on, Cohen would add a fifth category: the very technology-intensive "starship trooper". Referring to the novel by Robert A. Heinlein[41] and to Paul Verhoeven's movie adaptation[42], the model contemplates a RMA that would be technicized to the extreme and in which the current computer technology breakthroughs would only be the beginning of the intensive use of biotechnologies, nanotechnologies, robotics and genetic engineering. In such a context, the "true RMA" would occur around 2020–2030 and would be marked by the weight of innovation as well as that of the scientific figure. However, few authors fit into this school of thought. On the one hand genetics and biotechnologies have not yet led to direct military implementations and, for now, they belong to a prospective field, strongly tinged with futurology. On the other hand, this type of reasoning is generally subject to ethical criticism than praised due to the downward effects it could trigger [HEN 03].

---

41 In this movie, the hero an earthling from the 22nd Century, does his military service (which will enable him, in return, to exercise his right to vote). He finds himself involved in extremely violent battles against dehumanized opponents ("arachnids"). As soon as it came out in 1959, the book was praised (for denouncing an ultra-technological society, which adopts a political position standing in-between fascism and nazism) as much as it was criticized (for extending a construction of the adversary similar to the representations of the Japanese instilled in the United States during World War II). In truth, the author supposedly synthesises the political behaviors of his time in order to extrapolate towards a futuristic version. A libertarian (his next novel, *Strangers in a Strange Land*, is openly pacifist), he systematically stated that he was against communism as much as nazism. Let us note that the author and his work would go on to have a great influence on the sub-genre of military science-fiction, without much consideration for technology, but with a particular highlight on martial values [HEI 87].

42 Who takes (too) many liberties in comparison to the original work, to the extent of distorting its complexity.

All said and done, the ideal-typical opinions suggested by Cohen are inherently progressive. Thus, several authors who in 1997 considered that RMA was not happening will later review their opinion[43]. Finally, we can consider that the summary coming out of this analysis, and enabling us to distinguish institutional as well academic actors, remains relevant (Table 1.2).

	"Owens Clone"	Gulf War Veteran	Sceptic	Revolutionnary sceptic	Starship trooper
Where is RMA standing?	Already here!	Already seen!	What RMA?	Sometimes here, sometimes not	Beyond the horizon
Motor	Information technologies	Doctrine and human skills	Human nature	Integration of concepts and technology	Biotechnologies
Priority	Lower numbers	Keep numbers	Keep martial ethos	Testing and innovation	Invest in research and development
No. 1 threat	Inertia	Same size rival	Over-invest	Asymmetric retaliations	Intellectual conformism
Innovation	Aftermath	No interest	No revolution, evolution	Rises from the civil sector	Science

Table 1.2. *The types of RMA according to Cohen ([MUR 00, p. 241], modified by the author)*

1.2.4. *RMA schools at the turn of the millennium*

Opinions on RMA are very much split, all the more because the implementation of new weapon systems has increased, along with the interest for debating RMA. This results in an inflection in the position of the "sceptics", especially on relatively technical thematics. In this context, a work from O'Hanlon takes revolution for granted and offers a new classification for the schools of thought on RMA, based on the authors' technological preferences [OHA 00]. The first school of thought sends us

---

43 Such a review will occur, for example – given that it is not limited by it – with [GON 98] and [GON 99], but also with [MAR 01].

back to Cohen's "Owens' disciple". The second, called "dominant battlespace knowledge school of thought", bases itself upon the first, but considers that sensors' multiplication will enable a complete view on the battlespace[44].

The third school, called "global reach, global power" – a phrase first to appear in 1997 – sends us back to the position of the US Air Force, which considered that air power and long distance strikes will play a decisive role in achieving the process of *Transformation*. Here again, the place held by new technologies – meaning space-based lasers and other hypersonic bombers, for the most techno-optimists – is decisive [LAM 97, PER 95, GOU 97]. It finds many political and doctrinal representatives. If we follow O'Hanlon's thinking, we can think that a former Defense Secretary such as Donald Rumsfeld would be one of them.

Finally, the last school suggested by the author gathers part of Cohen's "sceptics" and considers that the American *high-tech* arsenal will be so powerful that whoever would try to attack the United States would use irregular methods. We can then see a variety of thinking being shaped. They either consider a dissymmetric threat based on weapons of mass destruction; or asymmetric threats, through the use of terrorist tactics, of which 9/11 would be the most completed example or the conduct of guerrillas for which American forces would not be well prepared[45].

Let us retain from O'Hanlon's classification that authors working on RMA often embrace a view that crosses the knowledge and opinions of different schools of thought, which are by definition ideal-typical. Following this thinking, we can consider that if O'Hanlon's assertion holds a heuristic significance, which is inferior to Cohen's taxonomy, it remains useful to help and understand the evolution of the "RMA/*Transformation*" phenomenon. As it is institutionally adopted and politically encouraged

---

44 This positioning is not limited to defense academics. The former military Chief of Staff of the US Air Force, Ronald Fogleman, could thus state in 1997 that "in the first quarter of the 21st Century, you will be able to find, localize or follow and target – in close to real-time – anything of consequence that moves upon or is located on the face of the Earth". Quoted by [HOA 00, p. 13]. About the concept, see [JOH 96].

45 This would be the case, among others, for literature on "fourth generation wars". Yet, let us note that some American weapons such as the *Marines*, are better prepared to this type of conflict than the US Army.

throughout *Transformation*, RMA is, indeed, called to generate choices (whether they are doctrinal or means choices), which would be much more complex, particularly due to factors that were underestimated in the literature such as acquisition and logistics costs and their consequence on the structure of forces. With this precision, we still need to note that this first approach of the notion of military revolution yet fails to examine its deep resources, which we will examine in the next chapter.

2

The Epistemology of RMA

The use of military revolution as a way to explain the integration of new types of weaponry and systems in the politico-strategic reality has been widely misused, as much in its definition as in the impact of its contributions to foreign and defence politics. The conceptual complexity of these definitions, or the enthusiasm for these technological evolutions were difficult to put into perspective, can be symptomatic of a partial, sometimes biased theoretical foundation of the phenomena of "military revolution" or "revolution in military affairs". Additionally, most literature does not consider RMA from an epistemological point of view, and rather focuses on its operational and technological aspects. Admittedly, what is traditionally understood by "the RMA" can be found in its own definition. But beyond this, relatively few contributions examine its relation to time or, more simply, to the notion of "paradigm shift", often referred to in order to justify the revolution itself. Epistemological elements prior to the creation of the concept are then most often scattered. Admittedly, in *The Structure of Scientific Revolutions*, T. Kuhn stated that a revolution implies a shift in the rules determining a (scientific) practice as the result of a confrontation of theories. Many authors who worked on RMA agree on this subject [KUH 72]. Therefore, in this chapter we will successively examine:

– the relation of different authors to the temporality of their subject (is it an evolution or a revolution?), particularly in view of Braudel and Ricoeur's viewpoints;

– the relation to a notion of paradigm, which is central in Kuhn's contribution.

Mentioning the notion of a *"fundamental breakthrough in technology, doctrine or organization"* in the given definition of RMA *supra* induces a relation to time, which is quite peculiar when it comes to military revolutions – here, we will discuss RMA as conceived in the United States. A revolution entails a connotation of production in a short period of time, inducing a break in the historical trajectory of "revolutionized" institutions, whereas they must inscribe themselves in a *continuum*. Yet, if Andrew Latham reckons that RMA benefits from a historical varnish, the phenomenon is not very well founded in its temporality [LAT 02]. The use of history by advocates of RMA usually appears to be instrumental, aiming at justifying its occurrence. From then on, when considering the current RMA, both viewpoints can be embraced.

2.1. *Longue durée*, *conjoncture* and event history ... outdated?

First, the "RMA phenomenon" can be based on an iterative evolution, in *longue durée* (to refer to the classification introduced by F. Braudel), and this in order to avoid the traps of an "event history" and to distinguish its major trends. From here, the positioning of advocates of RMA shows a gradation in linear or non-linear character of an evolution, which can conjecturally experience phenomena of acceleration triggered by organizational, doctrinal or technological innovations, or their combinations. Embracing a view that favors *"longue durée"* would in reality be minor and would be used by the most skeptical authors who are most skeptical towards the rise of an RMA. These authors would thus seek to put "revolution" into perspective. Yet, the quick series, in *conjoncture* and events history, of innovations in several technological sectors, have consequences for political and strategic conducts, and it is observed by the very same authors.

This is why, secondly, the same "RMA phenomenon" can be seen as an isolated product in *conjoncture* time, thus making it, strictly speaking, revolutionary. But can this detemporalization of RMA, outside of any continuity, find a true meaning? Isolated in a mass of weakly tied historical events, would RMA also become one? In his analysis of current sociopolitical conditions, Z. Laïdi gives an interesting lead [LAÏ 00]. He criticized Braudel's approach in favor or Ricoeur's, according to whom *"if history is punctuated of a series of events, some of them are more important than others.* Thinking that Braudel does not make any distinction between "event and fact" and underestimates the impact of a break in the historical trajectory of an object, Laïdi thus leads the way to exceeding temporal separation between *longue durée*, *conjoncture* and event history, indicating that "taking into account *longue durée* would not abolish the event"[1].

Yet, these two ideas, based on restrictive views on the temporality of a possible RMA, mostly have an ideal-typical value. So if we cannot get past the event, an analysis on the *longue durée* cannot either. Consequently, A. Latham states that RMA can be analysed on event history (RMA as a shift in warfighting), *conjoncture* time (RMA as a change in the *social mode of warfare*[2]) and in *longue durée* (war conduct based on feudal, modern and postmodern modes [LAT 02]). Then, RMA would become scalar, and with a variable measure of its extent depending on the chosen scale. Yet, the practice of the debate on RMA does not show the generalization of such a trisection. It rather shows the weight of views mostly focused on *longue durée* and *conjoncture* times on one part, and event history on the other.

2.2. RMA as a result of a long-term evolution?

In a long-term perspective, and in a more "evolutionary" view, authors believe – as others, including the most "revolutionary" – that RMA proceeds from historicity, the cornerstone of which is not the 1991 Gulf War (as several authors, usually techno-optimistic, had observed) [MAH 97], but the evolution of the American armed forces and, beyond this, the evolution of socially organized violence. At this stage, in the absolute context, this evolution could date back to the implementation of US forces in the 18th Century; to World War II with a logic supposedly implying the mobilization of all available technological resources; or to a "nuclear revolution", which would have started a dynamic of the proper RMA process; and, more generally, to the Cold War, which could have reproduced the mobilization trend of World War II. We can also stress the weight of methods of *operational analysis* and *operational research* and of an intent towards the "scientification" of war [GRA 97]. Beyond this, if Holmes believies that technology established tactics more than it disrupted them during World War I [HIA 99], indeed, it helped them evolve during World War II.

---

1 A concept he takes from Mary Kaldor and which refers to the way societies organize themselves and conduct wars [KAL 81].

From this viewpoint, if only *blitzkrieg*, naval air warfare or the nuclear weapon was unanimously seen as disruptive, the war in itself was not a military revolution. Following this thinking, it is interesting to note that only a few works on World War II, other than those on the German doctrine, have been used to historically establish RMA. Yet, the war sees the application of a series of innovations and will form a progressive sum, which will take part in the development of conventional doctrines during the Cold War. Ultimately, considering a historical "starting point" for RMA yet finds its roots in the works of military historians on extended periods of time, which remain minor in the restricted context of RMA debates. Indeed, if authors who embrace a new viewpoint work, among other subjects, on state transformations or on the evolution of notions such as violence, they do not examine RMA or the interrelations it can have with the state and its evolutions in depth. This is, for example the case of M. Van Creveld, whose book *The Transformation of War* makes the argument of a loss of relevance from the state, implying a depreciation of Clausewitz, the emergence of "wild wars" before which technology will not be of much use, or the (re)emergence of asymmetrical wars [VAN 98].

2.2.1. *From evolutionary to revolutionary* longue durée

In this regard, the author will be more careful before the numerous publications on RMA, just like historians like J. Keegan [KEE 94]. It will be the same for authors who, using Van Creveld's views, will work on the theme of violence degeneration and its deregulation in order to show that RMA is fundamentally unfit for the international environment. This is particularly the case for authors like Lind, Schmitt and Wilson and, more generally, for disciples of "fourth-generation warfare" [LIN 89]. Yet, this does not mean that their evolutionism is extinct. According to them, the current evolutions are the sign of the end of the modern era [LIN 94]. They maintain this opinion after the war in Iraq [LIN 04]. For them, "first-generation warfare" lasted from 1648 to 1680 (implemented by lines and columns tactics); the second generation was enabled by massive fire power, which was developed from World War I by the French army; the third generation is also rooted in the Great War, yet this time, in the German army and its development of what was to become the *blitzkrieg*.

The fourth generation is seen as the most radical evolution since the Peace of Westphalia and the emergence of the nation-state. According to this viewpoint, the true revolution is not so much the revolution that strategists have been calling RMA than a change in the profound nature of international relations and in the substance, connotations and views of the state and society. However, the authors' analysis is quite ambiguous. The first ambiguity is about the ethnocentric temporalization of their generalizations. Order and martial ethos induced in a first generation, and which will progressively split throughout the following generations, are by definition European characteristics, which can be discussed when speaking about other forces. Moreover, the series of these generations in time causes a problem: as it opposes, in the same timeframe, the second and third generations, their analysis does not take into account the possibility of irregular warfare (gathering guerrillas, terrorism and other indirect strategies), the history of which rather shows permanency, regardless of transformations. Moreover, while the series of generations suggested might be ideal-typical, it only shows a line of time periods without showing their structuring.

We can note that war is a phenomenon which is anterior to 1648. This fact is accounted for by the Tofflers, but not by Lind and his followers. In this way, as they always seek to locate their analysis in *longue durée* and, at the same time, to justify RMA, authors like T.L. Moore and R.J. Bunker offer a theory based on the use of energies, conceived as dictating exploitable technologies. Consequently, what is seen as "military revolutions" derives from a shift in the type of energy that is used and from a series of shifts impacting political, social, cultural and military scopes during the four time periods.

Time period	Energy	Classification	Expressions
First	Human	Hellenic and Roman	Phalanx and legion
Second	Animal	Middle Ages	Cavalry, knighthood, proto-artillery
Third	Mechanical	Modern	Mercenary armies, classic strategy, mass movement, firepower, mechanization, indirect strategy, *blitzkrieg*
Fourth	Post-mechanical	Postmodern	Professionalization of forces, advanced technologies, irregular warfare, information warfare, space strategy

Table 2.1. *Lindsay and Bunker's four time periods*
[BUN 94, BUN 96, BUN 97]

This viewpoint is particularly interesting since it sees "energy shifts" – and thus technological shifts – as times of radicalization rather than revolution. Thus, the authors see the time period shifts as transitions that can last up to 350 years and which enable the coexistence of different kinds of energy. The opinion developed by L. Murawiec is epistemologically close to this one. According to Murawiec, the United States – and more generally, the West – progress from a carbon-based economy to a silicon-based economy, even towards a dematerialization of our societies [MUR 00]. It tends to lead to an end of the analysis of theoretical categories (modes of warfare) in favor of material categories (energies, raw materials). At the same time, we detach ourselves from a liaison, which would be "*longue durée* = globality, therefore, evolution" to come down to a liaison "*longue durée* = series of *conjonctures*, therefore, possibility of revolution(s) or, potentially, evolutions".

Of course, this switch in the link between temporality and (r)evolutionary dynamics echoes the Tofflers, who established the characteristics of their three waves (agricultural, industrial and informational) based on distinguished economic (and material) production modes [TOF 94]. Yet, in doing so, they would fail to draw a clear picture of the interrelations and shifts between their three "waves". According to S. Metz, at the very most, they produced a theory without much demonstration [MET 94a]. Here, the data is crucial: their works will be profusely quoted in literature on RMA and will naturally lead the relation to time RMA specialists will have regarding their subject. Considered as a reference, the temporality they establish is also a techno-centered temporality based on factors chosen to demonstrate their hypothesis. Doing so, they establish a phenomenon in a longer historical trajectory while they only see its short-time effects.

2.2.2. *The eternal moment of changing epochs: RMA and postmodernity*

In this way, the positioning of the Tofflers is rooted in the *conjoncture*. According to them, technologies enforced within the specific doctrinal *corpus* during the 1991 war are based on an evolution that dates back to the questioning of American abilities to lead high-intensity operations following the Vietnam War. Besides, some think that this war saw the development of technological and doctrinal structures that were identical to those developed later and based on an overestimation of the importance of high technologies.

It would thus be the first post-modern war [GRY 97]. Yet, we must note that if the words "pre-modern", "modern" and "post-modern" refer to *longue durée* temporalizations, the last word should be used carefully and defined more clearly since, with its implication of technologies, it sets up a framework around RMA and transformation, which is not a neutral one. In the 1990s and at the beginning of the 2000s, this concept was used quite frequently in studies of strategies as well as in military sociology. It aimed at supporting the thesis of a shift, without really defining the nature of this new postmodernity:

Variables	Pre-modern military	Modern military	Post-modern military
Threats	Enemy invasion	Nuclear war	Subnational and non-military
Structure of forces	Mass army	Large professional army	Smaller professional army with reserves
Impact on defense budget	Positive	Neutral	Negative
Military leaders	Combat leader	Manager or technician	Soldier-statesman Soldier-scholar
Civil employees	Minor component	Medium component	Major component

Table 2.2. *Evolution of the characteristics of military organizations [MOS 94]*

By distinguishing pre-modern, modern and post-modern military, Moskos and Burk's typology illustrates the evolutions that were implemented in the past few hundred years and which always have complex relations to technology. The technical nature of the military field triggered a major evolution in armed forces. Indeed, armed forces were progressively marked by professionalization, evolutions of the specificity of the military profession and recruitment and by a redefining of their missions [MOS 94]. With the profound impact of technique, Janowitz's military sociology stresses the evolution of the soldier figure from a heroic ethos towards a manager model, before he becomes a post-heroic soldier [JAN 71]. This evolution was strongly stressed in the United States and tended to show a phenomenon of technologization, where the soldier's relation to its environment is defined by technological parameters, outside of the traditional military scope.

However, we must note that political and sociological literatures show that no definition of postmodernity was really reached, despite the attempts and characterizations[2] suggested by disciples, as many authors still contested the very relevance of the concept. In such a context, is the acceptance of "postmodernity" as the characterization of strategy "era" relevant? Following several advocates of this concept, Z. Laïdi states that the erosion and the fall of the notion of historiography, the loss of relevance of the notion of "project" – including an ideological one, the upcoming blurring of classic referents of temporality and reason, and the globalization phenomena supported by new technologies result in a society constantly updating the present. Post-modernity no longer shows the present as a break on a line going from the past to the future, but as a present caught in a net [LAÏ 00]. In this way, post-modernity would represent an omnipresent present, which would not deny the evolutionary nor revolutionary character of innovations, but which would go towards the end of a story generating a loss of senses. Appealing to this concept is not insignificant for us: such a view implies that the current technology is meaningful and becomes the only horizon for strategists.

As in other domains, post-modernity in strategy would mark the end of ideologies but also, simultaneously, the establishment of a media (and technical) time with which politics would comply, just like the generalization

---

2 In particular in the following fields (this list not exhaustive) [LYO 79]:
– Arts: the artistic forms of Dadaism and surrealism are considered as transitions towards postmodernism, whereas postmodernity would mark the end of a perspective metaphorically sending us back to that of modernity. Pluralism and aesthetic anarchy (chaos) would result from it;
– Economy: the emergence of a globalized "consumer society" would tend towards a constant reification of individual pleasure gained through exponential and erratic consumption;
– Sociology: through the emergence and then through the radicalization of indetermination, anomy, uncertainty, chaos and individualism;
– Science: through the interest for chaos theories, but also through the interest for genetics and aesthetic surgery transforming the individual, the erosion of ethics in business sciences (some literature claim to reveal *warketing*, openly advocating the use of psycho-technology) or also through a trend for constructivism, which individualizes the comprehension of a problematic. Simultaneously, who could deny the fact that the utility of social sciences – in a broad sense – is decreasing, as much as its budgets are not increasing, when they might stagnate?;
– Philosophy and religion: through radicalization of world's disenchantment which triggers complex and individualized opinions of "puzzle-like" borrowings of philosophical and religious concepts, even of mystical radicalization, which can trigger sectarian proliferations but which can also weaken the concept of reason.

of an opposition between civilian societies and the political world, or also the importance given to the sense of urgency. We could thus see the 2003 Iraq War as the translation of a strategic and technical urgency, and in this way avoid seeing Iraq equipped with weapons of mass destruction, also regardless of reason [HEN 04]. In truth, the political consequences of post-modernity are quite complex. They are declined on the internal as well as external state level, the distinction between these two spheres experiencing continuous erosion[3]. The role of new technologies – whether they are transportation or communication – is central to this transformation and considerably stimulates, in the international context, a globalization based as much on the rise of an almost-doctrinal individualism as on standardization.

We must also point out that, in its relation to international relations, post-modernity also generates notable consequences. Thus, for G. O'Thuatail, *"the condition of postmodern politics is a condition of world politics where the modern geopolitical imagination is openly challenged by structural geopolitical processes as globalization, informationalization, accelerated speed of interaction and communication and unforeseen consequences of technoscientific 'progress* [EK 00, p. 857]. However, the author admits the simultaneous co-existence of modern and postmodern conditions. This would not lead to a depreciation of the international relations literature "classics", yet it would trigger their amendment[4]. Eventually, such a posture of coexistence recalls that of the Tofflers, implying the possibility of simultaneity, within an international space as well as within a state, of the three "waves" they had defined. As the prefix "post", in post-modernity, suggests quite a clear break, there is no doubt that other terms would be more appropriate.

Paradoxically, post-modernity is thus defined as a constellation of representations and connotations of the present shaped in a mainly long-term perspective [LAS 90, TUR 90]; yet at the same time, it is immersed in a naturally technicized environment, innervated, among others, with information technologies. Yet, the possible operationalization of this concept is made difficult by its lack of establishment among strategists and by the fact that it is scarcely applied by politics and sociology specialists. It thus becomes the marker of a radical change, but its lack of definition instrumentalises it in favor of the predetermined project of legitimation of RMA and the

---

3 Here, we cannot account for the voluminous literature this question triggered. See also [BAT 03].

4 This view is shared by authors offering their contributions to: [GRA 99b].

technologies it implies. Yet, the drastic change "postmodernity" would imply can be openly – and, according to us, rightly – put into question. This way, postmodernity is not an entirely significant break. What is presented as the "post-modern condition" does not invalidate the range of concepts used in political science – the state, international politics, power, international system, balance of power, centers and peripheries, international relations or even strategy itself, without making it an exhaustive listing. With this mind, in political studies, Giddens suggests the concept of "advanced modernity" in lieu of postmodernity [GID 90], yet, he is not much quoted in strategy literature.

2.2.3. *An overused post-modernity, an assumed post-industrialism*

This concept could, however, be quoted by authors denying or showing a sceptical viewpoint towards RMA. Thus, for Giddens, advanced modernity is at the crossroads between the French and industrial revolutions. Yet, one of the leitmotifs of RMA advocates – including the Tofflers or Echevarria [ECH 92] – precisely suggests that RMA is deeply rooted in the post-industrial era, sending us back, once more, to a long-term categorization and witnessing the shift from and "industrial era, to and "information era"[5]. If it is understood by the authors in a spectrum going from revolutionary towards evolutionary, the shift implied seems more relevant, since it seems more perceptible and is shown on several levels:

– a managerial level, which, in the meantime, has become omnipresent in national military reforms, and which is based on computerization, the conduct of militarized civilian acquisitions. These aspects are included in the themes of *Revolution in Business Affairs* and of *Costs Off the Shelf Technologies*. This level is established upon the search for certainty, excessively focusing on mathematical methods and with a tendency to exclude more detailed analysis implying human factors;

– an organizational/structural level based on professionalized armies, which put a definite end to the patterns of masses rising, is technologically more intensive, substituting men for machines [FAI 88], even accepting the privatization of public violence by the growth of private security companies and the correlative emergence of a specific lexicon (*surrogate warrior,*

---

5 The bases of the concept of post-industrialism were established, among others, by [BEL 73]. Also see [BRA 93].

delegate warrior, private military/security companies) replacing the mercenary lexicon, which was too connoted [SIN 03]. It is doubled by a tendency towards automation/roboticization, with the risk of leaving behind the weberian referent of monopolization of legitimate violence by the state;

– an operational level magnifying the value of combat translated into diverse dimensions: that of precision [MAH 11], of *just-in-time*, of distant combat, and whose consequences are naturally international (subjects of *global reach* and of the forces projection, *full-spectrum dominance*[6]) and pertaining to the perception of the United States as a hegemon, or to the only superpower once again technologizing in the search for effectiveness, but also for efficiency;

– a level of ethos, in which the wrongly accepted perception of too strong a technical load[7] induces a compensation on the martial mode, tending to transform the "soldier" into a "warrior", thus technicized and foreseeing his environment through technique (see *infra*). This martial mode would not be a proper "regression" in the soldier's evolution; on the contrary, it would mean a new evolution, a hybrid of man and machine following the logic of "neo antique hero" [MUN 16].

The combination of these levels quickly triggered the idea of fundamental evolutions, which, in return, reached a political and symbolic level, thus making RMA and *Transformation* a conceptual framework, which, even if precarious, was presented as developing. Yet, in the meantime, globalization in which post-industrialism settles is also seen as a crisis carrier, here again showing the necessity of a debate. This is all the more the case that the perception of the notion of power, even if it was enriched by the advent of a "post-industrial era of information", remains fundamentally unchanged [REI 14]. In many aspects, military debates have been marked by operational, or even purely tactical considerations. However, Rupert Smith reminds us that very few debates have tackled the question of the utility of force, even if the latter is in coherence with a questioning of the impact of globalization or post-industrialism [SMI 07]. Classic rationality thus tends to

---

6 This means the capacity to win during all operations American forces would be likely to conduct.

7 Eventually, this question is not limited to the United States alone. The French debate of the 1950s and 1960s shows the polarization of positions between, on one side, the advocates of *technicized* army (Ailleret, Gallois) and on the other, those who think that it implies a weakening of martial ethos (F.-O. Miksche) [MAR 99, MIK 48, MIK 49].

be excluded in favor of a focus on technique. This is particularly true in the context where the use of devices reflecting the new "era" does not call the basis of military power into question [TEL 00, CHA 13a, CHA 13b].

Since the split is not entirely clear, post-industrialism does not validate post-modernism. Indeed, for others, "modern" means "current", thus erasing the aspects of temporality and characterization from modernity as well as post-modernity. Yet, we must mention that this approach is minor in strategic studies, as modernity and post-modernity retain their implications of temporal characterizations, not without ulterior motives aiming at legitimating the revolutionary implication of RMA. Yet, it does not fundamentally transform a strategy with a tendency towards post-modernity. Its main principles, or the importance of experience – including through military history – remain obviously valid[8]. Admittedly, it can become richer, yet it proceeds from an iteration progressing through intertextuality, but not in a linear way, on prior sedimentations, which form its basis and are the roots of its dynamism [WAS 10]. At this stage, the abundance of contributions of uneven quality on RMA brings out the question of coexistence, even of coextension of pre-modern, modern and postmodern eras.

Braudel thus indicates that *"war (...) does not have only one aspect. Geography brings colour to it, shares it. Several forms of war coexist: primitive or modern, as slavery, servitude and capitalism coexist. Everyone conducts the war the way they can and where they can* [BRA 73, p. 57]. This coexistence, in RMA, will almost become its main characteristic for J. Arquilla and D. Ronfeldt, when they state that the upcoming conflicts will be marked by "Curious combinations of premodern and postmodern elements (that) will appear in antagonists' ideologies, objectives, doctrines, and organizational designs" [ARQ 97, p. 4]. From a broader angle, this viewpoint sends us back to the Clausewitzian metaphor of war being like a "chameleon" in the contexts it passes through. Ultimately, it remains that notions of post-modernity as much as notions of RMA can be subject to criticism. RMA, as the avatar of a time which is constantly reproduced in a modern sense, would thus only be the rediscovery of old principles

---

8 The best proof being the *Traité de stratégie* and the *Bréviaire stratégique* from Hervé Coutau-Bégarie. With the exception of aviation or space, and excluding anachronisms, they could be read and understood as well by a Hittite general as by one of this "post-modern" fellow generals.

transposed into present time – adding technologies. This "rediscovery of the wheel", which we frequently hear from the "opponents" and other "sceptics", is to be found in many sectors of operational strategy, for example, in aviation strategy or in the concepts of operations of the US Army. Concepts presented as transformational and revolutionary would be nothing more than the rephrasing of prior principles, hardly adapted to new technological conditions – and even less often to operational environments.

2.2.4. The building of a revolution

Some critics have more impact than others, just like some events can reveal an evolution that had previously gone undetected. This is particularly true for the 1991 Gulf War, which progressed as a high-technology war from a political and media point of view and which supposedly induced, through its occurrence, the evidence of an RMA. Since 1991, this view – encouraged by G.H. Bush and D. Cheney, who stated in 1992 that a *"technological revolution in the art of warfare"* [DEP 92 p. 164] had been unveiled by the Gulf War – was denied and deconstructed many times [PRE 01, MAH 97]. Yet, it still gave birth to the movement of construction of RMA based on a technological fantasy. This construction of RMA would then be based on what we could call a "socio-political discovery of technological effects in the strategic scope". Despite the efficacy of the 1991 war as much as of the debates it brought about, the representations it implied more or less induced the entire development of RMA and then of *Transformation* as an intellectual movement.

This perception of radical shifts in the modalities of the conduct of warfare quickly appeared in the United States and sanctified technique right away, based on the fact that it drastically decreased the loss of allies[9]. Following the Gulf War, Eliot Cohen's works (in particular, the *Gulf War Air Power Survey* [KEA 93]) and a seminar conducted in 1994 at the *US Army War College* – which will give a consensual consecration to RMA terminology [MAZ 94] – echo Andrew Marshall's and ONA's most often private works and notes written as early as 1991 [KRE 15]. Prior to this, the

---

9 As it happens, it was limited to 240 people, most of them dying outside of combat operations. In comparison to the tens of thousands of Iraqi soldiers lost, the low rate of losses for the US will be a true shock for the military establishment, according to R.R. Tomes [TOM 07].

CSIS stated that "*the effects of technology (...) transform, and have actually already transformed the way armed forces conduct their operations*" [BAS 91b, p. 21]. At this stage, the process of shaping of RMA has not entirely succeeded. It implies, among other things, merging with considerations prior to the perception of RMA – specifically works the Tofflers' work on a "third wave" – before they themselves apply their viewpoint to the evolution of conflict and conflictuality.

According to them, distant combat, as it is quick, variably lethal but precise [OCO 94], is greatly enabled by the wider spread of a technology with collapsing costs, in all aspects of combat, and all the more by a constant management of adversary information. We will easily understand that the emerging view of technology tends towards the promise of short wars, which are cost-effective in terms of human lives, whether they be allies or civilian adversaries, conventionalizing – as it would create new rules for war and its prohibitions – the conflicts that had been uninhibited during the Cold War by the nuclear spectrum. Moreover, the promises described – with, we must admit, some perspicacity – were included in a very specific post-Cold War political debate. The latter would indeed favor the spread of the Tofflers's viewpoint in civilian and military decision-making groups. Within these groups, the subject of a politically promoted "new world order", based on economic interdependency and democratic peace, should favor a legal and international conflict regulation. This was particularly true of conflicts where vital interests of Western countries were not challenged by conflicts, which were recurrent, but geographically remote, thus favoring the endorsement options with high technological intensity.

In the meantime, the sociological context also led towards the adoption of revolutionary rhetoric as well as precision strike capacities. Edward N. Luttwak indicates that the decrease in birth rate in Western societies triggers a natural reaction to increasingly take into account the future of children which could serve the state. Soldier protection thus becomes a true political priority [LUT 95]. It even becomes an imperative within units. In the same way, C. Coker could state that "*the individual has become the center of the universe (and) a society promoting individualism tends to individualize each death – of its own soldiers as much as that of his enemies' soldiers*" [DE 04b, p. 162].

Yet, the notion of "zero casualties" is said to be no other than a myth from the misunderstanding of public opinion. This has been particularly true since 9/11 [MOS 02], when national vital interests were challenged. The "zero casualty" notion would also be a construction: the more exposed the public is to precision strikes in the media, the more it seems to dislike human losses, without necessarily developing the same aversion for war itself [HAR 97].

On the contrary, the notion of "zero casualties" suggests the illusion of facility and non-lethality for American civilians: the message of a targeting of opposing "miscreant" leaders is conveyed more easily, underlying the purity of American intentions and interacting with the strategic culture of the United States, extending older questions[10]. Let us also note that this phenomenon also affects targeted societies, the "message" of a targeted elimination of political regimes more than their societies. During operations in Serbia or Iraq, airstrikes did not really seem to disturb the life of populations. In return, this contributed to constructing the idea of a technological environment in which precision became the source of certainty – where war has always been a matter of uncertainty (see Chapter 4). In the meantime, this subject of the decrease of lethality was consistently taken into account in the RMA debate – we also find the first signs of a "clean war" – just as it contributed to justify the development of new weapon systems.

As a constructed revolution which, little by little, became the referral frame of strategic debate, RMA can in no way be isolated from its sociological, cultural, international or political substrate. On the contrary, professing a major change in the evolution of societies and in the evolution of their political conduct enables to justify changes in their practice of warfare. In this view, as the Tofflers themselves stress, RMA is the product of major evolutions in the scale of societies, or their modes of production and their comprehension of politics and economy, but also violence [TOF 94, ROB 67], which can be represented as follows:

---

10 This tendency towards the decrease of lethality has already inspired the evolution of American nuclear strategy when D. Brennan considered that the *Mutual Assured Destruction* was immoral (it targeted adversary populations) and that it campaigned towards a counter-forces strategy. Let us also note that, during World War II, the United States had refused to bomb German cities in order to better attack industry. Even with the development of the American aviation strategy in the 1930s, it refused to use chemical weapons or to bomb cities.

Type	First wave	Second wave	Third wave
Production mode	Agricultural	Industrial	Information
Historical trend	Pre-modern	Modern	Post-modern
Implied Institutions	Cities, domains	State	State, subnational groups (NGO, companies, terrorist groups), individuals
Threat	Invasion	Invasion Nuclear war	Subnational Military and non-military
Soldiers	Mercenaries, paesants, nobility	Mobilised civilians	Technicians, academics
Role of technology	Subsidiary	Central in management and production, secondary in combat	Essential in all sectors of strategy
Form of technology	Proto-industrial, handicraft	Scientific, industry	Scientific Small and medium-size businesses

Table 2.3. *Historical trisection of the Tofflers' waves and forms of conflicts*

The revealing function played by conflicts and highlighting the evolution of operation modes of conduct is indeed recognized. Nevertheless, following authors like Clausewitz, Fuller or Liddell Hart, the Tofflers recognize the link between a given society in a given time and its practice of conflictuality; a position which is ultimately quite consensual. Any understanding of a "revolution", even if it were constructed, would then be no more than the reflection of the evolutions experienced by this society. As it happens, when they were writing their work, the United States was marked by the subject of networks and of "information highways, the spread of computers in business and the transformation of modes of production. Thus, the American government will soon deregulate the Internet, thus signifying the emergence of the *world wide web* and the birth of strong cyber strategies and other varieties of "information war" in RMA" [RAT 01].

2.3. Confronting the distinctive aspects of military revolutions

The question raised is thus no more that of a construction of revolution – since its basis were established, even in a specific imagination – but rather that of an evolution, which would form, in the strategic field, an "acceleration of history". With this view, we can also consider a tendency towards complexity in expression of modes and of warfare technologies, which the Tofflerian trisection can account for, once it is adapted. RMA could thus include a series of changes with exponential complexity. Each war mode would change and, from one "wave" to the other, new modes would appear. Yet, while happening, would not such a position set the current RMA apart, as it would only be the product of a conjectural evolution? This is what Andrew Latham seems to indicate [LAT 02]. Thus, there is a second historical point of view on RMA, which presents it as an isolated phenomenon, produced by specific technological, cultural and political conceptions in a specific time period, when revolution is a matter of event history and no longer of *conjoncture* and *longue durée*.

2.3.1. *An anhistorical RMA?*

The analyst thus faces a more restricted historical scale. With this in mind, the trajectory of all phenomena, which, through military history, can be called "military revolutions", fall under a singularization which is specific to each of them, with the risk of seeing them disconnected or breaking the link between them. This is how total war, *blitzkrieg*, the appearance of the nuclear weapon and, we could add, the current RMA, were supposedly included in proper time patterns, each based on their own kinematic/dynamism, with multiple consequences. The first is that, following this sense, deducing a theory of military evolution could be problematic since the conditions in which it emerged systematically imply significant technological, cultural or political differentials, or differentials in their spread over time. Following this opinion, RMA would only exist in its peculiarity or, very simply, would be inexistent, according to the author. For example, E. R. Sterner, while observing the turn that the debate around some slogans was taking, will thus question the possibility of RMA [STE 99].

However, in practice, this viewpoint became less and less relevant through the evolution of armed forces and of its practices. After the Gulf War, the

Kosovo War became, from this viewpoint, the second "revealing link" of a radical evolution in the comprehension of the art of "transformed" warfare. It was also the most highly considered (as well as that of defense technologies) in European literature, acclaiming the theme of a European "*gap*" compared to the United States [DE 05b]. Deducing a theory of military revolutions remains possible by using a comparative and historical method, yet it can be a problem. In this context, the resort to historical analogy by American authors working on RMA, and who were more willing to take a limited historical viewpoint, is obvious. As they again take examples of the use of innovation from classic military history in order to justify their statements, they fail to account for the iteration these innovations experienced, and also, paradoxically, for the socio-political and historical context in which they appeared. If this disconnection does not incapacitate the impact of their contributions, it naturally favors the perception of RMA, resulting in a phenomenon throughout a historical event, and signifies an immediate turning point in proceeding.

The second consequence of an understanding of military revolutions in the Braudelian event history is that the said revolution can be transformed into a more or less auto-legitimating tale. The first part of the Tofflers' work, even if located in *longue durée*, is thus built on a mode which is close to epic, with strong hagiographic implications towards military reformers who could grasp the ongoing change and start what could resemble a myth with a science-factional outreach (i.e. impacting the collective conscience [SUS 05]), inhabited with its heroes[11]. Yet, in this work, the historical circumstances around the appearance of innovation markers are ousted, so that authors send their readers for further research in the book in order to find the causes of changes. We could also argue that myth can – and this is very minor within debates – give in to the mystique[12]. Beyond this, it is fascinating to note that this mythology becomes a history marked by truly real artefacts: "*vision*" documents like *Joint Vision 2010* and *2020* (respectively published in 1996

---

11 General Starry, or more generally "reformers" within the US army, the *Training and Doctrine Command*, but also… the United States and the freedom of thought they offer to their officers and researchers.

12 This way, a Colonel of Special Forces stated "you will discover two resources which are clearly going in our direction: God and microelectronics. The beauty stands in the fact that you can use microelectronics to project the mind… the brain works this way. Develop microelectronics weapons" [MCR 84, p. 124]. This viewpoint, caricatured in the movie *The Men Who Stare at Goats*, left some marks in the relations between the soldier and the "fighting entity" likely to be "raised" via technology.

and 2000) took their position in a spectrum going from a declaration of strategic intention validated by politics up to its implementation. RMA was then seen as the disruption in all military practices, in the context of a true fascination for the promises technology offered.

The third consequence of an evolution of RMA in event history – all the better if it is interpreted as a tale with mythical implications – is that it can appear as anhistorical; and even erase the historical approach. One of the most obvious symptoms in this matter is found in the way of considering technologies, seen as motors of RMA but which, in reality, are not new at all. The equipment used during the 1991 war had, for the most part, been conceived during the 1970s, in the context of the second *offset strategy* lead after the *reform movement*, which followed the Vietnam War [TOM 07]. A notable exception is that of GPS-guided weapons. It will also be the case during *Iraqi Freedom* (2003)[13]. Everything shows that wars too quickly qualified as "revolutionary" (in the meaning of RMA) show not only a poor knowledge and a poor understanding of the technologies to be used, but also a de-temporalization and a "de-historicization" of operations, failing to reconstitute their conceptual and doctrinal trajectories.

In return, this historical deficit thus generates incomplete spaces in the historicization of the generating process of RMA. It would then openly become anhistorical. This would be all the more true if the United States were to face a crisis in their military history, consubstantial to an extreme technicization and which could explain this deficit. In this way, according to B. Colson, in a naval and by definition techno-centered context, *"In the American naval thinking, the role of history experienced fluctuations tied to a periodic return of technicism and of the material school of thought. With this relation, history and strategy were always tightly linked. When the interest in history decreased, the strategic thinking would be impacted"* [COL 92]. Also, in the very context of RMA, history has yet to be used properly: in a context where American strategic thinking is marked by technique, J. Luvaas thus observed that history classes in American high schools were being replaced by *Western Civilization* classes, thus erasing every sign of historical culture to future American practitioners [LUV 95].

---

13 During which the British used Canberra PR.9 reconnaissance aircraft that made its first flight in... 1949 (!) [DE 07a].

In this way, even if there is still a full program of military history, implying several institutions with functions within American armed forces distinguished from the eminently normative role for armed forces elsewhere in the world, the historical reference is most often inscribed on a tactical level. Desportes thus reminds us that in the United States, there is a marked historical tradition dating back from the Civil War, during which *after-action reports* were automatically written, thus contributing to isolating lessons and the knowledge on broader operations [DES 02]. These initiatives were often based on personal initiatives[14]. This tradition was institutionalized throughout a *Center for Army Lessons Learned* (CALL), available online[15] and whose corollary practice is the prompt to both innovative concepts and self-criticism. Yet, the lessons collected are mostly of a technico-tactic nature and do not fully allow us to take some distance and to be fully conscious of the role of technique on strategy.

While noting the declining use of military history (as elsewhere in debates on RMA), or the evolution of American forces towards anti-intellectual attitudes [MUR 99], W. Murray stressed the lack of historical studies in the limitations of technology, which caused a risk of engagement of armed forces in non-conceptually studied context [MUR 98a, MUR 98b]. With the same mindset, the strength of technical factors in officers' training is seen as disadvantaging the resort to historical methods and, consequently, favoring the belief in "new wars", which no longer need history. Indeed, Desportes stresses that "*there is a tendency towards ignorance, a tendency to give in to the easy way and believe that wars are always new. The means are new, the ways are new, yet the very nature of war remains. (...) If someone makes the effort of going through the works of military authors from the past two millennia, he will discover two apparently contradictory phenomena. The first is that for centuries, we have been under the impression that we conduct new wars which have nothing to do with the previous ones; the second is that, with some distance, we are ourselves surprised by the stability of the main features of conflicts, by the permanency of their logic, by the mistakes which could have been avoided if the contemporeries of that time had simply had a less short memory [DES 01, p. 384].*

---

14 It is interesting to note that, during the Iraq war, many officers would have *weblogs* published on the Internet under the form of immediate lessons on lead confrontations.
15 http://usacac.army.mil/organizations/mccoe/call.

In the same way, A. Beaufre could state, more than 40 years ago and in the specific context of the nuclear revolution, that "*it is common to say that 'war has changed'. It has always changed through history. But what is new, and not very well seen by our contemporaries, is that something happened which is nothing but an evolution. We are witnessing a change which leads some to say that 'there will be no more war', a hope which is often disillusioned, and others to say that the changes we witness do not alter in any way the deep character of war* [BEA 72, p. 17]. In the context of a technical, or anhistorical RMA, we need to keep this thought in mind. In this regard, in a classic approach, J. Craig Stone shares the same reasoning and insists upon the necessity of redefining military education towards more historical than technological subjects, thus enabling a better understanding of the lessons history can bring.

2.3.2. *Breaks and discontinuities*

Beyond an approach favoring a historical positioning, the great majority of authors in favor of the notion of RMA think that it fundamentally returns to the occurrence of breaks and continuities in strategic history. Their differences thus lie on the level and extent of these breaks: the upsurge of a piece of information which afterwards becomes central to doctrines as well as to operations, the upsurge of precision weapons (the principles of which had however been set during World War II, even World War I), the upsurge of main changes on the international scene, a combination of them all? For Paul Ricoeur, the implication – whether it be evolutionary or revolutionary – these breaks can hold in event history is suspended on several conditions, regardless of the consequences that are seen from an understanding of the phenomenon in event history:

– the occurrence of an event triggering the perception of a new time;

– through this event, the implication of a break located between "before" and "after";

– all the most, "it must (…) establish a new time unit index [LAÏ 00, p. 155].

From this viewpoint, the fall of the Berlin Wall, that of the Soviet Union, the subject of a New World Order, or the re-discovery of low-intensity conflicts; and that of proliferation, represent many clues guiding authors towards a new historical era. Here, the complexity of causal channels in the international order is extreme and thus shows that Ricoeur's "event" must be understood in the broad sense of a combination of occurrences. Several authors consider that this break in the international order is doubled by a break in technological order. In this way, Martin Libicki comes up with a techno-dependent categorization centered on historical disruption, but which seems to lead the reader rather towards nuclear revolution than towards the current RMA [LIB 97]. According to him, RMA occurs with the appearance of a change in magnitude in the efficiency of well-led operations during a war, a change which is so deep that the end of a conflict is independent from the quantity of military systems belonging to the adversary; when the change is so fundamental that it pushes previous RMAs back into historical annals; when the entire strategic *corpus* but be conceptualized again; with the appearance of a change so deep that the understanding of the battlefield is fundamentally altered; with the appearance of an operational capacity altering the relations between the States. We will study this *infra*, we are yet far from it.

However, on a less techno-optimistic and more moderate level, even the most sceptical authors towards RMA admit that computerization triggers major impacts on armed forces and on combat. Cooper thus states that the increase in armed forces effectiveness, induced by the use of new technologies, causes in itself a break which is such that the pattern of "evolution in military affairs" is rejected [COO 97]. Yet, in reality, if the arguments legitimating RMA are quite widely spread in literature, they often lack theoretical conceptualization. This can be all the more serious given that the definition of RMA can almost exclusively be structured around technologies. Yet, if we look at it closely, technology might also have implied changes in the international order. With this thought, the upsurge of information technologies contributed to the fall of the Soviet Union. Starting the very intensive Strategic Defense Initiative (SDI), the United States forced the Soviet Union into a similar pattern, which would kill its economy as much as its political structures[16]. Nevertheless, the coupling "RMA" "changes on the international order" is not studied very thoroughly by RMA

---

16 This acceptation, praised by authors like Gaddis and Wohlforth, was strengthened by the opening of soviet archives and the work of V. Mastny, according to which the soviet view of the Cold War was deeply altered by NATO's disposal of high-technology weaponry [MAS 99, GAD 93, WOL 95].

advocates (beyond the dominant position in global power distribution RMA offers), these two subjects being most often detached.

The question remains whether RMA induces a new repertory of time unit, or whether in some way it recreates a proper historiography. If most authors in favor of RMA tend to semantically use the future tense in their works, we must also note that when studying the documents enabling implement action of the results of RMA, we notice the emergence of temporalities which are at the very least organized. Certainly, the implementation of the results of RMA within military institutions must follow time evolution and also the evolution of an international environment causing systemic pressures, and this despite cultural oppositions [KIA 03]. But beyond this, we can perceive two temporalities generated by RMA, and partially overlapping:

– *A temporality can be defined as a "delimited revolution"*. In this view, aiming at the implementation of RMA results, there is a profusion of prospective patterns and other implementation plans showing a bureaucratization of RMA, encouraged by politics. Even if the reality shows the incremental introduction of new technologies (because they are not all available at the same time, because some are submitted before others, because production does not enable the delivery of all ordered equipment at the same time, etc.), the mode of communication used causes the perception of a massive introduction. This imbalance between theoretical aspects coming from official documents for weapons meeting the characteristics of private businesses and practice naturally encourages to perceive a RMA. In the meantime, such a view aims at generating power structures and strategies of means finalized during a defined time period between 2015 and 2020. Let us note that the same kind of process is used by the United States in order to transmit RMA to their allies: this is the whole purpose of NATO's *Allied Transformation Command*. According to this viewpoint, politics itself generated a precise temporality. In 2001, in the *Quadriennal Defense Review* (QDR), D. Rumsfeld thus synthetized the conceptual aggregate formed by RMA, and rhetorically called it *Transformation*. If the word implies an evolution more than a revolution, authors quickly embraced it and brought into its meaning the concepts and theories resulting from RMA. In this way, the political scope is not the only one responsible: not only does the debate continue, it is also directed by a political determination. If some views are ousted, the search continues and is favored by the political sphere[17];

– Nonetheless, several authors speak of "post-RMA", defined as *"After-Next* RMA", which induces a *"temporality of unlimited revolution"*. Basing their statement on the fact that RMA would trigger doctrinal, organizational and technological consequences on the American forces, they gave rise to a questioning about its "after": not only about its maturation, but also about its possible futures. They identify several technological groups they consider suitable to cause new RMAs once they mature. Mainly considered as such are: biotechnologies, nanotechnologies, genetic engineering, robotics, and also breakthroughs which can still occur in the already existing fields of the "current" RMA. The "revolution" is consequently shown as open, sequentially reinventing itself as a result of technological breakthroughs likely to integrate forces.

An almost-permanent reproduction of the notion of revolution could come out of this. Yet, even if these new temporalities suggest quite anarchic agendas to different parties, they still keep the reality of a break present at the heart of their question. W. Murray and T. Gongora thus call to reason and try to temper "permanent revolutions", setting technological leaps as the only horizon of military revolutions. They thus consider that it takes RMAs several tens of years in order to mature, especially when they happen in times of peace [GON 99]. With this mindset, revolutions would only produce their effects out of steps with time needs. This is particularly true when RMAs go along with a consubstantial conceptualization of the international environment, modeled on the peer-competitor format both a symmetric competitor – yet without taking its specificities into account – and a self-fulfilling prophecy.

There is thus a great risk of having equipment and technologies which are no longer fit for an evolved environment[18]. An adaptation process is then

---

17 A typical example could be the works of the Army Colonel MacGregor. Examining the future combat conditions, he suggests to dispose of all *US Army* heavy forces in favor of high technology, partially airborne light forces. Rejected by the organization, the Colonel will immediately be recruited by Admiral Cebrowski's *Office of Force Transformation* [MAC 97].
18 For example the advocates of RMA argued that the rise of new forms of conflict would trigger the disappearance of tanks in favor of lighter armoured vehicles. Yet, in the end of the Iraq experience in 2003, these positions evolved greatly, considering a "return" or tanks.

implemented, equipment is reassigned to other missions, political and military organizations being the mediators of this adaptation through employment doctrines. "Revolutions" would then occur with some interval, so that the categories of "delimited" and "unlimited" revolutions would almost be coextensive. Not only because the conceptual sphere of political and the strategic implementation sphere are tightly linked – at least in the United States – but also because the political is naturally driven to managing techno-strategy. Facing diverse obstacles, programme cancellations[19] or their questioning[20] can follow. In the end, as they overlap one another, these two temporalities trigger a constant evolution in military institution. Yet, in the meantime, changes and discontinuities do not necessarily take place on the level of temporality of the strategic institution, but in its practices.

S.N. MacFarlane thus states that *"rather than being an evolution of pre-existing methods and instruments, they (RMAs) are transformative discontinuities in the way we make war, and in the way we think wars"*[21]. This phrase seems appropriate. With regards to their industrial, scientific or political counterparts, revolutions have not required abrupt changes other than ideal-typical changes. Yet, these "transformational discontinuities" require a new agenda, caused by the surge, in event history, of several technologies, which will alter the perception of actors who use them and who are likely to contribute, this time in longue durée, to another view referring to a new era. The anchoring of the most academic authors in generations, eras and other waves, refers itself to distinguished views of a generating time, depending on interpretations either of evolutions, or of revolutions.

If there is a revolution, authors have analysed it in almost-real time, sometimes without grasping one or the other of its dimensions or its long

---

19 This was the case for the very "RMA" helicopter RAH-66 or the self-propelled artillery *Crusader*. The first one was too expensive compared to an AH-64 it was supposed to substitute, but which kept presenting a superior comparative advantage. The second was not thought as being *"transformational"* enough and would only be the reproduction of a weapon system (M-109) dating back from the Cold War. In both cases, since the 1990s, no other solution than modernization of previous systems was found.

20 We consider in particular the F-35, which was supposed to be a model of managerial rationalization and a polyvalent device and which, in the end, had a non-mastered cost and whose superior abilities, essential to be classified as versatile were brought into question.

21 [MAC 99, p. 29].

term consequences. Throughout the years, each author's work shows an evolution of his positioning toward or his understanding of one subject or the other. Because of this, the only positioning of authors, in comparison with the temporality they choose to root their "RMA phenomenon" in the historical reality is not enough. This is why a further study is necessary regarding the "transformational discontinuities" tied to RMA and to *Transformation*, by deconstructing the theme of the paradigm shift often called upon by advocates of the effectiveness of RMA.

3

A Paradigm Shift

The "paradigm shift" is as much a recurring slogan in strategic literature on RMA and *Transformation* as it is a way to overcome questions on the temporality of military revolutions – *conjoncture* versus *longue durée*. In this study, it is also an opportunity to focus more thoroughly on the way RMA and *Transformation* concretely impact the act of warfare and its categories, be they practical or conceptual. Before going further, we must note that this "paradigm shift" covers different realities depending on authors, and also presents the risk of only developing the art of warfare under the influence of technologies, independently from strategic knowledge. This "shift" finds its roots in a disruptive conceptualization of action where the technologies and representations it carries play a major role.

3.1. A strategic consensus around the "paradigm shift"

For Hundley, RMA *"involves a paradigm shift in the nature or conduct of military operations (...) which either renders obsolete or irrelevant one of more core competencies of a dominant player (...) or creates one of more new core competencies in some new dimensions of warfare (...) or both"*[1]. Right after Kuhn, and in an attempt to extend his viewpoint, he considers that a paradigm is "a recognized practice which is a basic model for a section of military operations"[2] and that a core competency is a "fundamental ability that provides the foundation for a set of military capacities"[3]. Hundley had been – and will be – followed by other authors ready to allude to a

---

1 [HUN 99, p. 9].
2 See above.
3 As an example, he mentions the capacity of air forces to lead bombing missions.

"paradigm shift" in war conduct, thus giving RMA a revolutionary varnish [SUL 93, DAV 96, BAU 97], not without leaving this impression of embracing a rhetoric of technological determinism, usually found in business management [TAP 93].

3.1.1. *Paradigm pluralities*

In this way, at the beginning of the century, de Durand considered RMA as a paradigm in itself, which is true, focusing on the Republicans' political mobilization (and in spite of its using by Democrats) [DE 01a]. With the same intention, RMA as well as *Transformation* would be the conceptual reification of the regular art of warfare, and specifically that of the United States and their NATO allies. From this point, RMA is opposed to other forms of war conduct, be they regular or not, believing them to have a backwards reasoning. With regards to the Iraq war, Mary Kaldor thus considers that its insurrection phase represents a "new war", to be opposed to an "old" war, to which RMA would be tied [KAL 05]. In such a context, the confrontation to evolutions of irregular warfare – and this category is not historically new – would imply the downgrading of regular and techno-centered operations. We can note right away that several acceptations are given to the concept of paradigm in its relation to RMA. Sometimes, it means the way to conduct war, sometimes a specific war, or sometimes a political and bureaucratic model.

Few authors have defined the scope of application as well as the characteristics of this "paradigm shift". For many of them, the end of the Cold War imposed a "paradigm shift" for American foreign and defense policies[4] – which is convincing since the enemy is no longer the USSR – whereas Marshall notes it in the conduct of military operations. Krepinevitch considers that this shift is in the very nature of war [KRE 94]. This assertion is particularly motivating and will be used a lot in debates, but is fundamentally questionable. Embracing this viewpoint implies confusing the *character* and the *nature* of warfare [LON 04] while the strategist community consensually considers it as unchangeable. Beauffre's "*dialectics of opposing wills using force in the resolution of conflict*" thus strays from the forms it can take: whether it is fought with stones or with hypersonic missiles, war always comes down to the opposition of actors' wills. This is also where the whole

---

4 Thus making them embrace the concept of new world order and the search for peace through democracy.

relevance of Clausewitz's aphorism stands, since according to him, war is a chameleon whose colours are altered depending on the context, but whose nature is unique.

The view according to which the nature of war would alter with RMA is mostly techno-determinist: it depends on originally technological changes, where its nature is technologically determined, which is not without consequences for our perception and application of it. Technology is no longer just a tool serving the military, it becomes its main driving force and leitmotif: "progress" in this field is thus only understood in terms of technical and measurable performances. This position echoes the logic of "metrics", which are supposed to measure military performances and give war conduct a scientific varnish. Since then, this kind of position has been widely criticized, especially since RMA would only be an attempt to adapt to the nature of war in order to make the most of it[5]. This viewpoint seems more rightful: in this way, technology again becomes a tool and is no more an *ultima*.

Beyond this, the different shifts in the paradigm depend on the authors. For Pi Shen, the paradigm shift is cultural, within the military institution itself [PI 01], whereas for Patrick, it is organizational, altering the form of this very institution and its ways of functioning [PAT 94]. These assertions, as they send us back to Moskos and to the works in military technology, are more in tune with reality. Armies have always adapted their organization by switching "models" – an evolution which nourishes a great part of the literature on the adaptation process [GRI 15]. For Litton, principles of war gain a paradigm value, so that their evolution, under the influence of RMA, would indeed produce a "paradigm shift". This assertion is more questionable – as we will see later – even if indeed, RMA can imply a reorganization of the principles of war[6]. This plurality of meanings given to paradigm shift is to be found on other levels in the debate. For example, air or naval strategies can also experience radical changes in their practices (see *infra*).

Once it is brought up in debates on RMA, the notion of paradigm tends to become scalar, adapting to each sector that is mentioned. In a more general

---

5 In this regard, the abundance of the literature on the promises of lifting of the "fog of war" via technologies of the past 10 years represents in itself a negation of Krepinevitch's assertion.
6 Paradoxically, in his conclusions, he thus calls for a better understanding of strategic theory [LIT 00].

way, the "paradigm shift" has an impact on the majority of scopes of the art of war, of international relations and of military sociology. However, the very notion of a paradigm seems to be overused by "revolutionaries". Very few authors define it any other way than by quoting Marshall, Krepinevitch or the participants in the 1994 seminar. As it justifies said revolution, the plurality of paradigms supposed to change the art of war seems to become a marker, which allows us to identify changes in a conceptual and technological environment, which is at the very least blurred. Nevertheless, the "paradigm profusion" does not help the analyst: most of the time, it focuses on specific scopes and does not allow any overview of the shifts RMA would imply.

3.1.2. *The place of politics: scientific-rational and historical paradigms*

Following the works of Gat [GAT 91], Braillard and Maspoli state that RMA "*conveys a partial and misleading view on future wars, because of theoretical presuppositions it is based upon*"[7]. They base their criticism on the fact that, historically speaking, we can distinguish two strategic paradigms (here, they insist on redefining this term). The first, a scientific-rational paradigm – and which would refer to the material viewpoint – would seek a universal theory of conflicts, a complete control of the force it uses. In this context, "*theory is synonymous with doctrine; thus, it has a practical use and is focused on operational and tactical levels*"[8]. Most importantly, this theorization is such that the very specificities tied to each conflict are not be taken into account in the analysis. We specifically refer to authors like Bülow, Lloyd or Jomini, whose significance is well known in American strategic culture [COL 93, DES 02]. In such a context, politics is reduced to war politics and military politics; and has no influence on strategy. Moreover, this paradigm favors the perception of an RMA and highlights technology as a way of solving military problems.

The second paradigm, for Braillard and Maspoli, is a historical one. It considers war as a "*profoundly socio-political*" phenomenon, singular and fundamentally plural, where theory is not the same as doctrine and where there is "*great attention (*given*) to uncertainty, meaning the incapacity of*

---

7 [BRA 02, p. 631].
8 [BRA 02, p. 632].

fully controlling every aspect of war"[9]. Clearly, such a paradigm is based on Clausewitz – in its relation to the "fog of war", to uncertainty and to frictions – and on the eminently political aspect of a war which directly influences its conduct. Such an approach minimizes the resort to technology and finds its roots in a historical viewpoint more naturally than the previous approach did. If the previous paradigm seems to match the American approach of warfare, the second one would refer more specifically to a European approach. However, it is important to moderate the paradigmatic diptych offered by these two authors. It does not provide a full understanding of the RMA phenomenon in comparison with the paradigm shifts it would induce:

– first, on the question of the role played by politics in the production of military doctrines and the conduct of war. If, indeed, the relations to the two models differ, the authors underestimate the political character of Jomini's thought, as much in theory as in practice in American operations. In the same way, and beyond, the interrelations between political and strategic scopes are more complex in Jomini's thought than the authors suggest;

– second, the call for a universal theory of conflicts is refuted by the diversity of the literature, which still has not reached this goal. Nevertheless, we must note that while noting an outreach of the scientific-rational thinking, which is more easily operational/tactic than political, the authors lead the way to another explanation of the notion of paradigm shift.

Ultimately, and something worth noting, is that war as the *"pursuit of politics by other means"*, as defined by Clausewitz, is not fundamentally impacted by RMA, *Transformation* or the emergence of networks and other advanced sensors. Its technical/technological implication does not in any way influence the fact that it does not become independent from the political factor – which would come down to changing a nature which, as we saw, is unchangeable[10]. An extreme technological example – and maybe one which cannot be exceeded – is that of nuclear weaponry and its vectors, which was defined as a military revolution. It would alter the nature of war, making it impossible since its occurrence could potentially have meant the destruction of humanity, and thus of all political forms. However, when we take a closer look at it, dissuasion does not function like a strategic system since it is given credibility – which suggests that war is not impossible, under certain

---

9 [BRA 02, p. 632].
10 See the contributions of Christian Malis and Alain Joxe in [BAR 08].

conditions. We must add that the nuclear engagement – whether it is accidental or not – is itself the result of a political decision, just like the creation of arsenals and the validation of doctrines. Practically speaking, the choice of a global-scale suicide is not apolitical – it might even be the most absolute and the fullest form of politics. This is even truer when the history of nuclear doctrines shows that some *war-winning* conceptions – which consider the survival of human groups – were given some thought, or even embraced [FRE 03].

This detour via nuclear strategy is not just an extreme example aiming at showing the political content of any war, regardless of its technological intensity. It also reflects historical and scientific-rational understandings of war; its history and the concerns involved show that it cannot be reduced solely to logics of cost benefit calculations led on a rational basis. It is also essential in order to understand the context in which RMA appeared: as we saw earlier, many of its conceptual components and of its material artefacts are the result of the Cold War years, in the view of controlling a possible escalation, or a combat lead on the verge of nuclearization. The fact is that, with this regard, RMAs as *Transformation* did not incapacitate the conceptions of nuclear strategy, nor the perception of a need for these arsenals, nor even their integration in correlation of forces logic, with their conventional military systems. In this way, we cannot speak of a paradigm break between strategic practices marked by the nuclear order and the "new conventional order" of RMA/*Transformation*. On the contrary, there are many interrelations between nuclear and conventional powers, whether they are technical or strategic[11].

3.1.3. *The question of levels of engagement*

The viewpoint developed by Braillard and Maspoli thus meets several authors who consider that RMA is, first and foremost, a "new operational art" [GÉR 00]. As they note the weakness of the epistemological rooting of RMA, they also lead the way to a paradigmatic conceptualization of evolutions, on an operative and a tactic level. When considered as practices, these evolutions were conceptualized, even if their literature almost exclusively falls under the military scope and is rarely taken into account by political scientists. Two questions arise out of this. The first is that of the

---

11 This is the case – and we will come back to it – in the computer technology scope.

possibility of paradigm shifts in tactic and operation matters, which indeed seems recognized, particularly since the 1980s and the introduction of new technologies. From this viewpoint, the "paradigm shift" invoked by the advocates of RMA does seem real: in 2015, we do not fight, gather information or communicate in the way we used to in 1985. But this reality would somehow be hidden in politology, due to an understanding of RMA from the angle of a scientific-rational paradigm, which is significant for advocates of the said revolution and which partially "cuts" the relation between political and military scopes.

The second question refers to the future of relations between different levels of military engagements – despite the criticisms regarding the very relevance of a level grading [BIH 15]. Military strategies, as well as strategic studies, thus show an evolution in the positioning of these levels [MAC 92]. Indeed, the relation of the operative and the tactic levels with the political and strategic levels has evolved considerably, mainly under the pressure of technology and especially telecommunications, intelligence and the media, considered as central in RMA [FRA 97, DE 97]. And, at the risk of interfering more broadly with combat units for Odom [ODO 93] and of making those responsible in the military give in to the temptation of an existing micro-management, this was true even before RMA[12]. However, RMA implies a considerable shift in scale: in NATO's "transformed" forces, any Chief– and his superiors above him – is likely to receive a direct order from somewhere at the political level.

These questions were the subject of many warnings in the professional literature, around the creation of command and communication networks. The succession of these levels is no longer seen as occurring from the political to the tactical level in a linear way, as was the case until the 1990s; it is now blurred under the effect of technological impacts. Actually, we no longer talk exclusively about communication between the people in charge or the actors of these levels, but we also talk about the political intensity that is typical of these levels. Historically, political action filters through different levels in order to have tactical impacts, so that any military action

---

12 During the USS *Pueblo* incident in January 22nd, 1968, the American president ended up giving direct orders to pilots of the air and sea who were in charge of covering the rescue of the ship, in the purest tradition of the "Operations Room syndrome" denounced by Kissinger and according to which Johnson *"had given in to the romantic idea that in times of crisis, he could manage the world's affairs from this room, located in the underground of the White House"* [KIS 79, p. 327].

is both the realization and legitimization of political decisions. It is still true today – and it will no doubt still be true tomorrow – but the combination of communication technologies with networks, their tendency to become denser and multiply in civilian as well as in military scopes, implies that the opposite will also be true. Even the smallest tactical incident, apparently strategically harmless, can have direct political consequences[13]. This evolution is represented by Carlo Jean in Figure 3.1.

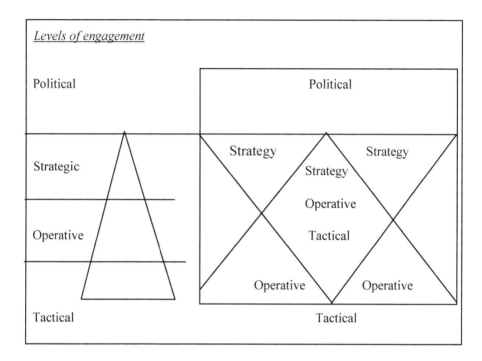

Figure 3.1. *Evolution of the levels of strategic engagements from the classic era to today (source: adapted from [COU 11, p. 145])*

Does this mean that tactics – meaning the level most likely to be influenced by technology – can end up leading operative, strategic and political levels? And, with this train of thought, is tactical art likely to subject strategic and operative arts? Several answers can be given here. From a historical point of

13 We remember that this way, the pictures of an American pilot who was captured and dragged in the streets of Mogadiscio lead to the retreat of American troops in Somalia in 1993. On the subject of "strategic corporal" which has a lot of success: [KRU 99].

view, tactics only determine the outcome of wars in their relation to political, operative and strategical levels. Tactical victory does not automatically become political victory, with the exception of a few cases of decisive battles [YAK 06]. In the same way, a series of tactical victories does not systematically lead to strategic victory either – this is one of the many problems linked to counter-irregular operations[14]. In the contemporary context, Guy Hubin shows how evolutions of tactics, which is revalued by a multitude of technological innovations, can improve the freedom of political and strategic manoeuvres, which is an asset [HUB 09]. However, Hubin will later state that the best military device and the best tactic are nothing without reachable war goals[15]. This way, we cannot escape the fundamentals of the art of warfare – and particularly the definition of Zweck and of Zielen, which influences the entire strategic process [STR 13]. We simply cannot reach a goal that does not exist.

Despite this, there is some temptation in thinking the opposite. With a more radical positioning, and in the specific context of the Cold War, General Gallois stated that "*today, speaking of strategy is studying the relation between populations' behaviors and the technical capacities of new weapons in depth*"[16]. Sceptical authors have noticed this trend in the proceeding debates on RMA. Echevarria thought that tatics were given too much importance in opinions. The way of warfare/battle would thus win over a way of war with its larger extent and taking into account the political level [ECH 04]. In the same train of thought, Colin S. Gray stated that technological innovations tended to over-represent the tactical scope in the detriment of political and strategic scopes [GRA 99a]. In both cases, Clausewitz – and mostly, the strategic paradigm tied to him – was revisited for help. However, institutions will never fully re-read him, and his thoughts in relation to politics will remain restricted by the American case [WAS 04]. The focus on tactics thus contributes to a phenomenon where a tight link is created between autonomization and the fascination for the effects of technology all along the debate.

If we do not conduct war for tactical stakes, it is still true that one of the main criticisms about RMA and the processes of *Transformation* are their examination from the angle of the logic of tactical efficiency, which confines

---

14 And in which, for the adversary, the sole fact of resisting is a victory, where the fact of not defeating in a decisive way is often seen as a failure for loyalist forces.
15 Interview with the author, 28 February 2007.
16 [DE 92, p. 148].

to a tacticization of stakes where, once more, only the political and strategic levels allow us to determine a military efficiency. This would be particularly true for armies that import American conceptions since it would "mean an impoverishment of the imported concept as much as of the doctrine of the army which imports it, resulting in the opposite effect of what was expected: a loss of military efficiency. This impoverishment usually takes the shape of an anti-strategic tacticization of the latter, meaning restricting it to its function of method of implementation of weapon systems, independently from the political conditions of this implementation"[17]. All said and done, armies importing American conceptions linked to RMA and *Transformation* are not the only ones that can endure this tacticization. This is also the case for the United States themselves, in the development of concepts such as Rapid Decisive Operations or AirSea Battle, which show a conception of combat based on technical parameters, outside of any political, or, even more simply, operative or strategic questionings [HEN 14a].

3.1.4. *A rethinking of strategy as an art*

All the same, we can consider that the validity of the paradigm diptych introduced by Gat and taken over by Braillard and Maspoli is not fundamentally called into question. However, in order to do it justice, we must still call the opposition of these two paradigms into question, even if it is ideal-typical and including in a context of informationalization/reticulation. We can also state that they form the extension of the old debate on the nature for strategy as science or art – which is far from being without any incidence on the way to consider (but also to conceive) new technological artefacts. Hervé Coutau-Bégarie allows us to go over this question by stating that "*strategy is an art, as it is a practice; it is also a science, as it is a knowledge which can be subject to a scientific study (in the understanding of social sciences)*" [COU 11]. Further still, some consider that strategy refers to "*sciences at the service of art*"[18], making these last two words ontologically coextensive. But are the scientific-rational and the historic paradigms coextensive as well?

If their ideal-typical characters suggest the opposite, the practice of American literature shows that "Clausewitzian" dimensions, with their historical connotations, appear as much in the works of advocates of RMA as in those of its opponents. For the first group, the goal will be to try and

17 [BIH 14a, p. 35].
18 [DES 01, p. 363].

uncover the "fog of war" contributing to uncertainty through technological intermediary [OWE 00, LIT 00]. For the second group, it is precisely because RMA does not take into account the Prussian's teachings that it must still mature [JAB 94b]. But in reality, the "projected shadow" of Clausewitz on the American military system has more complex features – actually since the 1970s [WAS 04]. Several of its concepts will be reused. This is the case for friction, which is still considered as a possibility in spite of technological breakthroughs. It must be countered by technological innovation, but Watts is lead to think that between two opposite conflict forces, the one experiencing less frictions is also the closest to success [WAT 96, WAT 84]. In this regard, his thinking is close to that of Boyd when he considers that the essence of strategy stands in manoeuvre, the primary rationality of which consists in generating as much confusion as possible in the adverse cognitive process.

Let us also point out the great attention given to the aspects of combat linked to uncertainty and non-linearity. These concepts were also stressed by Clausewitz, and RMA tried to regulate them. The theory of chaos, the search for the conception of software allowing the management of very complex situations – including in antiterrorism – thus show that the Prussian's works were taken into account, but mainly in its tactical contributions, as the political aspects of his thinking tend to be outcast – at least in the United States. On this subject, the American approach more specifically refers to Jomini. However, the Swiss is not necessarily as much of a "technician" as we might present him. He could thus declare that *war, far from being an exact science, is a terrible and passionate drama which, it is true, is submitted to general principles, but the result of which is subordinate to a great number of moral and physical complications*". In this way, and after all, the true cornerstone of a coextension between political-rational and historical paradigms is not so much the primacy of an approach over the other than the mutual connectivity they offer and which seems quite real.

Thus, the two scientific-rational and historical paradigms are in no way exclusive since they only act on different scales, which results in validating, at least in a conceptual way, the idea of strategy as an art built upon science. Still, the temptation towards a scientific strategy, in the understanding of "hard" sciences, is not historically new, from the geometrical vision of von Bulöw [GAT 91] to Soviet theoreticians in the 1920s–1930s [KOK 98]. Yet, if, for some time, the occurrence of RMA revived the debate, military institution itself quickly defines the questionings on the subject. We can be but appreciative of the numerous critical and sceptical publications on the subject, which were indeed published by researchers but also by members of the military, on many editorial reports, including in institutional reviews such as, in the United States, *Parameters* or the *Military Review* or also monographies published by military research centers. The mistrust deriving from experience was thus opposed to technical intentions, in addition to the questions of many strategists, noticing profound revolutions but no restructuring of their discipline.

The multitude of "paradigm shifts" RMA would not induce – and occurring depending on the scale of granularity on which we position ourselves – an anarchy, because of the intrinsically holistic nature of this very RMA/*Transformation*. For the majority of authors, RMA comes from the possibility of integration in the army of a relatively limited number of technologies and essentially referring to the full utilization of computer and electronic information[19]. Yet, what matters is not so much the sole introduction of systems than the multiple consequences on practices and conceptualizations that would break the (very precarious) consensus on the nature of "RMA" [COO 97]. For several authors, the outreach of the upsurge of information technology on all levels of security politics – whether it be interior or foreign – is such that the impact on political and strategic systems is also global, generating concepts of global outreach [JOS 99, GOM 98]. Specifically, if an argument which gives RMA a historical implication allows to justify it in the eyes of decision-makers – but also of possible sceptics within the military institution – it also seems to find an integration contributing to its occurrence in a self-justifying discussion [MET 95]. Indeed, several authors, A. Marshall among them, admit that one of the first conditions for RMA to exist is for it to be recognized by the institution and its actors.

In this way, it could also be seen as, at the stage of concept (for lack of being fully recognized as of a revolutionary nature), nothing more than a kind of declaration of intentions on the shifts to make within the military institution. However, given the political representation the movement benefited from, this fear did not become real. Yet, in this context, we can quickly ask ourselves whether the "revolution" must trigger a series of changes with or without them being mastered. This is therefore asking the

---

19 In reality, the question is more open. We will see this more thoroughly later.

question of strategy as a rationalized choice of factors linked to the creation of power [FRE 13] and of a process of adaptation, which is not out of control. Risk does exist: technological complexity can impose a determinist headlong rush with the risk of becoming a budgetary and operational trap. The FR-35 program, typically seen as one of the results of RMA and *Transformation*, is thus considered as "too big to fail" [HUG 15]. In reality, it has become the most expensive military program of all times. The question of keeping control over the adopted strategy is also raised in terms of internal security, where today the combination of electronics and *big data* allows a precise geolocation of people which was not even conceivable at the beginning of the 2000s and whose stakes exceed the sole operation efficiency by far.

Metz and Kievit will give a favorable answer to this question of technology control, stressing the necessity to systematically question the theoretical basis of the concepts used, as it happens, by the American army, but also its functioning, its culture and its organization [MET 94b]. It is thus a matter of self-objectivity in order to perceive the means technology can trigger on the governance of different "paradigm shifts" within national strategy. Yet, for Colin Gray, "American strategic and military culture is incapable of offering much resistance to the seductive promise of a way of war that seeks maximum leverage from the exploitation of information technologies"[20]. In fact, the question of operational and institutional practices is much more difficult than Metz and Kievit's recommendation suggests. Armies are still subject to a sociology of organizations where resistance to change can be very strong [LUT 84, CAP 99, THI 99, BUR 94]. Nevertheless, the deployment generated by RMA and *Transformation* induces a self-justifying discussion. The aim is thus to "defend" innovations, but also to become their incarnation – with the risk of focusing on them and not on their consequences, be they operational or political.

With the distance taken since its "declaration" in 1992, we can thus consider that RMA does not tend to be controlled, particularly in the United States – even if the phenomenon also impacts Europe, in a different way depending on countries. The consequence is the loss of control of the technological governance of institutions, but also an overestimation of technology's effects. What follows is that the subject of the use of highest technology is used by the institution in order to recruit (including through

---

20 [GRA 05, p. 20].

the intermediary of media[21]), to shape its image and to justify itself, but is also justified through politics. Technology carries its own aesthetics and implies new representations of power, which are fetishized, with the risk of a disconnection from the political as well as from its own stakes. In terms of what it brings in terms of technical parameters, technology is all the more uncontrollable than the military – as a subordinate but also as an actor in politics – tends to be seen as a "technician", whether it be as a result of a specific strategic culture (the United States) or of a more recent evolution (France and European countries). However, in the meantime, the political level can claim increasingly less to have a strategic knowledge likely to counterbalance this evolution.

The first Bush Jr. administration thus came into power with a true defense program, which was presented as being "reformist" [STR 03]. D. Rumsfeld's intention at the time was to take advantage of RMA's benefits and to radicalize them, thus leading to its end. As he considered restructured armed forces, replacing man by machine, looking for forces that would be more gathered but more efficient, he also questioned what could appear as political bastions within weapons. With this mindset, he suggested to give up heavy nuclear aircraft carriers or fighter plane programs such as F-35. In the meantime, he would suggest options like earth-strike space-based lasers. With 9/11, the program could not be fully implemented, yet many traces of it remain – in operations conduct as well as in the selection of generals in the highest rank[22]. The low number of men[23] sent to Iraq during the stabilization phase of operation *Iraqi Freedom* after May 2003 refers to this logic, as well as to a misunderstanding, which actually nourished RMA, of the difficulty of counter-irregular operations. During the planning phase of *Iraqi*

---

21 A sign of its time, a videogame like *America's Army* stresses teamwork (it can only be played online) as much as technology or, more generally, "surgically" administered violence. Prior to this, movies like *Top Gun* or *Firebirds* show, beside "human" heroes, "material" heroes – F-14 Tomcat and AH-64 Apache – in very divided, even almost-Manichaean situations (protection of the rescue of a US ship and fight against drug cartels) which do not really allow political criticism.

22 In this way, D. Rumsfeld and his assistants interviewed all officers applying for the positions of lieutenant generals or generals – the highest and most "politicized" positions in the army. In particular, generals who had been named under Clinton, even if they worked on RMA, were suspected of not applying what Rumsfeld saw as its consequences.

23 Estimates were thus made on the necessity of a land occupation rate similar to that in Kosovo at the end of the 1999 operations. For this to be possible, a deployment of around 400,000 American men would have been necessary. In practice, not much more than a quarter was deployed over the entire operation zone, including Kuwait and Qatar.

Freedom, D. Rumsfeld thus faced criticism from the American military establishment as the number of men involved was considered as being too low. In practice, *"he thought that they were old Army Generals rooted in the Second World War and who did not understand new forms of war"* [HAS 03].

In some aspects, we can also wonder about the effects of this technical-strategic hubris in the case of France, once we are able take enough historical distance. The multiplication of operations, from 2011 – Harmattan in Libya, Serval/Barkhane in the Sahelian band and then Chammal in the Middle East[24] – could thus have been nourished by the perception, on a political level, of a multiplying of the efficiency of armies due to the integration of new technologies and the representation of these technologies. These actions were not only taken because the political level overestimated the effects of technology, but this perception no doubt resulted in a failure to question operations on an ability basis. We understand that this problem of technological hubris represents major stakes, for the United States as much as for France. First, it is that of going to war and of the human consequences it entails. It is also the case for proper strategic stakes. The multiplication of operations weakens military presence, making it less fit for future operations, the stakes of which would be higher – British forces faced this problem at the end of operations in Afghanistan and Iraq. However, the logics of RMA/*Transformation* were firstly those of regular warfare as it was understood at the end of the Cold War, considering very intense but quite short operations, which were not adapted to the conflicts in which Western forces have engaged since the beginning of the 2000s.

3.2. Strategy of means and RMA

For researchers examining the evolution of Western armies for the past 30 years, the rhetoric carried by RMA as well as by the *Transformation* can seem puzzling. What are their truly new representations, and why are they interpreted as new? We could have doubts about this novelty when examining the technological projects conducted since the end of the Cold War and be quite sceptical: whether it is about weapon systems conceived in the United

---

24 But also an operation, aborted due to the lack of American and British support, in opposition to the Syrian regime following the use of chemical weaponry in August 2013.

States or in Europe, their specifications were written during the Cold War. This is also true for many combat aircrafts, ships, tanks, even soldiers' equipment – the uniforms of "soldiers of the future" – which were the results of thinking developed at the end of the 1980s. Be it in the United States or in Europe, many systems which today are called "transformational" were created during the Cold War, even if they could only be properly used during the 2010s. Comparatively few systems were created during the 1990s – apparently following the principles of RMA and *Transformation* – and effectively used. Several resounding failures thus occurred, especially in the United States.

3.2.1. *A hidden revolution? RMA and genetic strategy*

This is particularly the case for *Future Combat System* (FCS), which was supposed to experience a renewal of the whole range of American tanks, adding land-based or airborne robots, for combat as well as for support, while networking them. This is also the case for 6E-10MC2A (*Multi-sensor Command & Control Aircraft*), a land-motion detector (replacing E-8 Joint Stars) which was supposed to allow the correlation of information with an integrated capacity of electronic surveillance (replacing RC-135s) and of advanced airborne detection (replacing E-3s). In both cases, the systems were seen as "transformational" *per se*. They thus appeared as products and results of RMA in a perspective which was both managerial – extreme rationalization of forces – but also technological, forming the material crystallization of concepts linked to data fusion. In the end, both programs were given up as they were perceived as too complex (and thus technologically risky) and too expensive.

Still, the truth is that most of the main equipment for land combat, which will be used in the 2040s, will be the result of a reset and an upgrading of older machines, which appeared in the 1970s, or even before that, such as the 155 mm M-109 Howitzer. Its first versions were implemented during the 1950s, and it could become the first centennial tank. In the *US Air Force*, focus was on F-35, which was initially supposed to replace F-16 as well as A-10 – but in an imperfect way, and leading to many debates – whereas some equipment was either extended after being upgraded or reset. Beyond this, the appearance of drones is, in terms of platforms, the only notable evolution. Only the *US Navy* will have new systems which are not based on the evolution of pre-existing equipment[25]. In reality, this logic of equipment extension can be established in relation to its main functions:

Function	Available equipment in 1985	Hypothetically available equipment in 2030
US Army		
Main battle tank	M-1A1 *Abrams*	M-1A1/A2 *Abrams*
Infantry fighting vehicle	M-2A1 *Bradley*	M-2A3 *Bradley*
Troop transport vehicle	M-113, trucks	M-113 follow-on (to be selected) , *Stryker*
155 mm self-propelled howitzer	M-109A4/5	M-109A6/7**
155 mm towed howitzer	–	M-777
Attack helicopter	AH-1 *Cobra*, AH-64A *Apache*	AH-64E *Apache Guardian*
Reconnaissance helicopter	OH-58D *Kiowa*	RQ-7 *Shadow*
Maneuver helicopter	UH-60A *Black Hawk*	UH-60L *Black Hawk**, V-280 *Valor*
Heavy-lift helicopter	CH-47D *Chinook*	CH-47F *Chinook***
US Air Force		
Strategic bomber	B-52 *Stratofortress*	B-52 *Stratofortress***, B-2, B-21.
Air superiority fighter	F-15A/C *Eagle*	F-22 *Raptor*, F-15C upgraded *Eagle* *
Dual role strike fighter	F-15E *Strike Eagle*	F-15E *Strike Eagle** ?
Multirole strike fighter	F-16A/C *Fighting Falcon*	F-35 *Lightning II*, F-16A/C *Fighting Falcon** ?

---

25 In particular due to a logic according to which a ship is created right away to be used for 30–40 years, and in which it is quite easy to make it evolve. In this way, generations of ships will follow one another with clear breaks.

Close air support	A-10A *Thunderbolt*	A-10C *Thunderbolt**
Heavy airlift	C-5A/B *Galaxy*	C-5M *Galaxy**, C-17 *Globemaster III*
Intratheater cargo plane	C-130H *Hercules*	C-130J *Hercules***
Aerial refueling	KC-10 *Extender*, KC-135 *Stratotanker*	KC-10 *Extender*, KC-135 *Stratotanker***, KC-46 *Pegasus*
Airborne early warning and control	E-3A *Sentry*	E-3C *Sentry**
Reconnaissance	U-2R/S *Dragon Lady* (TR-1), SR-71 *Blackbird*	U-2R/S *Dragon Lady*** ?, RQ-4 *Global Hawk*, RQ-170 *Sentinel*
Electronic intelligence	RC-135 *Rivet Joint*	RC-135 *Rivet Joint*** ?
Tactical reconnaissance	RF-4 *Phantom*	R/MQ-1 *Predator*, MQ-9 *Reaper*

* Equipment first put into service in or prior to 1980.

** Equipment first put into service in or prior to 1965.

Table 3.1. *American equipment used in 1985 and their successors*

If it can seem paradoxical in a revolutionary environment, rationality adopted in strategy of means conceals much more radical evolutions. The center of attention is thus no more the platform – meaning the mobile component of the weapon system (plane, helicopter, tank, etc.) – but the systems it will be equipped with, be it sensors or communication/networking systems. In fact, RMA/*Transformation* does not show major disruptions in strategy of means, but rather the appearance, within itself, of a new stratum. In this way, the conception of a weapons system always meets the same logic of the definition of an expression of need and of the definition of specifications. It also meets the principles of genetic strategy – meaning the harmonization of a need with strategic environment – just as RMA does not nullify the two other components of the strategy of means – logistics and industrial strategies [HEN 12b]. However, the software stratum in weapons systems has become more significant. Genetics strategy of equipment thus evolves in order to almost systematically take into account the imperatives of reticulation and a different comprehension of the logic of intelligence, be it in the context of the upgrading of a system or the conception of new material.

In fact, if we only focus on weapons systems, we can consider that the revolution only shows itself marginally, and that it shows only once the access panels are open. Yet, doing so would mean denying a great number of major evolutions – which are still visible. This is particularly true of drones and the process of roboticization – which, besides, largely depend on computer technologies. Used in several armies in the beginning of the 1960s, mostly for artillery targeting means or as air targets, drones became, in the 1990s, major ISR systems [ZUB 12], creating new practices (the aircraft and naval persistence we will discuss later on *infra*) and varying from systems weighing a few grams to machines of several tons [SIN 09]. Right away, the question of a roboticization of armed forces was raised as an addition to or a replacement for current systems, and with the emergence of complex dynamics like fads or enthusiasm overcoming reality, or even contradicting it and thus showing the whole ambiguity of the realization of RMA/ *Transformation*.

We thus often heard that drones were the future of aviation, but this assertion has never been proved: to our knowledge, no publication on the economy of aviation or on the prospective of air power, whether it is scientific or not, allows to validate the implication that the piloted plane is condemned. Constantly repeated, the assertion has become a technological mantra, whereas most operational actors tend to foresee a future where drones and piloted aircrafts would be jointly used. The same type of pattern was observed in the scope of robots used for combat, surveillance, logistics or mine-clearing missions, in favor of land forces. By the turn of the 2010s, a generalization of robotics was thus discussed, in a kind of trend extrapolation based on the integration or more than 10,000 ground robots in the US Army, essentially assigned to mine-clearing and reconnaissance. Yet, once operations in Iraq and Afghanistan were over, the number of robots in service quickly decreased. In the same train of thought, a series of applications are not seen as a priority for the time being, in the areas of combat as well as in logistics, be it for technological tightness, budget priorities or mere military relevance [LAN 15].

The analysis of the process of RMA/*Tranformation* from the strategy of means angle thus implies embracing a nuanced approach and leaving behind any technological determinism based on "technological idols". It is also the case in the area of ammunitions, which is particularly sensitive since it refers to terminal effectors – meaning the last link of the continuance of politics by other means. While only 7% of bombs were guided during operation Desert Storm, they will be guided in more than 80% of cases for operations in Afghanistan [HEN 05] or against the organization of Islamic State[26]. In addition to laser-guidance weapons, electro-optical and infrared guided weapons, which have existed since the Vietnam War, GPS-guided weapons appeared with a decametric precision. Today, they are used so generally that the new version of the nuclear weapon B61 will be equipped with such a guidance system[27]. The race for precision also impacted the area of land ammunitions, with GPS-guided 155 mm shells as well as laser-guided or GPS-guided mortar shells. Here again, we must moderate the process of symbolization of navigation technology. First, because it is questioned on a tactical level, as well by the availability of GPS jammers deteriorating signals as by the fact that the spread of guided weapons does not imply the end of non-guided weapons – in particular on the land level. Second, because once more, technology mainly shows its effects on the tactical level and does not foresee the relevance of a strategy inducing the implementation of weaponry: *weapons don't make war* [GRA 93].

3.2.2. A failed revolution? RMA and industrial strategy

This time on the scale of industrial strategy – meaning on the level of military and industrial complexes – RMA came along with a series of speeches of a technical-managerial nature, linked to the transformation of modes of production of weapons systems. First, it is the case with rationalities of search for adaptability, as *"one size fits all"* becomes a slogan, which finds several realizations. It is the case for traditional logics such as the development of tank groups (for *Stryker* or FCS). Yet, this rationality can go even further in an attempt to counter contradictory environments of use, which comes down to "constrain physics" through technology. This will be the case with *Joint Strike Fighter* (JSF) program, which will come to realization with F-35. The chosen pattern will be to develop the aircraft by having it financed both by the United States and its

---

26 At least for Western aircraft.
27 Which of course seems redundant given the power of this weapon [GIA 14].

allies – in exchange of a return for local industries, but mostly, according to three main versions:

– F-35A for the *US Air Force* and allied air forces, requiring a traditional takeoff and landing. Initially, this version was supposed to replace F-16 and A-10;

– The short takeoff and vertical landing F-35B, which requires a specific setup (movable tailpipe and base exhaust, the volume of which requires a reduction in the size of the ammunition bay). It would be used by the *US Marine Corps* and the British *Royal Air Force* and, hypothetically, by the Italian and Spanish navy as a replacement to *Harrier* GR9 and AV-8B used by these forces;

– F-35C, meant to board on *US Navy* aircraft carriers as a replacement for F/A-18C *Hornet*, resulting in the necessity of a greater wingspan and a greater mass, just like all onboard aircrafts.

In addition to these obstacles, which are directly linked to aeronautics engineering, other difficulties emerge, which are linked to the "revolutionary" representations of future technologies. It is the case for radar stealth, which requires a specific design as well as the onboarding of weapons in the hold[28]. It is mostly the case for the machine's combat system, which allows data fusion coming from all onboard or remote sensors – information conveyed by an AWACS via, for example, data link – and to represent them through helmet viewing. In this way, a pilot would acquire a new degree of situational consciousness, unprecedented in history, as he would literally see through the cockpit, wherever he looks. Air or ground-air threats, fighter planes and friendly positions, position of supply ships and any other useful data would be represented in a similar way to *Google Glass* technology. Moreover, the pilot would have very powerful sensors. The sole AESA (*Active Electronically Scanned Array*) radar thus shows a capacity of simultaneous air–air and air–ground modes; it is more discrete, has electronic jamming, communication and also hacking capacities [HEN 13c]. The logistics of the machine must be integrated, thus allowing those in charge of its maintenance to be aware, in real-time, of the breaks and actions

---

28 Paradoxically, the fact that it is single-engined (to cut costs) requires a powerful engine located at the very back of the machine in order to leave enough space for the hold. While doing so, the infrared stealth of F-35 should be one of the weakest of all existing combat machines...

to take on the machine – the management of logistics stocks of the whole air fleet being correlated to the same system.

Yet, the promises of F-35, whose initial operational capability dates back to 2015 in the *Marines*, might never be kept due to the very breadth of the challenges assigned to industrials and to costs, which make JSF the most expensive military program of all time. The difficulties facing the design of F-35, regarding the platform or the combat systems, are such that the result was much criticised in literature [HEN 14c]. From a dynamics point of view, it is the less manoeuvring Western combat aircraft since the 1970s. The enemy's extended outreach engagement deriving from data fusion must compensate for this deficit, but the software, which is of more than 22 million code lines, is not fully written – and it is in a language which dates back to the 1980s, which is now only marginally mastered by programmers. Other problems are linked to the computing power[29], the representation of information[30] or to technical deficits of the platform itself[31], or also to its armament – so that it is considered as unable to replace A-10.

Mostly, the vision of an aircraft presented as information-dependent and not as information-attractive is contradictory to the very rationalities of strategy. Firstly, in some aspects, the aircraft is information-vulnerable. The complexity of its combat system is such that it could easily be altered by opponents – or by a technician[32] – even before taking off, which reverts back to Clausewitz's concepts of warfare as a dialectic of opposing wills and to the laws of reciprocal actions. In addition, if not connected to the system of logistics management and maintenance for 48 h – a system which is also quite vulnerable – the system must be reset through a heavy procedure, which could even imply a return to factories. If we can accept to take such a

---

29 Missile approach warning sensors must thus provide the pilot with night vision, but during trials at sea in 2014, the power of computer processing still seemed insufficient to reach this goal.

30 At the end of 2015, engineers were testing the third generation of helmets, but their mass was such that an ejection would be fatal to a pilot of less than 63 kg, which forced the US Air Force to change its logics of human resources management.

31 Since the beginning of 2016, US Air Force thus still recommends not to fly near a storm due to explosion risks. The solidity of engines and of some structural components was also questioned, here again forcing the US Air Force to give instructions on the necessity of reducing weight factors of the aircraft.

32 This is one of the reasons why the system source-codes could not be given to clients who, in order to evolve, have to either join one of the three factories building the aircraft, or call Lockheed Martin's technicians.

risk in civil aviation, we can obviously not in the context of a conflict, especially since cyber warfare has been one of the major features of RMA and *Transformation* since the beginning of the 1990s. Second, the promises of military efficiency of F-35, along with its cost, made air forces reduce the volume of their future fleet. The cost also considerably increased with time – it remains excessively hard to assess[33] – and the many of the buyer states had to reduce their target even more.

The logic according to which quality compensates a reduction in quantity, which is another mantra of RMA and of *Transformation*, is thus questioned and leads to tangible decrease in the states' freedom of strategic manoeuvre – where the very foundation of the use of military technologies is the increase of this freedom of manoeuvre. From this point of view, the case of the Netherlands is the most dramatic. When, in the beginning of 2000s, the plan was to buy 85 aircrafts to replace more 137 machines, a sealed budget purchase would only allow the acquisition of 37 aircrafts. In Great Britain, which is the first industrial partner for the project, the initial goal of 131 aircrafts, thus allowing the armament of two new *Queen Elizabeth* aircraft carriers, was subsequently reduced to 48. This called into question the very use of one of the two aircraft carriers, the building of which had been launched, and the contract of which had been signed. In the end, the target returned to 131 aircraft, but we can wonder about a series of costs linked to aircraft maintenance during its operational life and about the effects of these costs on the whole forces structure.

Another kind of discussion has to do with the *Revolution in Business Affairs* (RBA), which focuses on the generalization of the implementation of civilian technologies in the military (COTS – *Cost Off the Shelf Technologies*) [MUR 00]. It would have allowed a collapse in equipment costs while facilitating their conception, due to the dual nature of information and network technologies. The evolution also implied a redefinition of the relations between private and military sectors based on a greater interaction or even a partial privatization of a series of processes, specifically logistic processes, in order to reduce operational costs. Retrospectively, these different promises were only partially kept. The perception of economic advantages tied to RMA does exist, between logics of technicization/upgrade of the armies,

---

33 Particularly because much information given by the US Air Force or the manufacturer mentions the aircraft without its engine. In the beginning of 2015, the estimates were of a unit price ranging from $120 to $150 million per piece, whereas the goal set in 2001 was a price of around $50 million.

managerial/research vision of scale economies and the search for a positioning on the global market (meaning, an industrial *hubris*). It would thus allow to implement new production models such as *agile manufacturing* [GON 00] – the thematic of which is extended by questions inherent to 3D printing – or to bring out transposable innovations in the civilian sphere.

For some time, this reasoning seems to have been questioned. In the beginning of the 1990s, the reduction of defense budgets occurred along with the legitimization of a RBA in which civilian innovations would rather "pull" the military than they would thrive on it, as was the case during the Cold War. However, research conducted within the context of what, a few years ago, would have been called "*After-next* RMA", seem to confirm the reasoning of RBA. This would be the case for some applications in biotechnology or nanotechnology, or also applications deriving from a more thorough knowledge of lasers (surgery, communications, etc.). Yet, this logic is amended to become more interactive. In this way, the increase in budgets following 9/11 (for the United States) and following the invasion of Crimea (for several European countries) implied a new balance in the relations between civilian and military industrials – specifically due to a greater use of technologies linked to network security. In fact, if the use of COTS has become a true slogan in the 1990s, we must note that military applications require adaptation processes, which are such that specific equipment can cost less. Beyond this, if the typical example of COTS used in armament programs were the computer and its components, today, this kind of software tends to become an additional cost factor, restricting the impact of savings on *hardware*.

To some degree, the model of RMA also requires the privatization of some of the functions that initially come out of the armed forces. In its attempt to cut costs, RBA also gathered a series of speeches justifying the externalization towards private companies not only of basic logistic functions (supplies, infrastructure maintenance, diverse services), of equipment maintenance (up to operation theaters), but also of sovereign functions, from base security to combat. This question was subject to many publications to which we will not return [SIN 03, MCF 15]. Nevertheless, here, we must note that the promises of externalization and engagement of contractors were kept with some difficulties. The concept, which was promoted in the beginning of the 2000s, consisted of compensating for the weaknesses of "transformed" army masses with the support, expensive but limited in time, of private military entities. If, indeed, the daily costs turned out to be considerable[34], this structuring between armies and contractors was yet pulled down by the underestimation of the duration of operations: RMA's rationality is that of decisive operations, whereas the confrontation with reality in Iraq or Afghanistan showed engagements over several years.

If the use of contractors leads to serious ethical debates – especially fed by many exactions – it also raises the question of the capacity of "transformed" armed forces to carry out their missions autonomously. In 2012, in Afghanistan, American figures show that 110,404 contractors were deployed, against only 65,800 soldiers. However, right after the end of combat operations in Iraq as well as in Afghanistan, many actors of a sector which, for a time, was blooming – Blackwater even created its own combat vehicles – went bankrupt and are thus no more immediately available if needed. While coveting a greater accounting efficiency, managerial logic thus encountered the natural dynamics of operations and ended up reducing the strategic efficiency of force systems, through the reduction of their freedom of action or by its counter-productivity in counter-insurrectional engagements. Beyond this, if the problematic nature of contractors was underestimated in the effects it could cause and if we can doubt that they will again be engaged with as much importance, its managerial model also established itself. The information dependency on commercial software for many Western armies also implies a dependency to the sector's large private businesses [KRI 13]. It is the case down to their commandment systems, where there is a reduction in the biodiversity of software types on which states conceive their systems [DE 04].

RMA and *Transformation* thus require practice changes in the strategy of means, yet they do not appear as completely disruptive. The weight of factors such as technological culture or variables linked to economic policy still play a significant role in decision-making. In this way, when a program on new aerial refuelling tanker aircraft was to be launched, and after a first rejection of Boeing due to fraud, the choice of the *US Air Force*, in 2008, went to the European A330MRTT, which was at the time about to be implemented and appeared more technically fit to an American strategic position focusing on

---

34 In 2007, according to the US House of Representatives, a "mere" contractor cost $600 per day but, based on a contract reviewed by the Project on Government Oversight, a senior manager was paid $1,075, a manager was paid $945 and an operator $815. Comparatively, a single sergeant was paid $83–85 a day (depending on his seniority), versus $170 if he was married. As a general commanding operations at the time, David Petraeus was paid $493.

the Pacific. After Boeing protested, which triggered the freeze of the purchase process, a new request for proposals was launched as saw the final victory of Boeing, with an aircraft whose first refuelling trial only took place in the beginning of 2016. In this case, the main change in choice was not the adaptation to the strategic environment nor the technological maturity but, just as in the 1970s and 1980s, the choice favoring a national manufacturer. The standard analysis charts on the subject thus remain relevant [IRO 04]. This reasoning prevails in American as well as French network-centered systems, which does not exclude the possibility of transnational collaborations (such as Thales Raytheon Systems in the field of radars), or even of some external purchases (Thales Rifleman radios for the US Army[35]).

---

35 Here in conjunction with purchases of radios manufactured by Harris Corporation. The sources of supply thus became more diverse and imply a return on investment in the American economy.

4

Understanding (1): Piercing the Fog of War in Fluid Spaces

Conducting a critical review of the RMA/*Transformation* amounts to examining the relationship of these documents to the nature of war – which we have done up until now – and the prime components of war, the organs that make it a living phenomenon. In this regard, "revolution" is primarily a techno-strategic confrontation between several historical constants that it hopes to at least disperse, if not totally dissolve. The first constant is the Clausewitzian concept of "fog of war": the multitude of actors and their actions and the diversity of their abilities and intentions, from the tactical level to the political level, creates a complex, chaotic and fleeting situation, which is as difficult to understand cognitively as it is to understand practically. Following this, the second constant is an uncertainty and a deficit of structural ontological predictability. This complexity generates errors and inefficiency for armies as much affected by the sociology of organizations as by an adversary who, by definition, seeks to destroy them [COU 11, BAR 08]. The concept of "friction" takes into account the difficulty of operating in a contentious environment: "*Everything is very simple in war, but the simplest thing is difficult*". The combination of these constants, interconnected with matters of life and death, is specific to military operations and can be summarized by A. Wavell: "*war is disorder; it can only be that. There are so many unintended and unpredictable events in this uncertain business – a timing change that could not be provided, a message that goes astray, a chief killed at a critical time... – that even the best plan is rarely uneventful... the lesson is that it must be aware of and to appeal as much as possible against the uncertainties of war*[1].

Thus, this non-linearity characterizes war and its ontological conduct [BEY 92, LAW 14], raising the issue of an adaptation that takes the form of cognitively reconquering the environment and the stakeholders that operate within that environment. In a similar framework, the classically opposing response, which would distinguish the best officers, is articulated around two other Clausewitzian concepts. On the one hand, the *coup d'oeil* allows us to understand a given situation based on experience, observation and instinct. The *coup d'œil* corresponds to concepts of observation and – in an even more significant way, because it appears as the fabrication of cognition taking into account a set of complex variables – orientation in the OODA (Observation, Orientation, Decision, Action) loop of J. Boyd [OSI 06]. On the other hand, based on completed tasks, the "genius" of the military leader should allow him to find the most relevant solution that takes into account the nature of the adversary while seeking to manage resources or their own losses and thus be at once effective and efficient[2]. According to Boyd, the concept corresponds to the orientation and the decision phases, showing by effect of transparency that *coup d'œil* and genius are, at least conceptually, intimately linked[3]. These last concepts are the products of operations that appear just as fluid, fleeting and uncertain as war, so that even the greatest strategists have failed in their career.

In this is the framework, the mission of the upholders of the RMA and the *Transformation* consists of systematizing *coup d'œil* and genius, seeking in some way to smooth out what is non-linear and render the chaos intelligible. From "Kadesh to Kandahar" [EVA 03], this is certainly every officer's task but in this case the aim is to "bend" the nature of war to "transformed" armies by injecting a maximum of certainty into an environment that is by definition uncertain. The rationale is to control, cognitively at first, a phenomenon whose nature theoretically is uncontrollable and which tends, for Clausewitz, to rise to extremes. It consists of succeeding in mastering it "from the inside", or on

---

1 [WAV 46, p. 79].

2 A principle of war to which we will return *infra*.

3 This is not necessarily true in practice. Understanding a situation does not imply *per se* that appropriate decisions will be made to face it. On the contrary, the fact of poorly or not understanding a situation can be a determining factor in certain victories.

the level of its conduct, and not by the deflection that the political level naturally engages in for most of the operations, most often giving them a limited scope. This rationale intends to smooth out the natural differences between officers whose training is certainly identical, but whose human nature logically implies variations in the quality of their decision making. It consists of "augmenting" the person by seeking, ultimately, to make them a brilliant tactician or strategist by limiting the risk of errors they are susceptible to commit – an essential element when we consider the American origin of the RMA[4] – as well as searching for a means of optimizing their actions. The reality, however, is more complex.

4.1. Strategy of fluid spaces

Suggesting that the chaos and uncertainty of the battlefield can be controlled does not represent a *de facto* conceptual rift in terms of the history of the art of war: all military history, that of the command, tactics, strategy or even officer training, demonstrates a tendency towards this aim. The revolutionary nature of the propositions on this subject in the RMA/ *Transformation* stems from an investigation into the certainty of mastering the chaos not by a human-organizational intermediary – as was the case up to that point – but by a technological intermediary. The combination of sensors and networks plays a determining role in this vision, but the promises of the 1990s, founded on technological progress, must be placed in context with previous attempts. The RMA is not alone from the point of view of the history of technologies, as radically isolated from previous breakthroughs, but is the direct result of the technological history of the art of war itself[5].

---

4 One of the characteristics of American political culture, which stems from the pre-Independence period, is a mistrust of decision-makers likely to commit errors and drag the country into oppression. It translates by extension to a technological culture where humans are the source of errors.

5 From this point of view, it is interesting to note that the current approaches of the RMA show a lack of appreciation for the dynamic of the latter in time. The authors too often characterize themselves by considering their subject in a more synchronous than diachronous perspective. By doing this, they confine it to an approach affected by previous experiences, but not sufficiently influenced by more recent experiences. However, doctrinal publications do show a certain interest for immediate experiences [OHA 98].

4.1.1. *The fluid and the solid*

This technological archaeo-history, however, also demonstrates that the drive to control the chaos of war is expressed in what Laurent Henninger calls "fluid spaces" as opposed to "solid spaces" [HEN 12a, HEN 12b, HEN 13a, HEN 13b]. For Henninger, military environments, in the geographical sense of the term, can be described by these two ideal types, which present interfaces. "Fluid" environments require the appropriate technologies for their occupation. They refer to aerial, maritime, spatial and cyber spaces and constitute *mediums* traversed by power fluxes, which move relatively quickly, so no "occupation" in the military – or human – sense is possible. Comparatively, "solid" environments are more complex. If they belong to a variety of terrestrial domains, they are also "viscous" because of the presence of populations and the development of the flux of power is slow there. A comparison between these two categories of environments as ideal types can be represented as given in Table 4.1.

	Solid space	Fluid space
Human presence	Frequent, even systematic	Impossible or of very short duration
Relation to speed	Spaces of relative slowness: speed of progression on foot or in vehicle	Spaces of relative speed: from a few knots to supersonic or electronic speeds.
Relation to movement	Spaces of permanence	Spaces of transition: movement is a condition of survival.
Restrictions on movement	High, on average: the topography is itself an obstacle.	Low, on average: movements can be made between two, even three dimensions.
Military consequences of movement	Increase of options, from raid to occupation	Restriction of options, limited permanence
Relation to political-military control	Possibility of domination	Possibility of control
Polarity of the strategy	Facilitation of the defensive	Facilitation of the offensive
Necessity of technology for the investment of a space, life within it and combat	Not essential	Essential: an aerial or naval strategy cannot be conceived without planes or boats

Relation to knowledge necessary for its investment	Low	High: importance of navigation techniques, knowledge of points of reference
Segregation between civil and military spaces	Generally high from a historical point of view ("go on campaign"), now progressively lower (urban combat)	Generally low: spaces have the coexistence of civil and military actors
Examples	Countryside, mountains, urban zones, forests, straits, etc.	Surface and/or depths of seas, sky, space, deserts, railroads, roads, etc.

Table 4.1. *Comparison of the characteristics of fluid and solid spaces (source: [HEN 15b])*

More specifically, it is in the development of the aerial forces where the technological roots of the RMA/*Transformation* may be sought, since the aerial environment lends itself well to the clarification/rationalization of chaos in military operations. In fact, in Great Britain, the setup of a network of radars, regional command centers and aerial bases at the end of the 1930s constitutes a seminal form, with a simple rationale, which was only reproduced with more sophistication thereafter. With the arrival of this system, a patrol of planes randomly manoeuvring in the sky and searching for the destruction of eventual targets was no longer the first alert. That process did not systematize surveillance since patrols do not permanently cover all sectors, compared to radar, whose correct placement on the territory allows us to integrally cover its approaches [DE 11]. The information gathered – approximate distance, estimated direction, volume of the assailant – are transmitted by telephone to the regional command centers, where they are marked on a map by means of symbols as they arrive. From above, in the operations room, those responsible for air defense have a representation of the tactical situation and can command the take-off of fighters to intercept enemy formations, all the while modulating the volumes engaged in order to have reserves to face any surprises.

4.1.2. SAGE, the first network-centric system

The logic is to reduce the uncertainty while organizing the chaos of military operations – at this time, the one of air battles, not between pilots –

with direct results. However rudimentary it may seem to us today, if the C3I (Command, Control, Communications, Intelligence) system used did not win the Battle of Britain on its own, it definitely contributed. However, it is in the United States that the concept would be pushed furthest. As of 1949, less than 10 years after the first radars entered into operational service, the threat of a surprise attack by the USSR, recently armed with nuclear weapons, led the US Air Force (USAF) to use the work on what would be the first digital computer to implement the SAGE (Semi-Automatic Ground Environment) network [EDW 95, EDW 97]. Several technologies were already available: radars, interception aircraft, first generation air defense missiles. The true problem was in the articulation of all of these systems – or rather, what would today be called a "system of systems". The USAF did not have the experience of the British Royal Air Force in matters of aerial battle management. On top of this, the American territory was much larger than that of Great Britain and the potential advances of the Soviet Air Force suggested a diversification of its penetration routes: the transarctic route would not necessarily be the one used by Soviet bombers in the future.

The Massachussetts Institute of Technology (MIT) offered the first hints of a solution. In December 1949, George Valley – the father of the radar bomb sight system – met the members of project *Whirlwind* and its director, Jay Forrester. The program at MIT dated back to 1944. Supported by the US Navy, it designed an automated system that not only modeled the flight performance of new planes but also served as a central hub for flight simulation systems, which would serve to increase the speed of training of future pilots. Nonetheless, after the war, the budget allocations were reduced to the strict minimum and the program was no longer considered as important – even though advances in electronics had been considered essential just a few years before [CER 83]. However, that would change: Valley knew that a Soviet surprise attack, necessarily huge, would require a tremendous capacity for information processing. The capabilities of the *Whirlwind*, a digital (not analog) computer, would help. In a few days, Valley and Forrester hatched a plan: myriad radar systems linked via telephone lines to information processing centers acting as command centers, where orders would be sent out to effectors, planes and missiles.

Theoretically, the system was simple, but in practice, it was definitely more complex: it consisted of discerning civilian and military planes, friends and enemies, identifying them and noting the direction, altitude, speed; all that information for hundreds of planes and in real time. Once an attack had been detected and confirmed, it also consisted of alerting the political and military authorities or the civil defense. This was more problematic, especially because the mission assigned to the system was much larger: it also consisted of managing air battles. It required integrating other parameters, ranging from the weather to the type and number of interceptors (planes or missiles) available for each base, all the while taking into account their operational specificities and their tactical contributions. Until the intervention of a human, the system must also allow for an automatic guidance of defense vectors. This aerial battle must also be able to take place in a nuclear environment – not only due to the probability of enemy breakthroughs but also the allocation of nuclear heads to most American SAM batteries – which requires the resilience of the system. The program was a political priority and G. Valley headed it from 1952 to 1958, the year of the first deployment of the system, which would be fully operational in 1961 – the last one being used up to 1983.

SAGE was a true system of systems. Each control and command center housed two IBM FSQ-7 computers, directly issued from project *Whirlwind*, with a total mass of 270 tonnes and counting 58,000 vacuum tubes. The system had incredible power for the time: 75,000 instructions/second[6]. The computers were redundant by the time the system had to operate permanently. They were installed on the second level of a windowless bunker on 2 m thick walls, which made it possible to work in times of war. The third level was the regional command center, which included a giant screen showing the data. On the fourth level, over 2,000 m^2, were display consoles, telephone equipment and sectors reserved for identification. On the ground floor, the independent generating station was installed – the computers required 3 MW of power – as well as the production of water and the indispensable air conditioning units. At the console, the operator had a light gun – a technology developed specifically for this occasion[7]. *Life* magazine described the atmosphere of the control rooms with science fiction rhetoric: the computers "*summarize and present the data so clearly that men of the Air Force who manage SAGE can sit quietly inside these rooms to the*

---

6 As a comparison, the AMD FX-8150 processor used in an office PC exceeds 30 million operations per second.

7 It would make a fortune for the creators of arcade video games in the 1980s and 1990s.

strange light, facing their console, their minds free to take the necessary human judgments on the fight – when and where to fight[8].

SAGE had 25 of these sites, and the Canadian base in Goose Bay became the 26th when North American Air Defense Command (NORAD) was set up in 1957[9]. The different sites did not develop in the same ways. Some were set aside in the mid-1960s, with the final two still functioning in 1983. The effort was colossal. The development and construction of SAGE required the current equivalent of $90 billion, not including the radar systems and interceptors. Nevertheless, this segment represents only one part of the North American system of aerial defense. MIT also played a central role in the creation and expansion of the DEW Line (Distant Early Warning), a chain of 63 radar stations equipped with FPS-19 and mainly installed in the Arctic. Completing the Pinetree (39 radars) and Mid-Canada (90 radars) radar lines, located further south, the DEW Line was built in 2 years and 8 months, starting in 1954, in difficult weather conditions. The DEW Line itself represented an extraordinary technological effort, notably including some completely automated radar stations, others run by only three men and the main stations also serving as relays. The necessity of transmitting a large volume of information also required the setting up of communications reflected through the atmosphere (troposcatters). As of 1985, the DEW Line would be renamed and a number of stations closed, while others modernized with the installation of FPS-117 radar systems.

The *DEW Line*, a binational Canadian–American system, would also be completed by aerial early warning above the Atlantic and Pacific approaches to the United States. Three offshore detection platforms, the Texas Towers, were positioned in the Atlantic from 1958 to 1963. Likewise, US Navy patrols using old destroyers as radar pickets were also deployed, as well as the squadrons of WV-2 (later redesignated EC-121D Warning Star) of the US Navy, starting in 1956[10]. The complexity of the system was not without politico-strategic consequences. Paul N. Edwards saw it as a "closed world". For the author, it consisted of representing a huge complexity in an abstract manner while totally "locking up" the aerial space by representing it in a

---

8 [LIF 57, p. 62].

9 The center was buried at a depth of 210 m. The complex was completed in 1963 and remained in service until 2006.

10 The machine entered into services in the US Navy in 1953. The US Air Force only acquired its proper advanced early warning aircraft a bit later.

rational manner, setting aside political questions. Presented as a strategic defense system, SAGE was actually an extension of tactics, especially since the system was not without faults and not all intended targets were reached. The system, says Paul N. Edwards, was first and foremost a technological narration: a story prolonging itself on the possibility of a Soviet surprise attack with bombers [EDW 95, EDW 97]. In this sense, it includes the larger story of making the United States (and Canada) secure through an integrated defense system, a plan that was also proposed on the other side of the Atlantic in continental Europe, through NADGE (NATO Air Defense Ground Environment), which functions similarly to SAGE.

However, there was also an account that considerably embellished the military situation in several regards. First, in 1957, the USSR demonstrated its capacity to launch attacks over intercontinental distances using ballistic missiles, not bombers. Moscow also concentrated more on its missile forces than on its bombers, feeding another "nuclear panic"[11] at the start of the 1960s around the question of a *Missile gap*. Air defense batteries (Surface-to-Air Missiles – SAM) and radar systems put in place in the framework of SAGE were totally powerless to this threat[12]. At the time, the regional centers in which the network computers were installed and the operations rooms were located on aerial bases of Strategic Air Command (SAC), with the exception of the Canadian center in Goose Bay, which was cut into rock. The consequence was, despite the installation of centers in gigantic concrete cubes, a real vulnerability: the SAC bases would be among the first to be targeted by a Soviet attack. The system was also not very resilient. First of all, it relied on the national telephone line, whose cables and switching stations were vulnerable to electromagnetic pulses resulting from nuclear explosions. It also revealed itself to be quickly outstripped: the 58,000 vacuum tubes in each center were surpassed by the arrival of the transistor less than 10 years later.

Beyond that, the system showed itself to be extremely rigid: automation was still only in its early stages and the difficulty of accounting for all of the tactical scenarii possible in the programming of responses added to the system failures. In reality, the system automated virtually nothing. It became

---

11 The term "nuclear panic" makes reference to the term "naval panic", used in the 19th and 20th Centuries to describe the British reaction in the face of the rise of competing marine powers. These "panics" are equally exploited by the Royal Navy to take advantage of a surplus of resources.

12 For a summary of the debates at the time, see [BAU 09].

a system to represent adverse lines of attack; the orders and coordinates of targets ended up being given by voice command when they should have been able to be directly transmitted to the cockpits or launch the SAM BOMARC and *Nike-Hercules* developed and deployed to protect American territory. However, no sign of "parallel procedures" is revealed in the exercise reports. Officially, everything was going well and, if needed, the exercises were adjusted not to simulate the reality but to account for the limits of the system, which it was to preserve. In fact, there was a combination of varied interests to conserve the system:

– many scientists worked on the complex systems, establishing the bases of modern information technologies and giving an advance to the United States, knowing that the probability of the success of the military project was low. The same type of reflex was observed with the program for the spatial antimissile strategic defense initiative: though technically impossible, it permitted the injection of considerable sums into American Research and Development (R&D). Incidentally, not without industrial benefits, especially once they led to the current designs of portable computers;

– the system was a real lever of economic policy: with $90 billion injected, it constituted a surreptitious form of Keynesianism in a country that rejected it. Incidentally, for a US Air Force that was still young (the service did not become independent until 1945), it was out of the question to recognize the inefficiency of such a costly system;

– also for the USAF, the system constituted a concrete demonstration of the role played by the defense of American territory – a factor of legitimacy and thus permanence – while the years of the 1960s were also the years of Vietnam, which saw a crumbling of the legitimacy of the armed forces in the eyes of the general public. Likewise, the system justified the maintenance of several squadrons, armed with fighter planes – or the archetype of the combat aircraft, so important for the identity of the Air Force – of the Air Defense Command;

– politically speaking, the system responded to the anxiety, both political and social, of nuclear war. Objectively speaking, it responded little and poorly – the nuclear triad is, in fact, the best response – but SAGE was an example of a defensive system with a semiotic value, not only regarding the internal opinion but also the international opinion, including the Soviets.

As it so happens, SAGE incorporated a series of other innovations for the direct consequences on the processes of informationalization of armies, also in fluid spaces. The appearance of the system occurred while aerial defense had seen a small revolution with the appearance of detection systems on the effectors themselves. The British Spitfire was guided to a given zone by the operator at an air defence control center in a logic called GCI (Ground Controlled Interception); the eyes of the pilot then took over to precisely localize the target. But in the 1950s, this rationality of the *killer* transferred to the *hunter-killer*: we entered into a logic of GCA (Ground Controlled Approach) where the volume of the aerial space that a plane could search was incomparably more important. Moreover, the surface-to-air missile – the first true "killer robot" to refer to the fashionable terminology – could become a reality[13]. The gain of military productivity was radical but was only allowed by miniaturization. In fact, as we have seen, radar was not new and ground detection stations had been equipped since the Second World War. This was also the case for war ships. But these deployments required space to install a material otherwise excessive in electric energy – many factors implied until the 1950s, that the installation of radar systems would be limited to certain combat planes[14], which would disappear as soon as radar systems adapted for standard planes appeared – not, incidentally, without difficulties[15].

4.2. Fluidifying global spaces?

SAGE may have responded to a worse anxiety than nuclear war for Americans: that of a responsibility for security at all times and in all places, which marked the end of the possibility of an isolationist withdrawal. By positioning themselves as "leaders of the free world", they had to accept that responsibility and turn towards a logic of dispelling frictions, lifting military

13 Contrary to the rocket, the missile is, by definition, guided. The first missiles tested in 1946 used ground guidance, so the movements of the missile toward the target were effected via a radio command, the human assuring the information computation between the information (produced by a radar on the ground) and the action to distance on the missile steering. The solution, while remaining ill-adapted to attacks by saturation and vulnerable to jamming, proved to be considerably less efficient than the terminal guidance of the missile by radar or infrared.

14 This refers to the night attack planes, the "missing link" between the pursuit fighter and the all-weather fighter jet of the Cold War. They were larger (authorizing the increase of mass due to radar as well as its positioning), twin-engined (with among others for effect a larger production of electric energy) and two-place (the navigator is charged with using the radar).

15 A number of pilots who demonstrated the fire control radar of their F-86 Sabre considered that the mass reduced the manoeuvrability of their plane. In fact, the first reactors they were equipped with it were relatively unpowerful.

uncertainty in virtually all theaters on the planet. As Edwards noted, SAGE (and, more broadly, all automated systems) is the sign of a doubly closed world. Closed from within – a question of protecting against aggression – and shut to the rest of the world because of its techno-political commitment, the strategies developed allowed them to streamline this process through the representation of an electronic intermediary. In fact, the principles underlying the development of SAGE would spread to fluid spaces. It is, first of all and following a very similar design, the Ballistic Missile Early Warning System (BMEWS), which is still in service and which must detect all ballistic launches not only against the United States but the whole world. In 1991, commentators marvelled at seeing *Patriot* missiles fired against Iraqi *Scud* missiles, knowing that they had been detected by DSP satellites[16] – which directly contributed to the social perception of a RMA.

The logic was pushed much further in the 1950s and in the context of the Cold War. It became a matter of focusing the development of interception on ballistic missiles instead of bombers. The challenge was huge: other than the issue of detection, it included intercepting devices that were much faster than planes and had significantly more problematic interception profiles. If the United States was increasing the number of projects [BAU 09], then the culmination in terms of sophistication was the Strategic Defense Initiative (SDI) launched in 1983 by Ronald Reagan, which partially relied on spatial interception through an automated system that included lasers. In all cases, this required developing a robust processing power and drawing on the physical sciences. These capacities were indeed provided by the industry, but the programs' reliability was soon questioned. The fact is that fluid spaces are shared by both friendly and enemy forces, the threats are diversified, and applying a strategy to manage available resources involves being able to discriminate effectively [SLA 13]. The problem was not easily solved in the area of antimissile defense, nor did it fare much better in the field of air defense, where the tactical order is just as complicated. Often the only answer was to delineate kill boxes that segregate flight spaces, although this limited the flexibility of air forces.

---

16 Defense Support Program. From 1970 and 2007, the program allowed launching 23 satellites, positioned in geosynchronous orbits and capable of detecting the infrared flash of a missile launch. The program was preceded by MiDAS (Missile Defense Alarm System), with 12 satellites launched starting in 1960 and was followed by the SBIRS (Space-Based Infra-Red System) and Space Tracking and Surveillance System (STSS).

4.2.1. *Figures of the fluidification of aerospatial spaces*

Since the 1950s, the idea of advanced aerial detection equipment capable of spotting opposing movements and directing interceptors to them has been achieved by the American navy and the USAF with different versions of the EC-121 *Warning Star*[17]. The logic differed from SAGE in that the system was naturally mobile: contrary to the heavy network of air defense, a plane could be sent anywhere in the world to establish a "translucent bubble" in the air space. At the end of the 1960s, the design of the early warning E-3 *Sentry* AWACS (Airborne Warning and Control System) responded to the same logics but radicalized them[18]. The new equipment, introduced in 1977, was an airborne radar with which operators directed air battles. Although the firing orders given to pilots of fighter planes were left to air controllers who followed precise rules of engagement, the system also included a certain degree of automation. Once equipped with a data link – one of the products borrowed from the NADGE design[19] – the role of the air command post could be secured by performances far superior to those of the EC-121, above land or water, with a much greater range and the ability to detect smaller planes. Throughout their service, the radar performances of the E-3 increased as the search for an ever finer detection granulometry continued.

In the 1990s and 2000s, with the deployment of the *Link-16*, fighter jets dependent on AWACS automatically transmitted a certain number of results: fuel levels, weapon types and the number of shots fired, allowing the operators to make the most appropriate tactical decisions. The *Link-16* also transmitted AWACS radar images to the fighter jets: planes could turn off their own radar to carry out actions more discretely in an electromagnetic sense. The spread of the data link to a growing number of platforms (aerial, naval, terrestrial) allowed AWACS to act as an air command post for search and rescue missions or air/antimissile defense tactics, sharing information with SAM batteries or ships armed with anti-aircraft or antimissile systems. Used by the United States (32 aircraft), the E-3 was also bought by NATO (18), Saudi Arabia (5), Great Britain (7), France (4) and Japan[20]. Other types

---

17 However, it had several limitations linked to the capacity to process signals. The detection of planes flying slowly or in close proximity to the ground proved difficult [MOM 03].

18 Notably with in-flight refuelling, which facilitated expeditionary deployments.

19 The *Link-1*, developed in the 1950s, allowed the exchange of data between air control centers. The same logic would be used with the BADGE (Base Air Defense Ground Environment) destined for Japanese bases.

20 Four models of a modified version.

of planes were also bought by other states as the computerized management of aerial battles became a techno-strategic development norm seen as an inherent source of military efficiency – even down to the terminology, which classified the planes in the category of "force multipliers"[21].

Beyond air strategy, the rationales for networking forces were also employed in the historically complex field of naval strategy – another domain falling under fluid spaces [PAL 05]. In the US Navy, after World War II, there was an innovation by the CO (Central Operations), which allowed all of the information coming from sensors to be centralized in a single compartment of a ship where the appropriate orders could be given to all weapon operators. As it happens, the centralization of information and its interpreters – the operators – provided the commander with the most complete view possible of a given situation [WYL 14]. Also in the United States since the mid-1950s, it consisted of sharing information gathered by different types of sensors on different types of ships, since fleets used ships that were each specialized in a certain type of combat (anti-aircraft, anti-submarine, and the aircraft carrier being the main anti-ship weapon). The data links addressed the sharing of information and allowed a fleet composed of disparate elements to benefit from a common view of a given situation (common operating picture), which allowed for a unity of action.

By doing so, it decreased the friction that results from the presence of a large number of participants in a given action and reduces the risk that the fog of war will appear. Actually, in the naval case, this also means optimizing the "protection bubbles" (anti-aircraft, anti-submarine) offered by them. This logic calls for creating not only increasingly powerful – and secure[22] – data links, but also new types of integrated combat systems that exemplify the philosophy behind the SAGE system in the naval domain, albeit with much larger specifications and aims. These systems rely substantially on informatics and, like in air strategy, try to account for the

---

21 That is the case for these systems: the Swedish *Erieye* (in service, or about to be, in Sweden, Pakistan, Brazil, Thailand); the Israeli *Phalcon* (Israel, Chile, Singapore, Italy); the American *Wedgetail* (Australia, Turkey, South Korea); the E-2C/D *Hawkeye* (built into aircraft carriers and in service in the United States, France, Japan, Mexico and Egypt); the KJ-2000 (China); the KJ-200 (China, Pakistan); the A-50 (Russia, India).

22 The question is important. If the British had protected data links during the battle of Jutland (1916), they would have gained precious time and probably won the battle. All the same, because there was a risk of bugging by the German fleet, the instructions expressly mention the use of visual signaling when the ships were close.

possibility of saturation attacks with anti-ship missiles. To do this, the systems were developed to integrate all sensors and effectors (missiles, canons), so as to offer the operators the clearest possible view of their tactical environment.

In the case of the *Aegis* system, operational since the 1980s, the system includes extremely powerful SPY-1 radar and completely automated terminal defense systems (*Phalanx* canons were given their own radar systems and electro-optic fire controls). Based on the tactical situation at any given moment, the system also provides officers with action options, calculated by accounting for the rules of engagement and the recommendations of naval doctrine. To deal with a saturation attack, the *Aegis* combat system also has a totally automated mode that can fire the correct type of weapon at the most opportune moment without any human intervention. It can also slave other combat systems in a carrier group with intervening data links, commanding the launch of weapons positioned on other ships. Today, this system, which evolved incrementally, is equipped on most large American surface combat ships[23] as well as foreign navies[24]. The power of this combat system's radar even allows some ships whose software has been adjusted to engage in anti-ballistic or anti-satellite missions and occupy different levels of fluid spaces. With *Aegis* as an ideal type, most of naval powers have developed their own combat system – that of the *Mistral* landing ships to be sold to Russia is rightly one of the concerns about the sale – which all respond to similar logics.

4.2.2. *Fluidification by reticulation*

The culmination of the quest for the greatest situational awareness in fluid spaces is the reticulation of platforms operating in different strata. In fact, it has been in construction since the 1960s – long before the idea of an RMA – with the *Link-1* connecting the NADGE radar centers, the first data links in the naval and air domain. Since then, the logic has been largely expanded with systems like the *Link-11* and the *Link-16* – the replacement of

---

23 This includes 22 cruisers of the *Ticonderoga* class and more than 60 destroyers of the *Arleigh Burke* class. Incidentally, this system has a redundancy: each group of aircraft carriers is usually escorted by a cruiser and one or two destroyers. If *Aegis* breaks down on one ship, the second can take over.

24 On 1 February 2016, the system was sold to Japan, South Korea, Spain, Australia and Norway.

the former, the *Link-22*, is in development. The consequences of designing the first combat systems that were network-centric on command and control modes are as important as they are advanced. Its first application to the concept's fluid spaces is above all imposed by the logic proper to deterrence and nuclear strategy. The "nuclear revolution" was not solely due to weapons and their vectors, the appearance of a nuclear strategy, deterrence as no longer the determining strategy development of peace but instead of the survival of strategic actors, or a sustainable modification of conduct in the international environment and the international order. It was also the origin of RMA/*Transformation*. It may be because nuclear strategy is a fluid space strategy that it adapted so well to its encounter with network logic, newly founded at the time, and the appearance of cybernetics, in such a distinctive context as the years between 1950 and 1960 [LAF 04].

Command and control derive their meaning – and their political legitimacy – from a defensive approach: for the deterrence to function, its means must be credible and able to be protected while allowing the interception of enemy strikes. However, this outlook is very theoretical due to the nature of the war: the enemy will always seek an alternative route. Managing the complexity of a battle with clearly identifiable protagonists using informatics and reasoning – and, to some extent, distancing the human aspects of the battle –is facilitated by the fluid nature of the environments in which this occurs. The impression of control is necessarily misleading because it results from a more convenient representation of a part of a given situation and its changes. Yet, seeing clearly – and understanding clearly – does not necessarily imply being able to react more appropriately. The first network-centric systems responded to technico-tactical interrogations – where is the adversary, how many enemies are there – that revealed nothing of the real political intentions, masked behind representations of the possibility of an accidental attack or a ruse. They did not reveal which strategy would be adopted: would the first wave of the attack, where we are focusing all or part of our defensive forces, be followed up – or not – by another, or several more? In many ways, these questions persist today.

Nevertheless, an attempt to apply what were seen as efficiency factors in fluid spaces to solid environments was not long in coming. In the wake of the development of SAGE, the idea of an integrated command of forces emerged. As the core of the USAF project for national air forces, it was proposed in the strategic and the general domains: the SACCS (SAC Control System) allowed the transmission of secured and authorized launch orders to all the nuclear vectors while managing the in-flight refuelling necessary for the accomplishment of bomber missions. This idea occurs largely prior to the launch of ARPANET, which linked the largest computers in the country, though not, as we frequently read, in order to offer a decisional resiliency in case of a nuclear attack, but rather to share representations and increase speeds of calculation[25]. Concretely, the origins of SACCS date back to 1949 and the replacement of telephone communications between different SAC bases with a system that combined teleprinters, telephones, UHF radios, through a computerization deemed necessary because the initial system was too slow. The system, which included capacities of calculation, representation and data links, would be constantly modernized, notably by the integration of satellite links in 1968. Six years earlier, SACCS had already connected 85 bases and its program counted more than one million lines in a particular language – JOVIAL [EDW 95, EDW 97]. The system would be replaced in 1990.

The philosophy of SACCS and SAGE would be extended to the entire American forces with the WWMCCS (World-Wide Military Command and Control System), also operational before ARPANET (and much more interconnected). It would remain in service until 1996, when it was replaced by a conceptually similar system, the Global Command and Control System (GCCS). Like SAGE, the system was fundamentally restricted by the technologies of the time and its automation was limited. The incident of the USS *Liberty*, an American spy-ship attacked by the Israelis in 1967, is tied to the faults of the WWMCCS, when priority messages ordering a rapid engagement of the ship in the zone arrived 13 hours after they were sent. Constantly modernized following the lessons of this incident, it was a global network in itself: by the end of the 1960s, for better or for worse, it allowed 160 types of computers using 30 different languages to work together. The system operated from 81 nodes which dispatched encrypted communications to action units (USAF squadrons, ships, Army units and Marines). If SACCS still essentially operated in the logic of a fluid space – it consisted of managing combat planes – the WWMCCS and the GCCS accounted for the use of ground forces. These networks – of which a part are qualified as "*Big*

---

25 The idea was put to paper in 1962 and realized in 1970. Incidentally, the TCP/IP protocol and the work in "packets" proved more important than the network itself, which used classic telephone lines that are naturally vulnerable to the electromagnetic pulses of nuclear operations.

L"[26] – are not the only ones. For example, PACCS (Post Attack Command and Control System) was designed as a communication network including planes and ground stations and which allowed the American President to retain control over nuclear forces before, during and after a nuclear attack.

These systems are at the center of the Cold War and the American doctrine of flexible response, which calls for appropriate and measured responses to each adverse action. However, to respond this way, one must not only be able to control one's own forces – and prevent an inadvertent opening of fire – but also know what is going on. That part is definitely more complex. It requires relying on a radar trace that has a certain degree of probability of actually being an enemy plane or ship observed from a zone shielded from danger, and on human observation in the heat of combat. The inherent risks of poor interpretation – overestimation or underestimation – are increased by the very nature of the environment and are consequently very real. Thirty years before its theorization by Admiral Cebrowski, this was the midst of network-centric war. Interestingly, a number of issues raised in the 1970s around these systems are the same as those found in the literature of the 1990s and 2000s. This was also an engineer's war: the centralization of decisions in the United States signals the end of the powers of initiative for commanders of large units and instates *micromanagement* – in both cases, the end of a certain form of military art. President Johnson was not within this rhetoric when he ordered that not a single bomber would be launched on Vietnam without his approval: WWMCCS allowed him to validate the propositions of targeted plans.

4.2.3. *Operating in mixed spaces: generating political effect*

That the chaos and uncertainty of the field of battle could be controlled by an electronic intermediary represented a true breakthrough in the history of the art of war and an effectively revolutionary responsibility. At best, however, it consisted of an impression of control, which was necessarily misleading because it resulted from a more convenient representation of part of a given situation and its changes. It was also a material, and therefore incomplete, representation of the enemy, whose intentions and morale are difficult to represent graphically. Even if they could be, the best

---

26 In reference to the program codification: 416L (SAGE), 474L (BMEWS), 424L (the management system of NORAD), 438L (the management system of USAF's intelligence).

representation would never be a guarantee of a sound decision of a more relevant action since the more we know, the less we understand [BET 06]. In fact, the conduct of war – because that is what is in question – is not a purely rational domain. Passion and irrationality naturally influence it (to the point that Clausewitz made this one of the features at the center of his remarkable trinity) just like the permanent presence of human error, regardless of its origin. All the same, the irrationality can be feigned: the ruse is an integral part of what Luttwak called the "paradoxical logic of strategy" [LUT 89]. In a similar framework, the analogy too frequently made to a game of chess – one of the first computerized games of "strategy" – is questionable. In chess, the adversaries are perfectly symmetrical and we can see the position and movements of the pieces in real time according to intangible rules where cheating is not allowed, all on a perfectly delineated chessboard.

Nothing resembles war less than chess, even if they seem *a priori* easily equated to operations in fluid spaces, because they are subject to the individual constraints that can be easily understood (autonomy and endurance, payloads, number and quality of weapons, ceiling, maximum immersion depth, etc.). If this is true in the most fluid spaces, it is worth noting that it is not the case as soon as the space solidifies for any reason. Close to the ground, the capacities of airborne radar are reduced by interference echoes that the data processing system must manage to clear, or else the screens may become unreadable. At sea, the same thing occurs when close to coasts or in a strait. The sub-marine space is not homogeneous, not even mentioning the sea floor. Differences of salinity or temperature have direct impacts on the sensor performances – even cancelling them out[27] – imposing a greater capacity of data processing on combat systems. At the present time, a large part of the vulnerability of spatial systems exists, from a military point of view, in an attack on ground control centers. In many ways, this is equally the case in cyber strategy, which is about attacking cables and server clusters, getting at operators or using electromagnetic pulse weapons.

In this sense, there are also "mixed spaces", interfaces, which are notably those that allow forces operating in fluid spaces to take effective action on solid spaces –where the political decision-markers that we are seeking to defeat are located. An attack plane on the ground or a navy ship launching a cruise missile does not only operate in the tactical comfort of a fluid space.

---

27 The "thermal layer" (*thermocline*) separating the warmer waters from the colder ones can thus constitute a protection for submarines.

Thus, the conversion of the action into political effects – from the moment of a strike, when a military operation is not a goal in itself but an intermediary – depends on this "combat interface". Yet, the edges of these interfaces and of the mixed spaces are not totally defined. In effect, the fluid spaces are subject to the second law of Fuller, according to which each measure invites a counter-measure [COR 91, ENT 14]. On the contrary, the use of aerial electronic warfare appeared practically simultaneously to detection systems[28]. Thereafter, it would not cease to be refined and diversified (decoys, jamming, intrusions, deception, etc.), into different stealth techniques [PRI 01]. The latter was also representative of the historical relativism of the debates surrounding the RMA[29]. This evolution toward discretion is also valid for the surface and sub-marine naval domains[30]. Behind the use of counter-measures like electronic warfare, there are also attempts to "solidify" fluid spaces – aerial, naval and sub-marine, spatial and informational – that we want to make more opaque to electronic eyes.

In return, the weapon system – planes and ships – also evolved. The systems did not wait long to include counter-counter-measure equipment. The *hunter-killer* is therefore capable of varying the viscosity of fluid spaces imposed on it by reducing the mixed spaces. This evolution occurred through electronic warfare and a greater variety of sensors. In the aerial domain, the "all to the radar" was first questioned in the 1960s, in the framework of the Vietnam War, with the installation of a gyrostabilized telescope capable of visually identifying a North Vietnamese plane from a distance on a few F-4 Phantom II with AN/TSX-1 TISEO (Target Identification System Electro-Optical). Complex and delicate, this technology was not used systematically; contrary to IRST (Infra-Red Search and Track), which captured the infrared signature of an enemy plane if it was

28 The use of chaff to blind radar systems after an air-drop is only the prelude to embarking on more sophisticated jamming installations [HEN 05].

29 The first works on this question were launched in 1965 in the United States and gave rise, at the end of the 1970s, to the *Have Blue* demonstrator, which was used to design the F-117. If the attack planes (F-117, B-2) benefitted first from the new technologies, the fighter jets, more refined aerodynamically, had to wait until the end of the 1980s and informatics breakthroughs to benefit from them. In 1989, it was done: the YF-22 and the YF-23 were both optimized to reduce their radar signature.

30 Especially after the destruction of the Israeli destroyer *Eilath* by Egyptian patrol vessels in 1967. Most Western navies would equip their ships with decoys immediately after, with some equipping them with jammers in the 1970s. In the submarine domain, the use of decoys was more directly linked to the Cold War and nuclear operations.

oriented in the right direction. Abandoned by the United States after a few attempts, the technology was later refined by the USSR and then Russia and saw an increase, the United States later revisited it. The system had the advantage of being passive, contrary to most radar systems, so the pilot of the detected plane would not know he had been detected. Moreover, the detection of a target did not result only by detecting the propulsion system, but also from the friction of air (in particular at high speed), so that all planes, even "stealth" ones, were susceptible to being detected by this means. Also, as a function of the advances in the domain – notably the combination of capacities of flight calculation, IR imagery and wide angle systems – these types of systems were perceived as particularly useful for aerial combat [DE 14].

It was the same for the installation onboard planes of ESM (Electronic Support Measures) receptors that captured and classified adverse electromagnetic emissions (radar, data links, radio emissions) and which allowed a series of counter-measures. These developments were paired with the use of data links coming from AWACS, which allowed the fighter jet to remain electromagnetically silent, while maintaining a good situational awareness. To a certain extent, this was also valid for surface naval combat[31].

Actually, all these evolutions made combat in fluid spaces a techno-centric combat where networks quickly became essential factors. During operation *Desert Storm* in 1991, 34 air-to-air victories were recorded, of which 33 were in the coalition's favor and only one to the Iraqis. In 27 out of 33 cases, the targets were detected and identified by AWACS, often when it was at more than 70 nautical miles – and thus largely out of danger for coalition planes. Only four dogfights took place, the detection being systematically produced by radar when the coalition forces were more than 5 nautical miles from their target. Furthermore, 16 of the 33 engagements were led by BVR, with detection by plane radar occurring on average at 42 nautical miles and firing occurring on average at 10 nautical miles [STI 15a, STI 15b]. But, once again, we must be wary of determinisms when the technology produced also means an opacification of fluid spaces. This was

31 Practically, the ships face physical limitations: infrared detection such as the range of radar systems watching the surface is limited by the curvature of the Earth, where the field of vision of an AWACS operating at altitude would be much higher. However, the size of ships, the space and the available electric power facilitate the installation of sensors more than in the aeronautical domain.

the case, as we have seen, at the level of the platform – the combat plane – but this is also the case at the level of systems of force. The current trend, reified in the F-35, consists of thinking that the plane and its pilot matter less than networks that provide information, sensors, weapons and the fusion of data coming from these systems, which allow the pilot to make the right decision at the opportune moment. The fighter jet thus becomes an aerial defense platform where classical factors such as speed and manoeuvrability are absent[32]. The true manoeuvrability is instead cognitive: that which first detects the target has the most probability of taking it – in particular due to the speed at which engagements are conducted – as long as the set of sensors and effectors is functioning.

This vision was in accordance with that of the US Navy when it developed the F-111B and then the F-14 in the 1960s: a platform with little manoeuvrability but which had a very high fire power, capable of firing from a great distance, based on information provided by powerful radar systems and advanced detection technology. This logic also addressed the particular context of a large saturation attack against the American aircraft carriers using anti-ship missiles. When the *US Navy* noticed the growing Soviet aviation service, it saw the new F/A-18 *Hornet* as not only the replacement of the A-7 *Corsair II*, which was older and more specifically adapted to air-to-ground missions, but also a fighter jet to support its F-14s. The air forces were in a different position: they obviously needed to intercept bombers[33], but also shorter range combat planes. Operating above the ground, they also needed to avoid ground-air defense and be able to manoeuvre in air-ground missions. Above all, a technical determinism founded on the use of radar only – whether installed on the plane or AWACS – or other sensors and very long-range missiles could be hazardous in several ways:

– This presupposes that the radar carriers are immune, but AWACS is particularly vulnerable. Not very numerous in theaters of operation, they could be the first victims of long range missiles (Beyond Visual Range Air-to-Air Missile [BVRAAM]) launched en masse, or of attacks led by diverse means on aerial bases where they are located. Without AWACS, the fighter jets must use their own radar and are liable to be more easily detected, even with a low radar signature and even if the signature of new AESA radar

---

32 In fact, one of the lessons of "Desert Storm" was that no plane engaged a target over Mach 1.03.

33 This is the reason that the RAF hesitated between the F-14 and what would be the *Tornado* F3.

systems is lower than other radar systems. The space of battle, which historically has a tendency to expand due to the use of AWACS, would contract, while the probabilities of detection by the adversary would increase.

– It is increasingly the case that adverse means of detection are developed with wide angle IRST, eventually paired with radar systems operating on less frequently used bands, such as L, or ESM systems. This is also the case for "passive" radar systems networks, usable for the protection of a territory and using GSM network antennas.

– The best way to acquire air superiority may not be to engage adverse fighter jets directly. In 1967, during the Six-Day War, most of the Egyptian air force was destroyed on the ground. Likewise, a number of American losses in Vietnam and Afghanistan, as well as Sri Lankan losses against the Tamils and Libyan losses to Chad, were due to attacks on air bases by land routes. In 2012, a Taliban assault on Camp Bastion destroyed half of a squadron of AV-8B *Harrier II* of the US Marine Corps in a single attack. The threat is substantial and does not fall under fluid spaces: from 1945 to 1995, 645 attacks were recorded, leading to the destruction of more than 2,000 planes [VIC 95].

– The densification and the proliferation of air defenses, which can themselves operate in IADS (Integrated Air Defense System) networks with a rationale similar to that of SAGE, is a real issue for mixed spaces. The implementation of "double digit" (above SA-10) SAM systems that are increasingly sophisticated – and which can work on a diversified altitude ranges – is problematic [DE 14]. However, due to the cost of next generation planes, the volume of air forces can no longer offset eventual losses caused by any destruction not connected with aerial combat.

– We can also question the cyber-vulnerability of planes whose combat systems depend on informatics. Beyond bugs inherent to complex systems, there is a question of the infiltration of software during logistical sessions, or even a simple disconnection from these systems. Moreover, it seems that being offline from the logistics systems requiring the dispatch of private technicians to reset the planes is not very appropriate for war situations.

If the integrity of these programs was threatened over the course of a war and AWACS could only provide intermittent cover, the logic of engagement over ever larger distances permitted by networks would be destroyed. More traditional logics would take the upper hand. In the meantime, priority would be given to less manoeuvrable planes and the continued training of the pilot would concentrate on long-range engagements and the use of data fusion systems at the expense of short-range engagements or training centered on the simultaneous and "parallel" use of several sensor systems. The cost of these planes would moreover have consequences on the available mass, placing air forces using them in a situation of qualitative *and* quantitative inferiority. This would obviously be a significant threat to national security, a true failure of a determinist model that relies on the gamble that the adversary will be unable to conquer fluid spaces or at least render them opaque. Yet, the genetic strategy behind networks like SAGE, SACCS, WWMCCS or force systems combining AWACS and *hunter-killer* planes consists of steering the adversary onto technical ground: they will either find a display of the fluidity of air spaces, or they will be, linearly and almost mechanically, detected and probably shot. Just as before, combat in fluid spaces today depends on respecting the rationality associated with these spaces. Fluid spaces depend on solid spaces and by the interface of mixed spaces: planes and ships are inseparable from their aerial and naval bases.

Although fluid spaces are most conducive to a *"see first-kill first"* mentality where network-centric rationalities are the most easily applicable, they are the ideal spaces of deployment. But what is true for fluid spaces is even more so for solid spaces, which are naturally opaque. This is especially the case when they striate, introducing an extreme intensification, and literally channel the possibilities of movements of forces, as in mountains or cities. The real consequence of this hardening is the limitation of both range and penetrating power of sensors. The view from the cockpit of a combat plane moving at 6,000 m is several tens of kilometers, plus a hundred in good weather. In comparison, the thermal display system of the most recent generation tank is at best 6,000 to 7,000 m in a flat space, less at night or in bad weather. In a city, the majority of confrontations result at less than 200 m from engaged forces and the field of vision is especially restricted – not including smoke and the effects of light and stress on the cognitive capacities of combatants. In this context, how can we reduce uncertainty and clear the fog of war in operations led on the ground? How can we rationalize the chaos of battle in order to, through the implementation of networks, "fluidify the solid"?

5

Understanding (2): Fluidifying the Solid?

The quest to lift the fog of war is closely connected to the theorization of the art of war itself, the production of strategic thought considered in connection with friendly action but also – by the very fact of the dialectic nature of war – as it pertains to enemy action. The prevailing rationality to reduce uncertainty imparts a central place to both the art and the practitioner, but it also recognizes a permanent anxiety towards a rationalizing use of science and a predictive power. The temptation is not new in the history of strategic thinking: the geometric concepts of Von Bulöw, and even the attempts to define the principles of war (see next chapter), relate to this directly [GAT 91]. However, these ideas give way to the art and strategy that preserve a true freedom to manoeuvre. A first major turn appeared with the mobilization of mathematics in World War I, and a series of methods which would be refined until the 1970s and encounter along the way the development of informatics capacities. The techniques of *Operational Analysis*, *Operational Research* and *System Analysis* appeared successively. As of 1914, *Operational Analysis* could mathematically determine the main models of combat conduct, giving rise to the "Lanchester laws" (1916), a series of equations never truly demonstrated, which could specify the quantitative parameters of combat that allowed for almost certain victory [BRO 73, LEP 87].

Operational Research was developed next, which aimed to improve the study of operations using pure and simple mathematics to discover elements of predictability in social organizations, always considering mathematics as the central methodological tool. This technique is connected to the logics of fluid spaces, seeing as it was historically linked to the development of radar systems [ALL 87][1]. These techniques were primarily applied to the management of mechanized armies for which logistical demand was soaring [SMI 85, GRO 97]. They also optimized the conduct of bombing operations on Germany and Japan, before spreading to the social sciences or informing the conceptualization of nuclear war. Military personnel quickly criticized the approach defended by the supporters of research and operational analysis, who neglected human variables as not very quantifiable[2]. The civilians working on questions of strategy, more inclined than their military colleagues to use the operational research and analysis techniques, also had a tendency to linearize combat and strip it of its constraints and specifications. The role of the lack of experience in these models is central. These criticisms inspired *System Analysis*, which combined the results of operational research with results from the human sciences while seeking to determine the effectiveness of future weapons [KAP 83]. The Vietnam War was its most complete expression, while World War II was the triumph of operational research [GRA 97]. This approach remained largely restricted to the United States, while several NATO exercises make reference to techniques of systems analysis, notably when combat in nuclear environments was conceptualized, in large part by American think-tanks[3].

Above all, this new method remained, like the previous ones, largely dependent on quantitative variables that do not lend themselves well to conduct that is difficult to determine in advance, especially when history does not provide case studies [SIM 78]. The definition of *metrics* (number of bombs lost, percentage of hits, enemy soldiers killed or wounded, enemy infrastructures destroyed, etc.), is definitely relevant for matters of regular tactical combat – a question of exchange rates[4]. But this relevance is more

---

1 It was developed in 1937 through research conducted in Great Britain.
2 This refers to the critique of Paretto, who quickly sought to develop equations unique to sociology that allowed for the systematization of human, social and political conduct.
3 The website of the RAND Corporation uses several online studies and the simple consultation of a catalogue (which goes back to the 1950s) to clearly demonstrate the importance of the system analysis methods for the resolution of strategic problems.
4 Such as the ratio of friendly to enemy losses. This question was central to the definition of the doctrines of *Active Defense* in the 1970s and in the *AirLand battle* of the 1980s. It was also central to the design of the battle tanks of that period; each machine was supposed to replace a certain number of machines from the Warsaw Pact.

unlikely when the concepts are applied to a more complex situation. This reassessment, manifest during the Vietnam War, was called into question for not taking into account the dialectical nature of war: the enemy adapts to a context in which what we believe to be its weaknesses no longer necessarily are. The relevance of the idea of *metrics* was raised again during the war in Afghanistan [DE 10][5]. The main obstacle to the success of these methods, given their relative effectiveness, resides in a lack of dynamic knowledge of the enemy in relation to their adaptations and counter-adaptations. This aspect of the question is no less important than the more traditional view that only an officer's understanding of a situation can pierce the fog of war at a glance, whatever level of engagement he finds himself in.

5.1. The electronic battlefield

War can be understood as an enormous cycle of actions and counter-actions, even in solid spaces, which are considerably more complex than fluid spaces. In a similar framework, the primary question quickly becomes that of the monopoly of information, and then its conversion into intelligence – these two terms are not synonyms. The issue encountered is at once both technological and conceptual: in solid environments, the opacity is as much physical – mostly terrain – as it is intellectual when it comes to understanding enemy actions. The matter is relatively simple in fluid spaces where huge portions of sky or of sea can be surveyed and where movement often betrays intentions – the ruse and the diversion are only possible in even larger spaces. But, on the terrestrial domain, the main question is rightly one of the level on which one is positioned: supposing it is possible to detect all enemy actions, how can one represent them from the tactical to the strategic level? Can the movement of all of its forces reveal an enemy's intentions, their logistical and moral situations and everything else that can contribute to military efficiency? If the RMA/*Transformation* intended to answer these questions – if not totally, at least sufficiently to generate productivity gains – from this perspective, it is only a new iteration of a previous quest.

---

5 It is probable that it will be raised again at the end of an in-depth analysis of air strikes on the gas facilities of the Islamic State, which are the subject of the bulk of the institutional communication of the Western coalition.

5.1.1. *The Vietnam War*

If the conditions of the Cold War saw the development of rationalities meant to lift the fog of war in fluid spaces using networks, the Vietnam War played this role for solid spaces. On the ground, the operations quickly turned to seeking to control enemy movements through a logic of interdiction. It consisted of cutting off the supplies of the Viet-Cong through the Ho-Chi-Minh "path" – in fact, a multitude of paths – located for the most part in a dense jungle. For this purpose, the "McNamara line" began construction in May 1967, on the frontier with North Vietnam, Laos, and from the South China Sea to Thailand[6]. At 30 km long, it was a tactical barricade that involved a barrier surveyed by people. Most of the barricade was made up of mined areas packed with sensors whose activation would allow forces to locate infiltrations and make an appropriate decision, mainly the engagement of air forces. The information gathered would be transmitted, via relay aircraft, to the Nakhon Phanom base to be centralized and processed in an *Infiltration Surveillance Center* (ISC) [MAH 08]. The sensors themselves, some of which were designed to be stuck in the ground, others to be hooked in the tree canopy – were airdropped by planes, and several of them were just variations of sonobuoys used by the *US Navy* to detect submarines. The sensors could also be seismic, chemical – such as the *people sniffers* that could detect the ammonia in urine – infrared, electromagnetic or acoustic.

On paper, the system was a terrestrial extension of the logics used in fluid spaces. In practice, the centralization of tens of thousands of sensors – not simply hundreds – was a formidable task. On the one hand, the rate of false alarms, sometimes simply due to rain or thunder, was significant. Once discovered, they could also be used in tactical ruses by the Viet-Cong (such as releasing animals or placing buckets of urine). On the other hand, the relay of signals quickly became problematic: once the system was completely operational, requiring four permanent EC-121R[7] orbits, only 80%, at best, of the emissions were effectively passed on to the ISC. All of the information was transmitted to two IBM 360 Model 65 that represented

---

6 A prior project, dating back to March 1966, proposed a classic tactical barricade made up of barbed wire and minefields, which could be permanently surveyed. The army expressed their opposition to this project on the grounds that forces stationed there would no longer be available for offensive actions.

7 Note that these efforts were also at the origin of making small tourist planes into drones, which would become the QU-22B. However, their reliability was quickly questioned.

the activated sensors on an enormous wall map – a type of representation similar to that used in air control centers of the SAGE network. Four hundred analysts were posted at the ISC, which was installed in the largest building in the region, and they could decide to engage combat planes. However, carrying out air strikes according to this logic was a difficult exercise: once in the zone, the fighter planes had to locate their target, often in the middle of the jungle, so the effectiveness of strikes was quite variable. The strikes required the prior deployment of forward air controllers to "mark" targets for the combat planes, but by doing so, they lost the element of surprise. Increasingly, the Viet-Cong and the North Vietnamese adapted to this, coordinating convoys during the hours of least availability of American planes, taking a sea approach or operating at night, forcing the United States to expand their capacities to deal with this[8].

This was a decisive moment in the history of air-ground operations, with the implementation of the first nocturnal combat systems – FLIR (*Forward Looking Infra Red*) and low-light TV cameras. These onboard sensors, if they were not already widespread, would become essential for carrying out air operations in the future and were considered fundamental to the credibility of a "revolution in accuracy" as a component of the RMA/*Transformation*. However, the rationality of the McNamara line was also extended to all of South Vietnam, with sensors positioned in the periphery of American bases and along main communication routes to reduce the likelihood of attacks and ambushes. Nine times more sensors would be used for these missions than in the interdiction campaign on the northern frontier. However, not all American efforts in Vietnam can be reduced to the use of sensors, although this was a marked departure from previous practices. With more than 535,000 men involved in 1968, the operations were above all centered on sweeping the zones, on foot or in tanks, and the widespread use of more traditional and very human-intensive forms of intelligence and reconnaissance. This was largely conducted based on the models of regular war, despite being called a battle "for the hearts and minds", with a focus on the success of tactical operations. Colonel Harry Summers referred to these successes when he met a Vietnamese general after the war. When Summers pointed out that the United States had never lost a battle when they found themselves confronted by the North Vietnamese, his colleague responded that he was correct, but that was not the issue [SUM 82].

---

8 Sometimes to an extreme, such as the idea for a C-119 equipped with xenon lights to illuminate the jungle at night.

5.1.2. *The European model of the RMA*

Nevertheless, the war marked a turning point for the automation of intelligence gathering operations such as strikes in solid spaces through the intermediary of networks. In 1969, General Westmoreland, who commanded operations in Vietnam from 1964 to 1968, gave a speech at the *Association of the United States Army* that could have come 25 years later: *"I see battlefields or combat areas that are under 24-hour real or near-real-time surveillance of all types. I see battlefields on which we can destroy anything we can locate through instant communications and the almost instantaneous application of highly lethal firepower"*[9]. Westmoreland's vision would effectively be extended to the domain of regular war. The Vietnam experience served as a model for the *Mystic Mission* program, which aimed to transpose the rationalities of the McNamara line to the level of NATO and was tested in Florida in 1971 and in Germany in 1972. The principle was always the same: "unattended" sensors signalled the passage of enemy forces by transferring information to command centers for processing, analysis and decision-making. The director of American defense research revealed in 1974 that *"a remarkable series of technical developments has brought us to the threshold of what I believe will become a true revolution in conventional warfare"*[10].

The paradox is that the matter is actually very simple: in the context of a confrontation in Europe, it consists of distinguishing machinery whose characteristics are both known and specific. A T-64 or T-72 tank has a mass and a thermal and acoustic signature that are much greater than those of a truck or a bus transporting refugees fleeing the invasion of the Warsaw Pact. The detection of targets in the midst of the "noise" of movements in a country at war is much more simple than in Vietnam, where a truck was as likely to be carrying supplies for the Viet-Cong as humanitarian aid – without even mentioning how much more diverse the fauna is in Asia than in Europe. Similarly, we could predict a significantly reduced rate of false alarms. In the same way, sheltered from nuclear deterrence, the network of sensors could be positioned, tested and improved at will over the years, and not in the urgent situation of a war in progress. The issue, however, was the same: faced with a variety of potential routes of passage for the Warsaw Pact troops in West Germany, it consisted of determining the lines of advance and

---

9 [MAH 08, p. 112].
10 *Ibidem.*

volume of forces. In doing so, it was possible to identify if a diversion attack was being led, allowing for appropriate reactions while respecting the principle of the distribution of forces. In return, this type of action allowed for maintaining reserves which could be sent to where breakthroughs had not been detected. This logic ended up being validated from an ideological point of view in 1976 with the *Active defense*.

This theory did not touch on developments linked to networks of sensors. It consisted of modernizing structures like the equipment of the American armed forces, notably equipping tanks with their proper target acquisition systems which augmented their performance in operations led at night. On the ground, the *Active defense* involved leading a defensive, delaying combat on enemy penetration lines followed by counter-offensives while ensuring that friendly forces consistently covered each other. The theory was built on the then-recent Israeli experience during the Yom Kippur War and the delayed German battle against the Soviet troops during World War II [DUN 93]. The support of new technologies had radicalized the tactical efficiency observed in these two experiences[11]. It transformed conventional war into a game of chess that it had not been up to that point, but the game soon developed into something much more complex than the covering of carefully delineated geographical sectors in West Germany by forces of NATO member-countries. It was not only about networking sensors; it was also about forces maintaining continuous communication. It was around this time that the acronym "C3I" (*Command, Control, Communications, Intelligence*) became widespread.

The term "information warfare" appeared in 1976, coined by Thomas Rona as an analyst at Boeing [RON 76]. Twenty years later, he defined it as the "*destruction, the incapacitation and the corruption of the ennemy information infrastructure*"[12]. The same year, Paul Dickson titled one of his works *The Electronic Battlefield* [DIC 76]. According to Dickson, this consisted not just of the automation of intelligence gathering, which became fragmented due to the multitude of sensors employed, but also the automation of the retaliation, notably by the use of "intelligent" mines capable of determining if they ought to explode in proximity to a particular

11 Despite the strategic failure of Nazi Germany in the second case. The possibility of a failure of the *Active defense* was accepted, in fact, in a Cold War context where the engagement of conventional forces was only one of the rungs on the ladder of violence.
12 [RON 96, p. 10].

vehicle. For the author, this evolution was made possible by three revolutions:

– the electronic revolution, with the arrival of the transistor, the miniaturization of components, TV cameras and IR, and the widespread use of computers;

– the development of systems controlled from a distance, whether for observation or firing;

– the development of bionics, or more precisely, according to the meaning that the author gives it, the application of originally animal characteristics to sensors[13].

The first and second of Dickson's "revolutions" would occupy a central place in the second *Offset strategy*. Formally launched in 1977 by Harold Brown (then the Secretary of Defense) and William Perry (a future Secretary of Defense), the initiative led to the design of systems that would be considered central in the future RMA/*Transformation* and which also reified the tactic-centric logic of "detection-processing". The quantitative superiority of the Warsaw Pact on NATO and American forces had to be defeated by a qualitative superiority. One of the flagship programs of this effort was the *Assault Breaker* [HEW 82]. Launched by the *US Army* and the *US Air Force* in 1978, it combined airborne detection with Soviet shielding provisions and processing at a safe distance. The *Pave Mover* radar system could detect movements of vehicles on the ground as well as determine and categorize lines of penetration. The radar could also survey large zones and detect movements as well as zoom in on a more restricted area, producing a high-resolution synthetic image to identify stationary targets. Initially, it was a question of equipping F-111 twin-jets. These could transmit the data to a ground station because the radar also served as a communication link. Another plane, whose existence was not revealed until the middle of the 1990s, was also designed.

The F-111 operated on the front line and had a radar range limited to a 100 km, so the issue of detecting at great depths into the enemy position was raised. The *Tacit Blue*, a very stealthy single-jet aircraft constructed specifically around the *Pave Mover* radar system, was also engaged over the Warsaw Pact countries, using its radar to transmit data in real time to the

---

13 This meaning came first, historically, dating back to a conference led by the US Air Force in 1960.

analysis stations on the ground. The US Army's small twin-engined OV-1 *Mohawk* reconnaissance planes were also equipped with a less complex version of *Pave Mover*, completing the network of sensors. The analysts posted in the ground station had to identify the lines of enemy penetration and activate the launch of strikes against tanks. If the "system of systems" effectors were diversified, two single programs were indicative of the overall effort. The T-16 and T-22 missiles should have the capability to be fired from zones far away from the front line of the battle zone (*Forward Edge of the Battle Area* [FEBA]) in the direction of forces detected by the *Pave mover*[14]. At the end of their ballistic flight, they dropped terminally guided sub-munitions which were then directed toward the tanks individually.

One of the system's innovations was that the missiles themselves had a fairly simple guiding system. Because of this, however, they were liable to deviate from their course. So, through the intervention of the ground control station where operators followed the entire tactical situation on their screens – including the progression of enemy forces and the missiles fired at them – *Pave mover* also had to be able to send instructions to rectify the trajectory of the missiles. Another vector, the NV-150 cruise missile, was also proposed at the time. As well as having stealth forms and being precision-guided, it was equipped with the same sub-munitions as the T-16 and T-22 in order to reduce the cost of the system by making the most of scaling. An air launch variant of the *Tomahawk* missile, the AGM-109 MRASM (*Medium Range Air-Surface Missile*), also carrying the same sub-munitions, was designed and tested. In the end, this true system of systems did not enter into service in this configuration, but several of its components were a success and therefore deployed. The *Pave mover* radar system was installed on the E-8 J-STARS (*Joint Surveillance Target Attack Radar System*) planes, of which one of the prototypes was used with success during operation *Desert Storm* in 1991. However, the ground station was abandoned and the operators relocated to the consoles in the cabin of the E-8. As a joint program of the US Army and the US Air Force, the T-16 and T-22 missiles were abandoned (much like the AGM-109) but the Army continued their efforts and developed the MGM-140 ATACMS (*Army Tactical Missile System*), used for the first time in combat in 1991.

---

14 The missiles themselves are sub-versions of the *Lance* and the *Patriot*. They were launched from trailers as well as from F-16 or B-52 bombers.

The end of the Cold War put a stop to the project of arming the plane with terminally guided sub-munitions, but it was equipped with 950 or 275 typical sub-munitions or a unitary charge of 227 kg and was exported on a large scale[15]. The development of the NV-150 missile continued until the 1990s under the designation of the AGM-137. Abandoned after that, its missions would be taken over by the AGM-158, now in service with the United States, Poland, Finland and Australia. For the most part, these sub-munitions programs would also be maintained:

– The US Army tested the TGSM (*Terminally Guided Sub-Munition*) at the beginning of the 1980s, of which 6–12 models (16 kg each) were equipped to the T-16 and T-22. Once dropped, a parachute and wings deployed and the munition descended while its infrared sensor sought a target. Once detected, the parachute released and the control surfaces activated through the use of a calculator in order to rectify the trajectory, permitting *in fine* to hit the target on the roof, penetrating it with a shaped charge. The program would be adapted with the inclusion of acoustic sensors and became the *Brilliant Anti-Tank* (BAT) sub-munitions, which then became the GBU-44 *Viper Strike* and were equipped to drones;

– The *Skeet* sub-munition actually entered service under the name BLU-108/B. When dropped, this sub-munition is slowed by a parachute and begins to rotate, deploying four projectiles, each equipped with infrared and laser sensors. Once the target is in range, the weapon explodes and pierces the roof of the tank with a preformed penetrator. For the time being, the weapon is only loaded on an aircraft bomb, the CBU-97 SFW (*Sensor Fuzed Weapon*), which contains 10 BLU-108 and is capable of covering a surface of 460 by 150 m. A similar sub-munition, the SADARM (*Sense and Destroy Armor*) entered service in the mid-1990s, equipped with 155 mm shells[16].

In fact, the logic at work was to obtain the largest transparency possible, up to the infra tactical level of a strike on a single tank. Faced with uncertainty about an effective strike, the matter became a question of elementary mathematical probabilities: the saturation of sub-munitions in targeted zones should minimize the possibility of seeing enemy tanks go

15 Purchasers include Bahrain, South Korea, the United Arab Emirates, Greece, Taiwan and Turkey.
16 It would also be equipped with rockets for the multiple-launch rocket system MLRS. Similar systems have been designed since, such as the French-Swedish BONUS and the German SMArt 155 (*Suchzünder Munition für die Artillerie 155*).

untouched. This is a true lifting of the fog of war by the search for an overkill of the enemy, directly permitted by electronic progress[17]. While the *Assault Breaker* program was a major component in the second *Offset strategy*, it was not the only one. We owe the progress in electronics, informatics and miniaturization to the efforts launched at the end of the 1970s, a series of developments that were also fundamental to the future RMA/*Transformation*. This was the case for works on stealth, which produced first the *Have Blue* demonstrator, then the F-117 – whose first flight took place in 1981 – and the future B-2 bomber, which began development at the end of the 1970s. In fact, if stealth did not disperse the fog of war for the forces using it, it did thicken the enemy's fog. Beyond the formidable effort made in the domain of precision-guided weapons, the second *Offset* also introduced the GPS (*Global Positioning System*).

It is remarkable to note that development of GPS is fundamentally linked to fluid spaces and the fluidification of solid spaces. One of the most ardent defenders – and one of the fathers – of the design, Francis X. Kane, was a colonel in the *US Air Force*. He joined Virginia State University as an associate professor in engineering and stayed in contact with the Pentagon by remaining specialized in spatial issues [KAN 71]. Kane also co-authored the book *The Strategy of Technology* with Possony and Pournelle, which initially appeared in 1970, and which is the clearest formalization – and also certainly, the most radical – of a technological determinism on military operations [POS 97, HEN 12a, HEN 12b]. As head of the 621B spatial navigation program since 1963, he also played a central role in the development of spatial sensing capacities for the firing of ballistic missiles or anti-satellite laser weapons. The launch into orbit of the first 10 satellites, between 1978 and 1985, suggested the possibility of precisely locating any unit equipped with a receptor. Better yet, the use of GPS receptors on long-range missiles allowed them to be guided with more precision and ease than any other device that had existed up to that point. The first use of the system for this purpose was during *Desert Storm*, when about 30 AGM-86 missiles equipped with conventional loads were fired with the greatest secrecy [HEN 05]. The miniaturization of electronic components had a central role in this as well[18].

---

17 The NATO norm considers enemy forces to be destroyed when they have been reduced by 66%. Yet, the saturation of battle zones with sub-munitions would only leave a few percent of enemy vehicles intact.

18 The first GPS receptors weighed more than 25 kg. By 1991, they had decreased to under 1.5 kg.

5.2. The fragmentation of intelligence

The different developments examined here are not the only ones. Since the Vietnam War, substantial progress was also made in the domain of electronic war, through ground systems and especially air systems (RC-135, RC-12). The capacities of spatial intelligence also expanded considerably. As a result, the strictly tactical logics were abandoned for an operative angle and the focus of planners shifted away from the idea of reconnaissance, still central in the 1980s, and onto surveillance. This is the framework for the development of drones and air systems. Although not really on the agenda at the end of the 1980s[19], after 10 years, they had become central to the American rhetoric of intelligence collection. There was a multiplication of the types of platforms, regulated as a function of their level of engagement, which replaced reconnaissance planes, at least in the United States[20]. This transition toward a rationality of surveillance, which had been developing since the Vietnam War, was not strategically neutral. Reconnaissance is transitory by nature. A plane or a specialized unit can capture an image of a target and its position, which is liable to change over time, but neither the plane nor the unit cannot remain indefinitely in the area. On the contrary, the idea of surveillance suggests permanence and persistence. The conduct of each target must be observed in real time if possible. The philosophy of the relationship to the Other passes from a sequence of snapshots, from which the strategist can interpret a dynamic, to a panoptic.

5.2.1. Fragmenting and network-centering

The implementation of this panoptic should definitively "pierce" the fog of war given that "*From Plato to NATO, the history of command in war essentially consists of an endless quest for certainty*"[21]. This rationality is at the center of the strategic project – if not the center of gravity – of the RMA/*Transformation*. It is a meta-narration that is sustained by its own

19 Actually, Western forces have used drones since the 1960s, essentially as systems of observation for the benefit of artillery. It was in Israel that their use became widespread in the 1970s, in border surveillance missions.
20 Several hundred RF-4 *Phantom II* were still operational in the 1980s in the United States but they were not replaced; the R/MQ-1 *Predator* and -9 *Reaper* drones took over from them. Similarly, according to the original plans, RQ-4 *Global Hawk* drones were supposed to replace the U-2, although this was later abandoned. In Europe, air forces combine drones and reconnaissance planes if possible.
21 [VAN 85, p. 264].

fiction, necessarily centered on networks and the computer processing of considerable volumes of information. From the first works in the 1990s up to the current debates on *big data*, the theme of this militarily significant panoptic has not changed. One aspect of this issue, which can be found throughout the work of Owens, is its potential to be bureaucratically legitimized for the purpose of obtaining the necessary budgets [OWE 00][22]. From his perspective, 90% of what is militarily significant for a given zone will be able to be detected in 2025. This vision is without a doubt a bit optimistic in view of the current progress of both armies and manufacturers, although the progress of manufacturers is not small. The variety of sensors as well as their sensitivity has increased considerably.

The fact remains that this is unlikely for several reasons. The first reason pertains to the dynamics of the nature of war and its impacts on equipment strategy. Since the end of the Cold War, the majority of conflicts that Western forces have engaged in have been irregular. These conflicts have been characterized by a double phenomenon of dispersion/ disappearance of the enemy. Emerging from the population, he does not stand out – thus he "disappears" – and his conduct means he is potentially present everywhere, making identification from a distance virtually impossible. During the war in 2006, the Israeli general Reuven Benkler called Lebanon an "empty battlefield" where populations spent most of their time going about their peaceful business. But, for a few hours a day, certain inhabitants supported the Hezbollah or completed missions in their name. The tactical consequence of such a mode of action is that this switch must be identified and can only be acted on when it is operational [BEN 07]. Even within the category of irregular conflicts, this is very far from the logic of a Che Guevara or many of the opponents of the colonial wars who operated more or less "full time" and remained in groups.

This rationality is completely contradictory to that of regular operations for which most armies continue to equip and train themselves. A narrative of the ideal conflict remains vivid because its foundations refer back to strategic cultures that support it. It refers to clearly identified armies engaged in "campaigns" and facing each other in "fields" of battle with heavy resources, easily detectable and identifiable. In this sense, the works of the 1990s around the ISR and new sensors intersects the works of the 1970s and 1980s: in several regards, the ideal enemy of the RMA is the USSR.

---

22 He was vice president of the United States Joint Chiefs-of-Staff.

Similarly, the qualification, historically quite quick, of China as a *peer competitor* – or a competitor of equal level on the strategic scene – seems to reify the disappeared enemy, extending the regular and technological temptation to which Western strategic cultures are inclined. In certain respects, the Napoleonic fictions join those of Cold War, albeit in a way that is frequently uninformed about history or strategic subtleties. The Napoleonic wars were also marked by irregular phases – the peninsular war, in Spain, is only the most well-known – just like how a cold war, becoming hot, would have seen the use of attacks, the widespread use of agitprop, of armed opposition groups or special forces raids behind enemy lines. The detection/identification would have been more difficult, even in a framework primarily marked by phases of regular combat.

The issue is in the separation between the physical representation – the combatant or the civilian liable to be a combatant – and their intentions, whereas the presence of an enemy tank in friendly territory combines both representation and intention. It is about generating intelligence that is sufficiently discriminating, which is only possible in irregular conflicts by cutting oneself off from the rushed chronostrategy towards which the RMA/*Transformation* leans. It consists of observing conduct long enough to determine a *tactical pattern* and deduce the intentions behind it. During operations in Afghanistan, armed men – a common feature in this country, even for civilians – were not considered legitimate targets until they had been observed for more than 30 min while they buried what was clearly an IED (*Improvised Explosive Device*) on a road. However, the logic at work here is doubly problematic. On the one hand, the maneuver depends on specific rules of engagement unique to each state member of the coalition and is liable to result in targeting errors, with civilian losses on top of that. On the other hand, the electro-optical sensors currently used involve a "tunnel vision", through which only a relatively narrow zone where the sensors are directed can be observed.

To resolve the issue of "tunnel vision", an "absolute" panoptic was attempted through a computer intermediary. It consisted of equipping a drone with several optronic systems so that it could, by processing the data, survey a zone of several tens of square kilometers. The first missions of the system, dubbed *Gorgon Stare*, which can track all relevant movements, were conducted in 2009. However, the concentration of data did not produce the expected result. On the general image that resulted, black triangles appeared and moved around, and no one was able to correct the bug. The second phase of *Gorgon Stare*, capable of surveying 100 km², was tested in 2014. The *Autonomous Real-Time Ground Ubiquitous Surveillance Imaging System* (ARGUS-IS) produced a continuously refreshing 1.8 billion-pixel image produced by 368 cameras. The whole thing represents several terabytes of data per minute and therefore involved an in-depth analysis. Intelligence from other sources must be added to this image-based intelligence, such as wire-tapping of communications, especially cell phones – which are not under the exclusive purview of Western forces or any armies[23].

From a tactical perspective, the representation of a zone of operations appears fragmented, dependent on a multitude of sensors. The forward movement of a company on the ground can also involve a tactical drone, a medium altitude drone, the designated pod of a combat plane "covering" the unit, and the scouts of this unit or other units carrying out the monitoring. The commander of a company finds himself obliged to juggle with several facets of the zone in which he is operating before even making any decisions. But this fragmentation doubles as reticulation, in particular when it is a question of an operative perspective. Images taken by the MALE (Medium Altitude, Long Endurance) drone or a pod can also be transmitted to a commander by a ROVER (*Remotely Operated Video Enhanced Receiver*) liaison and be simultaneously relayed to the commander of the battalion or even higher levels. This reticulation involves intelligence and also relies on unit data: their location, potentially automatic (by *blue force tracking* systems) and the state of the men or the stocks of munitions. Although the commander of a company may have a fairly good understanding of the state of his unit, this is not necessarily the case for the upper echelon, who find themselves in a situation of uncertainty not just in relation to the enemy, but also to their own forces.

As it happens, this logic of compensatory reticulation of the fragmentation of intelligence sources is not new, historically speaking, and was first expressed technologically in the radio. The military ingenuity of the German *blitzkrieg* was not due to the combination of tanks and planes as much as it was to the radio. The use of radio communication enabled units to coordinate over huge spaces and increase their speed of adaptation while being able to quickly command back-up from engineering or artillery. This

---

23 In 2006, Hezbollah was capable of listening to the telephonic communications of Israeli soldiers.

logic is still at work but has seen a decrease in the number of participants in the network, whether human (managers at all levels, subordinates) or not (sensors). Today's military units have thus become roaming information producers, networked in the most significant force systems, to the extent that there is a risk that the aim will become generating information instead of generating political effects. Complex and naturally procedural machines, armies see their processes of adaptation/modernization through a series of practices with technical responsibilities whose objective is easy to forget. The question remains as to whether the rationalities developed in the past 40 years will allow us to effectively clear up the fog of war.

It is difficult to answer this because the logic at work since the 1990s is repetitive and makes it difficult to step away for perspective. As early as 1998, the formal recognition of network-centric logics of war [CEB 98] raised the issue of the relationship of the tactical, operational or strategic leader to information. He is liable to be drowned in information – at the risk, aided by fatigue, of not being mentally capable of worrying about a reasonable image. On the contrary, the vision, technically normalized with information, risks creating a "tunnel effect" where what is perceived as real is what is presented – at the risk of bypassing other essential information. These issues, which make up the contradictory poles that an officer must balance, occur throughout the literature on the matter [DE 06] and have not yet found a solution. Above all, as Brian Steed notes, "piercing the fog of war" does not only involve intelligence, which is in the end only a technical component – and tends moreover, as Keegan shows, to be overvalued [KEE 03]. On the contrary, because the fog matters less than uncertainty, all components of the art of war play a role in uncertainty generation for the enemy. This is also the case for aspects that tend to be left aside by armies who are too sure of themselves technologically, and too centered on tactics, such as the fact of having reserves, or the study of history as a way of knowing the enemy [STE 09].

5.2.2. *The network-centric man*

Seeing better – or even understanding better – does not necessarily imply acting better: in a certain number of defeats, the defeated side had a perfect understanding of the situation. Now, the question of the relation of information to the military realm also concerns the first and the most intelligent sensor used by armies: the combatant. The soldier has become a technical subject and, with the automation of sensors, which subordinate the human element, this raises the issue of the mechanization of the soldier, which is commonly represented as either an anti-thesis or a complement to the automation of the battlefield. For the last 30 years, this question has mainly been considered as referring to science fiction, but new publications about the mechanization of the conduct of soldiers from psychologists, philosophers, sociologists or political commentators have demonstrated that this mechanization is not only real but observed [HEN 03]. It seems that technology very quickly dehumanized the combatant, who became mechanized by the continuous repetition of destructive acts. The machine-gun of World War I became the archetype of a death that was itself mechanized and led to a routine "mechanizing" of offensives. These mechanizations gave rise to a lack of moral standards in the combatant, placed in a situation of stress and disconnected from his environment. Theweleit concluded that technology was heading in the direction of exceeding the limitations of a human who is exposed too much on the battlefield, opening the door to him being overtaken by technology [THE 89].

Practically, the soldier first changed physically, through standardization. Where traditional strategy only paid limited attention to the equipment of the combatant, the end of the 19th Century witnessed a transformation that would be completely expressed as of 1914. The flamboyant uniform colors of the start of the century were abandoned for khaki battle dress. The helmet made its first appearances, only rank and unit numbers made it possible to make distinguish between the men. The armies engaged the soldier in a closure of his space: if he lost his armour, he was exposed to shots. The history of his equipment up to the present day is that of the restoration of that armour, psychologically reassuring but technically imperfect [HOL 86]. Faced with this search for absolute efficiency opposite which the combatant seemed limited, concerns about "post-human future" appeared at the intersection of political science, strategy studies, sociology and philosophy. From this perspective, authors like C. Cocker, C.H. Gray and D. Harraway undertook to examine a "cyborgology" that had relevant implications for the military domain [GRA 95, GRA 97, HAR 92, COK 13].

They estimated that man was no longer in the midst of allying with the machine, but of becoming a hybrid with it – at the risk of robotizing a human who is already, in fact, in the midst of "augmentation"[24]. Prior to this, the works of Norbert Wiener drew philosophical conclusions in his theory of the cybernetic glimpses of a post-human future, colored by a concern about the control of technologies that become out of control [WIE 00]. Although we do not consider these concerns well-founded, they partly informed the Cold War. In the civil domain as in the military domain, several examples of loss of control of technologies were observed[25]. The risk continued to generate anxieties and concerns at every level and only increased with the consideration of the increasing automation of military systems creating a *cybernetic empire* through the accumulation of automating and, for man, automatizing, systems [LAF 04]. C. Lafontaine was drawing on the previously cited authors when he showed that a "thinking machine" was being designed bit by bit through a cybernetic empire. If we are, at this stage, far from HAL[26] and a total autonomy of the machine, it implicitly shows several facets of the desubjectivization of the individual [EHR 95] by bringing it back to the stage of a self-regulated information processing entity, which, in fact, is the product of the humanist schema supported by modernity and the emergence of apoliticism[27].

While this interpretation, whose upholders generally operate in the frame of a critique of the Western technological model, is relatively pessimistic and does not take into account *a priori* the legal and political modes of combat regulations, it is notably based on the American and European experience of the evolution of the soldier. This is partially detailed and relayed by the work conducted in the frame of the RMA and that of the development of systems supporting the combatant. On the historical schema, very quickly, the United States, through an institution like the *Human Resources Research Office* (HUMRRO), would work on the theme of human engineering. HUMRRO works on a vision where it seeks a "(...) *training*

---

24 The *Défense & Sécurité Internationale* journal dedicated a special issue to the question in 2015 [CUS 15].

25 Citing, among others, cases of air accidents (an Airbus of the Romanian TAROM crashing due to an incorrect option choice by the automatic pilot) or military demonstrations. C.H. Gray reported a presentation of self-propelled anti-aircraft artillery DIVAD during which the target acquisition unfortunately targeted the stand of spectators.

26 The oft-cited – in reports about the sociology of techniques – computer animated by artificial intelligence in *2001, A Space Odyssey* by Kubrick.

27 The relationship between cybernetics and apoliticism has notably been taken on by Philippe Breton. He showed how Wiener attempted, by conceiving of what is considered as a cybernetic revolution, to stand in the way of totalitarianism.

geared to the system that a man is to be part, whether it be a "rifle system", a helicopter or a missile battery, The HUMRRO approach – and subsequently the Army's – is to look at men as integral parts of a weapon system with specific missions" [DIC 76]. *A contrario,* the French position is to consider the weapon as a prosthesis of the combatant. The relation is thus inverted by the Clausewitzian schema: the weapon is a continuation of the soldier, himself a bearer of a power that is only conferred to him by the situation of war, itself a continuation of the political situation.

Inversely, after the weapon has "absorbed" the man, the American logic tends to eliminate it as soon as it becomes dysfunctional or becomes an obstacle to the efficiency of the weapon system. This perspective also results from the political: war has its own independence in the United States, once the political has decided that it will be conducted. This idea doubles that of R. Hofstadter, who thought that American culture saw man as the source of potential faults. This perspective goes back to a time when the British Crown Counsellors steered the new state into maintaining a heightened degree of suspicion with regard to its political representatives, in a more or less conscious way [HOF 65]. In fact, this leads to a slightly naive anxiety towards the automation of combat – because the technology does not make itself. Rather, it is developed by humans, who cannot be "far". American political culture also contains the foundations of the processes of robotization. Nevertheless, this is only an anxiety. The place of man remains all the more central in American works because he is also the most sophisticated sensor available to the armed forces, the very foundation of the information system. He is also primarily protected and equipped as a function of his missions and, it is interesting to note, the United States are systematically positioned as normative influencers in this matter as regards other armies. It is equally remarkable to note that the increased attention given to the equipment of a soldier is similar to the RMA/*Transformation*.

Western soldiers now receive bullet-proof vests and more appropriate uniforms that allow the skin to breathe and have good thermal properties. In the 1980s, the "Fritz" helmets reappeared, protecting the neck and the ears from sound shock waves, but in Kevlar this time. The lashing, magazine carrier and other small equipment were designed to be ergonomic, like the main armament. Protection goggles appeared in the 1990s and have since been equipped with protection against lasers (of range finders and combat): the eyes are the main sensor of the combatant. Faced with biological threats, cocktails of vaccines were refined, though not without being called into question. Faced with chemical threats, the soldier was equipped with syringes of atropine and pyridostigmine tablets that should protect one third of his nervous centers in case of absorption of neurotoxins. Combat rations were also studied in order to optimize them nutritionally[28]. The use of drugs, alcohol and caffeine (the coffee of American GIs contains three times as much as commercial coffee) is a historical constant. It goes back to the search for intellectual concentration and lower fatigue – the use of amphetamines by *US Air Force* pilots and *US Navy* or the complements of food rations – or the disinhibition to violence – recurrent use of khat or coca leaves by African and South American guerillas. Drugs that repress violence must be added to the list as well, used individually to handle stress, which remains one of the limitations of humans[29]. In this way, each sector of the soldier's combat environment would be optimized.

The second development takes shape in the years following 2010, with the entry into service of equipment dubbed "the infantry of the future" – and which are the fruit of the discussions held by NATO beginning in 1989. This consists of including the soldier in the widespread process of informationalization. The search for informational domination involves surpassing the network of vehicles to reach the men. GPS, individual radios that allowed communication with the rest of the unit (and transmitting data) and night vision goggles are included in the kit of every infantry soldier. Previously, it was rare that units other than special forces would be equipped in this way. The soldier might also see his weapon equipped with an electro-optic that has various functions, whose images are projected on a small screen positioned in front of the eye. This allowed them to "shoot around corners" and verify *a posteriori* that a firing error had not been committed or to give the unit leader an idea of what different soldiers see to help him understand a given situation. The unit leader is himself equipped with a computer that allows him to transmit and receive data or command an attack. These evolutions have radically changed infantry combat. The connections between combatants mean that they can distance themselves from each other. So, for B. Cummings, *"when a dozen men launched an assault on an enemy position, they tend to stick together, looking at each other all the time, this is a very strong natural reflex. Now* (benefiting from new equipment) *they disperse*

---

28 At one time, it was a question of dosing his meals with enzymes that, when exhaled, allowed him to be tracked.

29 83% of US soldiers operating in Italy in 1944 saw their neighbor "crack" and endure *battle stress* that manifested as either complete silence or a hyperactivity that was just as problematic.

more easily, they are more adventurous as they remain in close contact despite the distance. They launch offensives not only better coordinated, as expected, but also bolder and more inventive" [EUD 03].

They could fight day or night, which had true military significance: war would never have to stop again. However, these evolutions are not without limitations. The transported equipment – and the batteries necessary for them to function – involves a weighing-down of men. In the beginning of the 2000s, an American soldier, completely equipped, carried 63 kg. The limits of what is physically supportable over reasonable distances were soon reached. The technicization of the combatant raised the question of his development. At this stage, two categories of models – non-exclusive and similar to the process of automation – appeared. The first can be qualified as the *neo-conventional model*. It aimed for the use of proven techniques or those in the midst of development and its integration to the equipment of a soldier who remains fundamentally integrated with the weapon systems that he uses. The use of nanotechnologies reduced the weight of carried equipment while research around battery efficiency augmented their performance by reducing their mass and their bulk. Insofar as the capacity of each person to occupy terrain increases, a lower number of combatants are needed to complete a given mission. On the front, men were spaced 2.5–5 m apart during the American Civil War. The division of World War I controlled 10 km of front, against 30 km in 1986 [GAR 95]. The terrain is more "controlled" by computer connectivity than by the geographical proximity of forces. It follows that the general format of forces can be compressed, reducing the troops but raising significant issues when it comes to conducting reconstruction operations, stabilization and the anti-guerilla struggle, all considered very human-intensive.

Data	Antiquity	Napoleonic Wars	American Civil War	First World War	Second World War	Yom Kippur War
Area occupied by 100,000 men (km²)	1	21.12	25.75	248	2,750	4,000
Front (km)	6.67	8.05	8.58	14	48	57
Depth (km)	0.15	2.5	3	17	57	70
Men/km²	100,000	4,970	3,383	404	36	25
m²/men	10	200	257.5	2,475	27,500	40,000

Table 5.1. *Evolution of the dispersion on the battlefield (source: [DUP 84])*

The adoption of a new state of mind – or, according to the accepted meanings, a new culture of war – was not problematic for the soldier. For B. Cummings, *"I thought that they would need weeks to feel comfortable, but it took them one morning. Young recruits belong to the generation of video games and the Internet (...) However, the supporters of the old school worry, war is still a tiring and messy task. There is no question of transforming the American infantrymen in small technicians with clean hands, on the contrary. Our goal is not to make the soldiers' life more comfortable, but to increase its ability to kill"* [EUD 03]. While this model is similar to what we observe today, it also involves giving the soldier back their mobility, a guarantee of tactical ingenuity and protection. The combatant would be equipped with an exoskeleton capable of evolving in contaminated areas but that would be capable of automatically giving its position to information systems. They would also receive continuous medical follow-up and nanotechnologies, run automatic translation systems, automatically adopt their camouflage and receive new weapons while they await directed energy weapons that use lasers or microwaves. The trials conducted on the "infantryman of the future" show men equipped with integral combinations and capable of fighting in highly lethal environments. In these representations, everything is done to present what the popular imagination identifies as a robot – dehumanized during all military action in a battle zone.

However, there is still a question of a potential limitation to this neo-conventional model, which critics say does not noticeably improve the physical performances of the combatant. This leaves a space for the development of a second category, the *cyborg model*, which aims to exploit the progress in matters of biotechnology, medicine and genetic engineering. It also touches on prostheses replacing limbs and the development of artificial organs. The knowledge of virology and genetic matters are such that the possibility of "reprogramming" the human body is discussed. At this stage, we are no longer in the techno-human connectivity proposed by the neo-conventional model but the bionic integration or, according to J. de Rosnay, to a "biotic" hybrid of man and machine [DE 01a, DE 01b]. While we are still far from that, certain concept models have already started and show a human system, conceptually packaged as *wetware* (hormonal, cardiac and cognitive sub-systems); *software* (training, acquired and innate reflexes) and *hardware* (muscular, bone and entire body sub-systems) [GRA 97]. This trisection normalizes the combatant of tomorrow, himself become a system of systems on which the adaptation of prostheses is only one extension of the system among others.

As the logical continuity of the vision of HUMRRO, this model dilutes the combatant in a pool of disciplines that should optimize each of their functions. Thus, the Americans have worked since the beginning of the 2000s to render the combinations of infantry not more intelligent (the regulation of the ventilation or its exterior), but "brilliant". Connected to the suit, the soldier is injected with trace elements or alimentary components. According to de Rosnay, the biocompatible nanotechnologies allow man to network with the exterior, and with himself, through biochips – once dissolved in the body's proteins – which can be communicated with and physically improve man at the atomic level, involving a network of transmitters, including hormonal in order to modify metabolic functions. These same biochips could produce the medication whose dose would be applied in real time. It does not consist here anymore of *Human-System Integration*, but of *Human Performance Enhancement*. The overtaking of man is within easy reach and has been conceptualized since the Cold War. The PITMAN program, led at the end of the 1980s, sought to develop an exoskeleton of 100 k capable of resisting 12.7 mm bullets and which would be directed by the nervous influx of the soldier through implants [DAV 87]. While the experiments involving such implants have been led since the 1970s on dogs and rats at Stanford in which the *US Army* was the most interested, it must be noted that the search for implants both nervous and muscular was consistently promoted, as much in the United States as in Europe.

However, such a combatant is not the ultimate step of the bionic combatant. The genetic engineering breakthroughs allow a glimpse of the militarization, because "*we count on genetic engineering to develop the ability to learn, skills, and improve the performance of the sensory apparatus, through the development of stimulants*"[30]. The widespread use of DNA tests suggests the possibility of selecting the best candidates for a precise military function, even manipulating embryos in order to make them acquire these capacities, in tune with a more and more invasive informationalization in military practices. But if this is the peak of technoscience applied to infantrymen, a "militarized eugenics" or even a military-cyborgologism does not seem guaranteed in strategic practice. Even the most fervent partisans of an excessive technologization of the American

---

30 [MUR 00, p. 187].

forces tend to reject this, as much for ethical factors as for the lack of attention given to more traditional concepts such as morality or training. This is the view of R. Peters in particular [PET 95]. Above all, the fact remains that the soldier tends to become "the tip of the lance" of the *Transformation*, and is himself susceptible to reifying the concept of technological superiority: his entire combat and attack environment has been "transformed"; there is nothing left to do but "transform" himself.

In filmographic terms, a *Universal Soldier* who is human rather than the robotic *Terminator* seems more probable. In any case, whatever model of combatant development that armies turn to, the soldier is only thought of from a network-centric angle. As a producer and consumer of information, it becomes a challenge of informationalization processes – with the appropriation/militarization by the manufacturers of defense of systems of the *smartphone* variety – as well as a generator of military effects. This is especially the case when the environment itself is stimulated by information and when the least smallest could have repercussions on a global scale. From this point of view, it is not a coincidence to see the idea of "strategic corporal" emerge at the end of the 1990s [KRU 99]. While the Web 2.0 had not yet emerged, the informational dynamic that it falls into was already well-anchored. This is not without consequences for the political representation and the ethos of the combatant himself. The reinforcement of individualism puts pressure on the cohesion of the units – which is their cement and their main force, because it equalizes the strengths and weaknesses of each – all while raising the issue of a military identity. The American soldier no longer addresses his superior, but "the network".

By doing this, the chain of command is less and less identifiable and, if we are not careful, the soldier risks becoming somewhat distanced from the political reasons for which he is engaged in combat. Yet, while the literature shows that they fight above all for their unit and their comrades, legitimation factors also play a role: he must also know why he risks his life and why he may die. The challenges of the informationalization processes are not insignificant for military structures, all the more because we are not certain that the gains of military efficiency are as systematic as studies from the 1990s led us to believe. The first feedback of the experiments of the "infantries of the future" is not necessarily positive. The increase of the mass of materials is such that all of the equipment is only used in certain cases. Human engineering, whether it consists of cables or the distribution of mass on the bodies of men, is not always considered optimal. Above all, the nature of the engagements carried out by the infantry does not seem to have evolved. The dispersion of combatants due to their "informational control" of the terrain does not compensate for the loss of physical protection (the mutual cover of men) that results. These two factors cannot simply be compared, by the very nature of war, and cannot be modified by a technical intermediary: while the network can affirm that no threat is present, it cannot guarantee that this is the case, because the adversary can adapt and may have set a ruse.

5.2.3. *Uncertainty and new armies of the old regime*

War in solid spaces is naturally complex, all the more because it tends to develop in increasingly striated solid spaces, which R. Peters qualified as "new forests" – urban and mountainous environments. It favors the defensive, which Clausewitz estimated to be the stronger form of war because the defender tires less than the assailant and is able to counter-attack in more favorable conditions. Similarly, the fog of war has not lifted and the uncertainty is reinforced for three reasons. First, the technologies create new conditions of uncertainty not only by the fact of their proper complexity (breakdowns, etc.), but also due to their rationality. Thus, in the "solid" environment of naval mines, it is a question of replacing the current combination of "detection by sonar, confirmation by human eye of the diver" with an automatic detection/confirmation installed on sub-marine drones. Yet, many mines were designed to be confused with rocks and a sense like touch can be necessary. This is what is reflected in the declaration of a French officer working according to the traditional method at the end of an exercise with American sailors working with the drones: *"That day, the French recovered six of the eight mines that had been placed in their area. The Americans found no mines, but sixty targets needing identification..."*[31]. The analogy between the operations at the bottom of the sea and those in an urban or mountainous zone seem relevant here.

The processes of technicization/informationalization are costly and involve reducing the volume of forces that can benefit from them. Yet, the rationalities examined in the last 40 pages do not seek, openly and formally, to exclude the human from war, even if there is indeed an anxiety regarding automation – or the externalization towards the private – of a maximum of

---

31 [SAR 08, p. 60].

functions. The search for an "information lock" of battle zones, which seeks to "fluidify the solid" in order to reduce the uncertainty, was constructed from the perspective of a close interconnection of the human in order to increase its freedom of manoeuvrability. From this point of view, the RMA/*Transformation* is not dehumanized – from all points of view, including moral, for that matter [COK 01] – and, on the contrary, revalorizes the place of the combatant. A certain number of the effects of technologies are counter-intuitive: drones, robots and reticulated "future soldiers" do not "dehumanize" war, they reposition human decision (and human perceptions, war being a dialectic) at the heart of tactics and the production of strategic effects. But the combatant wavers by turns between the figure of the operator and the elite soldier; between the procedural technician and the judge of situations so humanly complex that they become "over-political" – with the consequence that the national political level does not want to hear about it.

This leads to two outcomes. On the one hand, it reduces the freedom of political manoeuvrability when it is a group of human minds that confirms what electronic eyes detect. The same group that is likely to apply the rules of engagement – the military translation of political intentions as regards the conduct of conflict. On the other hand, the issue raised is the qualification of armies "*transformed*" into "new armies of the old regime", an expression that I owe to Laurent Henninger and Benoist Bihan, and of which the characteristics can be more worrying than the specter of the automation of war:

– As a result of the processes of professionalization and the suspension of conscription, armies composed of highly trained professionals appear. We notice that, these last few years, special forces – the peak of elite forces – are without doubt over-valued, to the point that the political can engage them in light infantry operations for which they were not designed, nor equipped, nor trained.

– This logic prioritizes quality over quantity, at the risk of being outflanked by a more numerous adversary and where obtaining victory is hardly possible any longer. The concept is hardly used, contrary to the figure of "success".

– These "new armies of the old regime" are otherwise engaged in operations which we would wish to confine to the "lace wars" of the 16th–17th Centuries, by applying completely controlled violence. Obviously, they can no longer be – as they were at that time – detached from the violence of war.

– These operations do not imply vital national interest, at the risk of suffering from a lack of legitimacy, as much at the level of national as local populations and up to the political ranks. In so doing, the appropriate means cannot be granted, which does not favor success and reinforces the temptation to conceive of forces that are even more qualitative. The military operations are closer to an "armed diplomacy" than a war properly speaking [SIM 12, SMI 15]. The logic at work is that of a "management of chaos" or a containment of threats. But the "management" is a managerial category more than a strategic one[32]; because a containment does not resolve the base issue.

– The last point can vary depending on the national institutional structures, but it implies a disengagement of the legislative level – and thus of the national political representation – faced with the executive, which intervenes more and more frequently within the scope of urgency.

Finally, this uncertainty reinforces the dynamic character of war and the appearance of hybrid forms of combat, between regular and irregular operations. Forces are thus capable of combining quantity and quality and inserting these into modes of action, such as the techno-guerillas, defeating our forces. Certainly, the classification of the issue as a "hybrid war" is relatively recent, although it has certain historical anchors [MUR 12], and it will undoubtedly raise the issue of the adaptation of our forces. The hybrid war combines "the worst of both worlds", putting advanced technology in the hands of actors who are more determined than us to win, capable of maintaining themselves in the long term and able to carry out both regular and irregular actions [HEN 14b]. By doing this, just like mass armies made up of conscripts have definitely removed all relevance from armies of the old regime, we can question whether hybrid forces will play this role for our "transformed" new armies of the old regime.

---

32 This prompted Hervé Coutau-Bégarie to write that the term "crisis management" was quite inappropriate when "we only manage the things we want to grow". The term "crisis maneuver" may be more relevant.

6

Waging War in
Network-centric Conditions

Since the appearance of the RMA/*Transformation* – or, more precisely, its portents – impacted the way in which war is waged by applying rationalities initially linked to fluid spaces to solid spaces, was the grammar of strategy also affected? It could be estimated that if the nature of war is invariable, its conceptual mechanics is equally invariable, but this would deny the dynamism of the character of war. The conduct of military operations has continued to introduce conceptual categories that have become norms – such as the principles of war or the notions of deterrence and interdiction – but the relationship between these different categories has evolved. We will not examine all of them in detail in this chapter, but it should be noted that our relationship to war developed as a function of the consequences of the RMA/*Transformation* on the way in which war is conducted.

6.1. The kinematics of operations

This is especially the case concerning what is connected to the kinematics of operations, or the manner of understanding their proceedings in relation to time – which is the essential dimension of strategy, not geography[1] – or space. The RMA/*Transformation* focuses on the hope of operations carried out at a very quick pace, destabilizing the enemy by literally compressing the time available for decisions and actions; this is not without consequences for the manner of contemplating the relationship to victory, defeat or legitimacy. But this view also has a double translation in space. On the one hand, this is

---

1 Geography is the primary dimension of tactics.

due to the expeditionary character of contemporary operations. The "transformed" armed forces thus see themselves designed to be projected onto geographically and culturally distant theaters of operations, symbolized by the war in Afghanistan – which saw, among other things, the deployment of Estonian and Swedish troops – or the operations in the Central African Republic, where the Georgians were engaged. On the other hand, this is due to the search for a fluidification of the solid through attempts to reinterpret ideas linked to maneuvers, offensive and defensive.

6.1.1. *On the conquest of time: chronostrategy*

Time is the poor relation of strategic literature, qualitatively and quantitatively. It must be stated that "time" is a concept with different meanings for different (sub)disciplinary fields, from Braudel (short-term, temporary, and long-term time) to Laïdi, who aptly demonstrated, among other things, different understandings of the idea of urgency [LAÏ 00], to Virilio, who demonstrated the development of a "dromopolitics" [VIR 77]. The translation of this view into the military domain has been undertaken by Christophe Prazuck. He showed that there are several forms of this inscription. Over the course of his intellectual thought process, he showed how much time could impact political perceptions and the acquisition of technologies. He looked at *resource time* – in the acquisition of their control, their deployment and in the correct understanding of what they can represent politically; *tactical time* – in their comprehension and potential adaptations; *ideological time*, showing their evolutions throughout history; *perspectival time*, seeing their successive evolutions; *strategic time* (which he associates with indirect strategy) and finally a time in strategy, an example of which would be the American policy of containment during the Cold War [PRA 97].

In international relations, authors like G. O'Tuatail or J. Der Derian have demonstrated that the appearance and large-scale spread of information technologies has led to a compression of the distribution time of economic, political and strategic information, which, in turn, model the understanding of distances and power relations, even the way in which the power relations are applied [TUA 98, DER 01]. There are even more extreme positions on the matter: for W.B. Wriston, information technologies cancel out time and space [WRI 05]. What is true in international relations is equally true from a socio-political point of view. From the 1970s, even before Toffler's writings,

D. Bell and Z. Brzezinski predicted a *technetronic society* [BEL 73, BRZ 70]. Next came a perspective in which information became an aid for decision-making that compressed the time reserved for the latter: we could do more in the same amount of time and decide on the best course of action. This is typically the reasoning that is upheld by partisans of the RMA. Subsequently, with the advent of projection technologies, these partisans adopted Paul Virilio's words that *"the real time of action and reaction impose itself on the real space of geography"* [PIE 00]. This reasoning was echoed by the supporters of the RMA, who used it in the search for speed through intelligence and command/control systems that allow the "transformed" forces to ensure complete control of time [SIN 96].

We can also ask whether these new technologies, applied to defense, provoke the strategic attempt to make time the ultimate strategic space. Concurrently, its control would be a gauge of success. The logic at work here spans both perception and action and was theorized by John Boyd, whose famous "OODA loop" (Observation, Orientation, Decision, Action) is one of the most oft-cited ideas in works about the RMA and the *Transformation* [FAD 98, OSI 06]. Stating his views in a series of briefings that were widely distributed before being formally published, Boyd thought that the ability of a given military system to react more quickly – physically, mentally and morally – than its enemy through the continuous process of self-adaptation, would lead directly to victory. He also considered military units (regardless of their level) to be organizations searching for survival and prosperity in a competitive environment. The adaptation process results in the simultaneity of multiple decisions, with cultural roots, whose structure can be explained by the OODA loop. From this point of view, Boyd produced a theory of action by cognition, or a manner in which a series of events can be understood.

From this perspective, conflict is the sum of the interaction of a multitude of OODA cycles that reflect the adaptation – or not – of antagonistic military systems in a continuum of the mind, time and space and whose intermediary is physical action. The practice of this loop reveals not only a tireless repetition at all action levels (it does not distinguish between tactical, operational, strategic or political levels) but also at all enemies and observers involved. Conflict is thus a complex process of combinatorial logics, in harmony with the Clausewitzian laws of reciprocal actions. This decisional dialectic between enemies that interpenetrate their OODA cycles has accelerations and decelerations. It is the correlation and the interaction of all the decisions taken on all parts that lead to a coherent maneuver of forces. But his meaning is not linear. What Boyd defines as the crucial phase of the OODA loop, orientation, is also the one where the relativity of time is the most significant. It consists of collating facts and diverse ideas in order to deconstruct them and better integrate them into decision-making, according to a multidisciplinary process that he calls "destruction and creation". For Boyd, all use of the OODA model must refer back to a combination of guidelines:

– "speed", a direct consequence of the model, must allow for "catching the enemy off guard". An idea and an action that are quicker than the opponent's, though equal in quality, must go into its decisional cycle;

– the "variety" prompts a range of options such that the uncertainty of the enemy must be reinforced;

– the harmony is the re-transcription, in time, of the principle of unity of command, that ensures the coherence of the combination of all cycles of the OODA and in effect defines efficiency as the absence of friction within the forces[2];

– initiative determines the acquisition of surprise, which practically allows one side to impose a desired pace of operations on the enemy, while depriving them of the ability to be proactive.

However, the control of time is only a tool to be manipulated. Boyd uses it for maneuver: his entire work is centered around maneuver, the famous OODA loop being simply a tool that was secondary to his purpose. From his perspective, the control of time was the prerequisite to imposing cognitive and physical chaos on the enemy. Boyd seeks to thicken the disoriented enemy's fog of war and maximize the probability that it will be subject to frictions that make it less and less capable of acting. This understanding goes back to that of B.D. Watts, for whom the side, which suffered the least friction, had the greatest probability of winning [WAT 96]. Generally, this logic is perfectly compatible with the strategic project of the RMA/ *Transformation*. On the one hand, the origins of Boyd's ideas go back to the 1970s and 1980s, models of the RMA, which itself played a large role in the theoretical debates of the day, specifically around maneuver and in relation

---

2 The question is even more crucial since the search for the best adaptation led Boyd to prefer a command style centered on *Auftragstaktik* – command by intent, centered on the initiative of the lowest echelons – rather than command by the plan, centralized. We will return to this question.

to technologies. On the other hand, there is a natural harmony between Boyd's view and that of the RMA/*Transformation*, which sought to impose its rationalities on an enemy – at the risk of negating the dialectic of opposite wills.

Yet, Boyd himself was Clausewitzian and did not absolutely negate the possibility of a counter-adaptation of the enemy, capable of bringing them to victory. In this sense, the RMA/*Transformation* made Boyd an absolute, reduced to the point of casting doubt on the critical plan of the theory that he had called into question. This unfair simplification is inaccurate, however, due to another chronostrategic logic: that of the irregular enemy. Where Boyd tends to exemplify the very Western preference for decisive operations [HAN 90] that quickly result in clear and neat victories, the contributions of Liddell Hart and, more broadly, theorists of small war and revolutionary war, show distinct uses of time in conflicts. They demonstrate the necessity of provoking a slow attrition of the enemy in order to make up for the inability to concentrate adapted forces. A long-term action, considered as such, is the result, which leads to a strong degree of coherence between political and military actions. There is a fundamental contradiction between a decision imposed in the short term and a decision constructed in the long term, there being an almost chemically pure opposition between regular and irregular modes of war.

This is the incapacity of the American Rapid Decisive Operations (RDO) used in Iraq in 2003 – which targeted the collapse of the enemy's strategic disposition by drowning it with crushing fire power[3] – to face the appearance of several phases of guerrilla warfare and rebellion. The example is extreme, but it effectively demonstrates the unsuitability of a strategic system faced with operations in which it may become engaged. The system must manage to question and set aside its cultural preferences for a regular mode of war. The difficulty, at this stage, is that the structure of force, its equipment, its theories and the training of men must develop under enemy pressure with successive adaptations. This is a long way from imposing a will on the enemy. Only the Clausewitzian "tribunal of force" can resolve this, although its judgment criteria do not depend on the degree of transformation of engaged forces, but rather on factors related to strategy itself. The differential of wills between enemies has direct strategic implications, because they increase with time – and perhaps this differential will increase

---

3 For a history of the concept and its criticism, see [HEN 07b].

more rapidly than the realization of promises for decisive results by transformed forces. In this framework, it is the idea of victory itself that is questioned. It can no longer be decisive because the very conduct of the enemy does not allow for decision making. The very fact that the enemy is able to resist technically superior forces for a long time is itself like a victory.

Only success can be considered in this way, at best. But again, this must be put into perspective from the moment it is obtained according to complex criteria and subjected to interpretation because of often poorly or little-defined objectives. We cannot reach an objective if it does not exist: that is a never-ending and atemporal strategic rationality, on which the introduction of networks or new technologies has no influence. This problematic is even more acute given that the objectives can, inversely, be unwisely expanded. It does not consist of only winning, but also stabilizing and reconstructing. The appearance of the figures of *state* and *nation-building* or even the general approach in strategic debates are concurrent with the use of expeditionary operations of "transformed" forces. The intervention made possible by *high-tech* networks and means of projection must also be politically ethical. But strategy is stubborn: the mobilization of human and financial means to attain such objectives is such that it is unrealistic if the supreme national interest is not involved – which is the case of several expeditionary operations launched in the last 20 years [SMI 15]. The asymmetry of wills cannot simply be bypassed by technology, and, while networks can compress time – which is already a great achievement in itself – they cannot expand it. Now, the major concern is the resilience of systems of force. While networks can help very indirectly – especially in integrated logistics management – they cannot remedy an incompetent political decision or the fog of successive evolutions of the phenomenon of war.

The long-term efforts of "transformed" force structures are not yet totally understood. The low volume of equipment bought – until it is considered more efficient by an action unit – goes hand in hand with an extension of its lifecycle, from its design to its service discharge through processes of "mid-life modernization" or incremental evolutions. Today, air forces that plan to revolve around 40 combat planes, which are designed to be operational for 40 years will no doubt be ill-suited for action then. It is not inconceivable that even just the attrition resulting from flight accidents will reduce the volume of the fleet by 50 or 60%. These extended cycles also conflict with the speed of enemy tactical adaptation. This is the main problem with military systems that have become techno-centric and only think in terms of technology: in addition to a quantitative deficit, they also suffer from a delayed reaction. The typical example is the American reaction to the arrival of the IED in the Iraqi theater. A new generation of 4×4 and 6×6 vehicles was designed in less than 2 years and 27,000 models produced, but in the meantime, Iraqi insurgents used preformed penetrators, more powerful and able to destroy the new machines [VIV 11, VIV 14][4]. This question of adaptation in time is also a difficult organic question. Great Britain increased its "operationally urgent" purchases in order to adapt to the Iraqi and Afghan theaters, but this exhausted budgets and destabilized the management of a number of other programs.

As a consequence of the logics resulting from the RMA/*Transformation* – and by networks – and also resulting from the weight of expeditionary thinking, the place of strategy in Western military machines was re-evaluated. It was no longer synonymous with war conduct in a given theater but tended to become a set of more or less managerial practices focused on preparing for the future. It consisted of seeking to reduce uncertainties – around the nature of future operations, for instance – as well as preparing to implement the evolutions of force structure with appropriate planning. The logics associated with networks play an important role in the matter: as of the 1980s, the management of logistics stocks, the planning of equipment maintenance and the management of human resources and soldier career plans were computerized in many armies[5]. Although the visibility of military staff in a certain number of sectors – certainly essential – increased, this was not the case for their potential capacity to evaluate threats or adopt a strategic position. There was also a temptation to only focus on the aspects that were most immediately caught by the networks – because they were more easily detected – rather than on the problematics that were subtler. The defensive plan, a naturally perilous exercise, was made even more complicated by a projection in time [DE 15].

---

4 The paradox of the matter is that the mass of the MRAP (Mine Resistant, Ambush Protected), larger because of the installation of the armoring, forced their users to use main roads rather than backroads. This made their movements more predictable.

5 Incidentally, not without showing the weaknesses of this logic. In 1979, the informationalization of the logistics stocks of the Iranian air force were incomplete due to the Islamic revolution and the departure of American advisors, leaving Tehran in a very poor condition.

6.1.2. *War and movement, war and command*

The temporal dimension is essential to the exercise of strategy and this is also the case in relation to movement, although less in the geographical sense of displacement than that of the application of armies. Networks play an essential role here because they enhance the two main modes of command historically used by forces, regardless of the level of engagement considered:

– the command by the plan is very directive and means that each actor has a precise mission to execute meticulously, with the complete orders forming a rigid plan. The task of adaptation is mostly assigned to commanding ranks once the plan has accounted for both friction and potential enemy reactions. In a similar way, the lower echelons essentially have an execution role;

– the command by intent, or *Auftragstaktik*, means that the upper echelons give very general directives to lower ranks, who must be aware of the purpose of the action. So, they become the echelons of execution and decision, and initiative is essential.

Both approaches have advantages and disadvantages. Command by the plan is very effective, especially for large armies, because it has the potential to execute very complex actions and takes full advantage of the forces of each unit engaged. However, it is also bureaucratically heavy and its implementation is vulnerable to every kind of friction, such as unexpected enemy reactions. Specifically, this type of command is important in the United States [BIH 14b], albeit with a few significant variations from time to time[6]. Because of a normative influence on the ideological framework, it also tends to be used by NATO member-states. In comparison, command by intent is especially suitable for smaller units but is less appropriate for the category of armies that are primarily complex systems and require specific back-up and support. On the other hand, this command system is more flexible when faced with frictions or the enemy. Historically, this type of command was used more in Great Britain, France, and to a certain extent,

---

6 This is the case of the Marines and within the US Navy, where the air and sea group – or the submarine – are relatively independent actors.

Germany[7]. Nevertheless, it also involves "getting everyone on the same wavelength", a real problem that Boyd tackled in his briefing, *An Organic Design for Command and Control*.

He demonstrated that the American philosophy of command and control has consistently favored a technological response. However, he considers an army to be a system operating on different levels whose coordination occurs through implicit links and interactions between the different components of a force. It is perceived as an organic whole where what is implicit in actions must prevail over what is explicit in orders, structured communications and hierarchies. From his perspective, the term "monitoring" is more appropriate than the term "control" and the concept of "influence" is more suitable than "command". Boyd tends toward a logic of command by intention and is based on the principles of harmony and initiative – which must also play a role in synchronization [BIH 12]. However, this perspective is more theoretical than practical: the reality of the use of networks shows that if they are actually playing a role in synchronization, they reinforce the American inclination – and, for that matter, NATO inclination – of command by plan. The information technology tools themselves, which include databases, spreadsheets, chat rooms and e-mails, are also tools for processing substantial volumes of information in real time, or nearly. The main problem related to command by plan – its lack of adaptability in the face of circumstances – seems to be resolved by this. Nonetheless the application of command runs the risk of *micromanagement*, interference between levels. This type of reaction is not new – J.F. Kennedy had direct access to the commanders of ships ensuring the Cuba embargo, taking control of military personnel – but the logic can be systematized, regardless of the echelon under consideration.

There is another criticism to add, which is associated with the spread of a logic of command by networks and implies a dependence on them. The processing of a mass of data is more than adequate intellectually, even more so because technological progress assures that the orders transmitted are actually carried out in real time – or nearly. At the beginning of the 2000s, the computers in the command network SIC (System of Information and Command) of the French land forces posted tactical situation

7 The Schlieffen plan, applied in August 1914, is a perfect example of command by the plan, integrating the data related to train times, volume of troops transported, the location of a certain unit at a certain time, etc. Refined by generations of staff officers, it was eventually defeated.

refreshments with a delay due to the movement of units [SAR 06], but the orders were given in real time. Today, the presentation of the tactical situation and the generation of orders are simultaneous. Similarly, the mobile command posts of the US Army no longer need to stop being used [DE 07b]. This means that in Western armies, the decision process – the OODA loop of the commander, regardless of his level – can be continuous. However, as discussed earlier, the RMA/*Transformation* is a discourse that tends towards a unilateralism and negates the dialectic of wills on the basis of imposing a direction on an enemy through technological superiority. However, the enemy is in reality liable to lash out at the decision system with attacks on the command system. The idea is evidently not new: the priority of "striking the head" appeared as quickly as the first definitions of the art of war itself.

The widespread use of the radio by the military, around 1910, was quickly followed by the development of wire-tapping, encryption technologies and radiolocation (which could be used to find and destroy command posts), as well as jamming and, later, intrusion [BON 14]. During the Yom Kippur War, Arabic-speaking Israelis infiltrated Egyptian radio networks, giving artillery batteries coordinates that led them to destroy their own forces. From these points of view, the "war of command and control" is not new [PLE 00]. However, it is being renewed by the increase in the possibilities of interference with the decision process, in several respects, which M. Libicki organized as follows.

Form	Sub-type	Innovation	Effectiveness/counter-measures
War of command and control	"Anti-head" (decapitation of command)	The targets are the systems, rather than the commanders	New technologies suggest that the protection of systems is possible
	"Anti-neck" (elimination of communications)	"Hard"[8] lines of communication	Redundancy and networking allow the pursuit of operations
War based on intelligence		Is easiest to conduct at the present time	The United States constructed this system but allotted too little attention to the ruse
Electronic war	Antiradar	Since World War II; *developments due to Suter*	Possibility of disconnecting emitters and receptors
	Anti-communications	Signs during World War I	Frequency hopping, larger spectrums, directional antennas
	Cryptography	Implementing facilitated digital codes	The current production techniques of codes favor the producers

8 Such as optical fibers.

Psychological war	Anti-will	No	Propaganda must adapt (1) to information in real time and (2) to "*me-TV*" (or the individualization of information sources).
	Anti-forces	No	Necessary adaptations to propaganda
	Anti-command	No	Calculations for deception are always complex
	Kulturkampf[9]	No	Towards a clash of civilizations?
War of hackers[10]		Yes	Every society becomes *potentially* more vulnerable
Economic war	Blockade of information	Yes	Several societies must still rely on information fluxes
	Imperialism of information	Since the 1970s	Businesses and war use information but business is not war
Cyberwar	Terrorism of information	No	The threat can justify better protection of private life
	Semantic attacks[11]	Yes	Too soon to say
	Simulated war[12]	Virtual reality approach	If the two enemies are so civilized as to simulate war, why conduct it?
	Gibson's war	Yes	Science fiction

Table 6.1. *Forms of information warfare according to Libicki ([LIB 00], modified by the author)*

Several authors understood very quickly that the power of Western forces exists primarily in a mode of command that is preoccupied with information technology resources. As early as 1991, military use of information technology viruses to paralyze command was theorized by an Indian author, V.K. Naïr [NAI 91] – before it developed into a thriving literature on cyberwar. For the moment, it consists of work centered on the cybersecurity of networks, which prompted Thomas Rid to write "*Cyberwar will not take place*" [RID 13]. However, the possibility should not be entirely excluded:

---

9 Libicki clarifies that the question remains as to whether or not an instrumentalization of culture (in a broad sense) exists in the framework of a conflict.

10 A war of hackers aims, sporadically or permanently, to undermine the operation of information systems.

11 Semantic attacks seek to make the information technology systems function normally, at least on the surface. In reality, this type of action allows giving incorrect responses to the system by manipulating data and software.

12 Just like "Gibson's war", simulated war implies a projection of the war act in a virtual reality. In the second case, this project operates through science fiction. Practically, these types of conflicts seem to have been placed in this taxonomy only for memory's sake.

because the technological dynamism in the matter is paired with an increasing dependence on information technology tools, it is likely that a strategic actor would seek, if it was not already available, to develop a new ultimate weapon capable of electronically eviscerating its enemies [LON 04, STI 15a, STI 15b, WIT 15]. Besides that, the historically constant search for the physical destruction of nodes of communication and command in zones of conflict and behind the lines is widespread and extensive.

This type of mission has even become especially legitimizing for special forces, air forces and the design of cruise missiles, whose commercial presentations consistently demonstrate their function in the struggle against strategic targets and their command centers. The development of conventional EMP (electro-magnetic pulse) weapons, which create an electrical overcharge on non-protected computers, also directly responds to this [HEN 05][13]. This is also the case for carbon weapons, notably used during operations in Kosovo in 1999. Upon release, the fibers that they contain infiltrate electronic systems, creating short-circuits. The debate about the vulnerability of networks of command, control and communications has also changed considerably. In the 1990s, the network (intended as a distributor) was perceived as a mode of certainty, with redundancy offering a resilience that would be able to keep an attack from reducing the ability of the network to function. Paradoxically, networks have become the enemy of the network: the reinforcement of intelligence capacities also introduced opposing electronic battle orders that were much subtler and more precise, offering a map of a network and its nodes in a more relevant military way because it allowed the clear designation of targets.

6.1.3. *Controlling and dominating*

Beyond the chronostrategy and the way in which the command is connected to it, the command must project power over a given zone. The concern is to find out what its expression will be. At this stage, two ideas evolve by trial and error. The notions of domination and control refer to complex and partially antithetical realities. On the one hand, domination was quickly invoked by supporters of the air force, citing the technological

---

13 A first system, the CHAMP (Counter-electronics High-powered Advanced Missile Project) was tested in 2012. The load, which could be activated several times, was equipped on a cruise missile.

capacity to eliminate all air threats[14]. Then, it became the stated objective of a combination of information warfare and precision weapons, demonstrating the inability of the enemy to carry out any movement without being detected and eliminated. On the contrary, control historically refers to a rationality that is closer to that of the US Army, leaving a margin of maneuver to the enemy by virtue of structural constraints: the fog of war is taken into account and it is less the intention to establish a domination that matters, than whether it is physically likely. The distinction between these two expressions of the projection of power is based on the stress placed on the interdiction on the freedom to maneuver imposed on the enemy – total in the case of domination, partial for control.

While these expressions – observed above in the framework of the American debate around the RMA/*Transformation* – have not yet been the subject of an in-depth analysis of their connotations, they are thought-provoking, because they refer directly to the logics linked to fluid spaces, which suggest that domination is possible, and solid spaces, which are more favorable towards control. Although we can also gauge the attempt to fluidify solid spaces by the figure of the network – of intelligence, command, strike – it must also be said that the French debate retains the notion of "control", which accounts better for frictions (compared to an overly optimistic domination) and results in more operational flexibility (compared to an overly defeatist control). However, the ideas of domination and control are also the results of a debate that sought to reconsider the nature of conflicts and their deployment in the spectrum of conflicts, or the field of different military interventions. This idea of the conflict spectrum became one of the major bases of the American ideological reflection. Historically – once again – this notion goes back to the Cold War, when the conceptualization of military operations planned a series of stages for the use of violence, politically steeped in the ideology of the flexible response which envisaged "*a reaction capability against all possible forms of attack, from general attack to the diverse types of aggressions and infiltrations that can be conceived*"[15].

The nuclear origin of the conflict spectrum was developed in the 1980s, as seen in the different editions of the FM-100.5, before being developed in

---

14 Note that this idea is partially linked to the development of the F-22 *Raptor* air superiority fighter. As the successor of the F-15, it combined stealth, advanced avionics and guided missiles, and quickly qualified as a plane of "air domination".
15 [POI 88, p. 205].

the *Discriminate Deterrence* report in 1988[16] and was then partially reconfigured at the end of the Cold War. Arquilla and Ronfeldt stated that a new era corresponds to a new conflict spectrum [ARQ 97]. As soon as there was no longer a designated enemy, the reflection focused, almost technically and in a depoliticized way, on the responses to be provided for the categories of missions, that can be presented as follows.

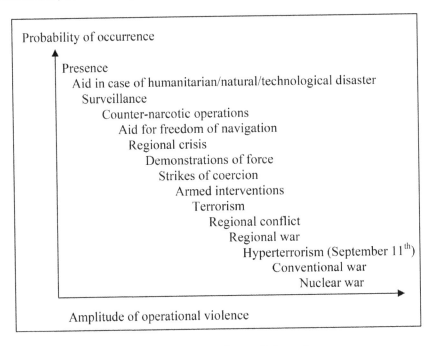

Figure 6.1. *Example of a conflict spectrum*

This classic representation of the conflict spectrum corresponds to a simplistic vision of war that favors a technical environment where the types of operations/conflicts appear easily classifiable and refer to a mechanical notion of operations. It does not highlight the complexity of interactions that can exist between these different conflicts, including when it is a question of "low-intensity conflicts" whose dynamic can rapidly develop into high

16 Which marks a departure from nuclear power as a referent of force, with some tactical nuclear missions being taken up by conventional forces. In this war, the Americans proceeded to increase the nuclear threshold.

intensity. A *comprehensive doctrine* has also been proposed [DIX 89], but it has also been criticized[17]. It also does not define a certain number of operations, that are intersecting and led to a more or less permanent manner. This is especially the case of operations pertaining to information warfare and counter-terrorism. However, the concept of the conflict spectrum also refers to specific rationalities. So, American ideological literature developed the notion of *Full-spectrum dominance* according to which, regardless of the missions being carried out, the American forces must systematically succeed, controlling and dominating by turns, regardless of whether the environment in which they find themselves is fluid or solid. The function of technology is central, from a tactical point of view – no spatial progression is feasible without technology – but also from an operative, strategic and political point of view.

When the authors were developing *full-spectrum dominance*, their argument focused almost invariably on information warfare, precision-guided munitions and stealth. Very quickly, it appeared that the construction of this type of research about the "domination of the conflict spectrum" relied on technology and its artifacts. Yet, as too few authors point out, this is precisely why a *full spectrum* approach is rich in the type of missions that it cannot consistently carry out technologically and why the rationalities focused on by networks are not consistently adapted. On the contrary, there are many more authors who denounce the results of such an approach, which include: culture blindness and a lack of adaptation to local constraints [KAP 05], greater attention paid to high intensity combat, ideological weakness in the conceptualization of counter-irregular and peace-keeping operations (including in the case of failed or collapsed states around which substantial debates were constructed), and vulnerability in asymmetrical operations. A focus on the art of technological war includes what appear increasingly like "operators" in a specific rationality, detached from realities. Talking about "control" and "domination" once again implies unilaterally imposing strategic behavior on an enemy who is discredited because he does not share the same course of action.

---

17 According to Colonel H.L. Dixon, there are four categories of low-intensity conflicts: insurrections and counter-insurrections, anti-terrorist operations, peace-keeping operations and Peace-time Contingency Operations (PCO). However, the variety of missions that fall under these categories is not very substantial and uses so much knowledge that we can question its relevance.

6.2. Waging war in networks

The discrediting of the enemy can take a very subtle form as a critique of a model that focuses on war centered on technology. It hinges on three concepts that appeared in the framework of the RMA debates in the 1990s: asymmetry and its consequences, symmetry and dissymmetry. Initially, the concept of asymmetry was mobilized as a critical instrument of the RMA. It generated an extremely large body of literature and while it has been given several definitions, they all revolve around the idea that American technological power can be circumvented "from the bottom" through an enemy's implementation of a series of appropriate strategic measures [MET 01]. Nevertheless, this concept quickly left the domain of academic debate, which incorporated an institutional narrative centered on an alteration through an inversion of its meaning – a type of movement that is also observed in the present day in debates around hybrid warfare. Concretely, the asymmetry is interpreted from an almost exclusively technological angle, which characterizes an enemy as having a lower level of technology. Yet, once again, technology matters less than its use and its essence when it is a factor of tactical order, carrying the seeds of a biased view of the enemy.

6.2.1. *The paradox of the enemy: the (non-)responses to asymmetry and hybrid warfare*

Consequently, the asymmetrical enemy is systematically defined as "weak", because the symmetrical claims to be "strong". The paradox of the debate revolves around the fact that the "strong" may be beaten by the "weak" without truly challenging the reasons for which the "strong" is perceived as such. The debate is the same as the one that took place at the time of the Vietnam War. The military personnel started from the principle that "he who can do more can do less", so it was assumed that counter-guerrilla operations would be easily dealt with by combatants trained in regular warfare, which was thought to be more difficult. This logic is evidently reprehensible from an operative or strategic point of view: even if tactical knowledge was identical in regular and irregular war, tactics alone have never been enough to ensure victory. The concept of asymmetry also underscores the ethnocentrism of the RMA: historically, only the most developed states have ever waged war in a symmetrical/regular way. Practically and on the contrary, asymmetrical and irregular warfare is more the norm. Irregular war and the procession of ruses, betrayals, misalliances and non-respect of rules and conventions do not constitute a kind of strategic trickery or militarized deviance. On the contrary, it is the essence itself of a war waged in a rational manner [LAM 03] – if only because war is still, networks or not, the *"confrontation of opposing wills"* of Beaufre.

The problem is made more complex because the integration of technologies by the actors can be different. Western states have, little by little, put in place a norm of technological distribution that is sometimes imitated by other states (Russia, China). However, this norm is the translation of a fundamentally linear positivism into the technological domain. As a consequence, technology, mythologized, is only considered in relation to a constant increase in performances – regardless of the system considered – and in support necessary for its implementation. The use of armed forces has become very technical, involving logistics and heavy support, because the systems of combat have themselves become very complex. However, it is not the same case everywhere, just as it has not always been at the core of Western forces. Any given strategic actor can break with this logic and seek to create a new balance between the contributions of technology and the constraints it introduces. As a result, the technology is no longer structurally obliged to engage in a very costly mode of regular war – in terms of budget and knowledge – and withhold a strategically profitable irregular mode of war. This is the whole problematic posed by techno-guerrillas engaged in hybrid wars that combine "the worst of both worlds" and also use networks and advanced technologies [HEN 14b].

The organization of forces and their relationships to discipline and professionalization, fire power, irregularity (and, from there, to the rights of armed conflicts), as well as the fact that they reveal new mixed orders, positions them at a break with the "new armies of the old regime". Paradoxically, an asymmetry is, in fact, created but it is only tenuously connected to what was meant by "asymmetrical threats" in the 1990s. Hybrid war suggests an asymmetry of wills and equipment (like all war), but also an asymmetry between modes of conduct. However, the reinterpretation of the operational, organic and declaratory fundamentals of resource strategy – and thus of the pillars of military strategy – is not the subject of such close attention as asymmetry. Asymmetry, interpreted through a technological angle, can be processed linearly, although this seems to defy logic: the technologically strong must win over the technologically weak. It is completely contrary to hybrid warfare. Its interpretation by institutions –

NATO, as it happens – showed that an actor having a comprehensive strategy is a tautological perspective once all actors hold a comprehensive strategy used in a more or less appropriate way.

Thus, the term "hybrid war/warfare" was used to describe Russian strategic conduct in Ukraine, as well as ambiguity and *proxy warfare*. But to twist the concept in this way totally pushes aside the contributions of the concept to strategic theory [HEN 15c, TEN 15]. Above all, this interpretation perpetuates a perspective wherein "transformed" forces remain seen as efficient, because their technological superiority has not been threatened. Faced with this type of operation, as when faced with irregular enemies, "transformed" armies have a hard time offering satisfactory tactical or strategic options. Admittedly, this is because nothing can replace strategy and its prime factors, such as will, and because only tactical excellence can counter the absence of strategy. It is also because the posture adopted can, quite simply, be rational and result in the study of the probable enemy and its vulnerabilities. So, the models of hybrid forces, if they were historically controlled by the enemy – and the result of the evolution of a very specific war [MUR 12] – are increasingly the result of a deliberate choice. Faced with "new armies of the old regime" that are fewer in number in order to be of a superior quality, it consists of combining quantity with a surfeit of quality. Of course, the qualitative level does not reach the level of Western armies, but it sees the acquisition of equipment and knowledge that were initially unique to Western armies.

This is the case for night combat, coordinated infantry assaults coming from multiple directions with back-up, anti-tank and anti-air combat by means of portable devices (what Rosenau called the individualization of power), control of a refined propaganda at a global scale (including social media), capacities of command, control and communication as a means of systems available in trade, or even the capacity to develop rudimentary chemical and biological weapons. In a certain number of cases, it consists of true *"competitive techno-regressions"* [ZAJ 15], to use O. Zajec's term. Some equipment is seen as useful either because it will allow for a roundabout use (the theme of *sidewise technologies* [BRA 05]; or because it is so old that the counter-measures to it have become out of reach[18]. The

---

18 In this case, the example comes from Hezbollah who, in 2006, used old field telephones linked up with copper cables for their communications. Contrary to radios, they could not be cut, bugged or scrambled unless the cables were actually found.

examples of use of a hybrid warfare have recently increased, at the level of non-state groups as well as States, including European conceptions of alternative strategy from the 1970s and 1980s; the quasi-conventional force of the POLISARIO Front in the 1980s; Tamil Tigers developing a navy and proto-air force in the 1990s; the anti-ship missiles, ballistics capabilities and ground combat tactics of Hezbollah in 2006; Chinese conceptions of popular war or coastal naval warfare; or even Iranian conceptions of coastal warfare [BRO 79, HEN 14b]. In this regard, a major break in the art of war is without a doubt developing. We will come back to this idea in Chapter 7.

6.2.2. *Future wars and wars in networks*

Faced with hybrid combinations and a strategic solution opposed to regular forces, Murray and Mansoor gave a clear warning: *"do not fight a hybrid war unless the most fundamental interests of the State are at stake"*[19]. The recommendation is even more clear because hybridity is only one type of enemy structure by which "transformed" armies will find themselves confronted, whether in fluid or solid spaces. In this respect, we can assume that they will deal with operations that have three main characteristics. First, a hardening can be observed. Historically, the firepower deployed by armed groups and states tends to increase and render military operations riskier. This tendency would continue and even accelerate. Access to relatively advanced technologies by combatant groups doubles by States adopting irregular modes of warfare. Beyond this, the hardening also passes through a series of evolutions: proliferation of navies (ships and submarines) and air forces in Asia-Pacific, renewal of conventional Russian, Chinese and Indian forces, and capacity increases in Africa and the Middle East.

A deregulation can then be observed. The conduct of military operations by the probable enemy would respond less and less to classic rules of the art of regular war, for which European states are trained, equipped and organized. As a mode of war historically used to support one-time or symbolic political objectives, terrorism – intended as an act of political violence led by a group of irregulars and targeting populations or civil infrastructure – would be widespread within groups using other types of irregular actions (insurrection, guerrilla or techno-guerrilla) or conventional actions at the same time. Beyond that, this deregulation equally affects all

---

19 [MUR 12, p. 307].

states, who are far from all respecting the rights of armed conflicts or who consider those rights as secondary to their interests. This has led to the cities of Aleppo (2016) or Grozny (1999) being literally razed. Similarly, the use of "improvised" chemical weapons by irregular groups, not subject to international treaties, that has been observed for about a decade would increase[20]. Practically, we must realize that only a fraction of forces "transformed" by networks and their logics are actually subject to law and ethics. While "transformed" war is perceived as ethically superior – because it allows for carrying out better informed and more precise (and thus more discerning) actions[21] – this view is not universal.

Finally, future wars will be marked by the process of "glocalization", on local and global levels and in a unity of time. The hostile strategic actors no longer work according to local logics. They have become global and target Europe in particular. They notably pass through strategies adapted to information warfare (cyber-actions of propaganda and influence), recruitment actions and also, potentially, destabilization, intelligence or cyber-strikes on European or American soil. As it happens, the technological advancement of "transformed" forces is projected on this glocal scale in the first place. This is certainly the case, as we have seen, with the global deployment of networks of command and control. It is also the case with deployment from a distance of means of reconnaissance and strikes. Without even coming back to the image of the *Predator* or *Reaper* drones operated from Nevada and monitoring Waziristan or Yemen, the inherent logics of air or naval strategy refer to this directly. During the operations in Libya in 2011, raids originated directly from British or French bases. In Kosovo, the American B-2 took off in Barksdale to go to hit Belgrade [HEN 05].

In all cases, this triple movement is not "a-reticular". On the one hand, this is because networks play an important role in this as systems of communication. On the other hand, and this is even more important, the way of thinking about the grouping of forces calls on new forms of rationalities, particularly pronounced in the debate of ideas since the 1990s due to the spread of the metaphor of the network. For Forget and Polycarpe, social relations are naturally reticular and are marked by the connection of nodes for interaction and producing power and influence. The network naturally

---

20 Thus, 17 chemical attacks occurred in Iraq from 2004 to 2008, with others occurring in Syria and Iraq since 2011. In 2016, material destined to make home-made bombs contaminated with tetanus was also found in Morocco.
21 See Chapter 7.

incorporates a set of actors in the relations of power (whether economic, political or military) by making them more fluid, more easily established and more resistant to attacks to which they might be subject. A reticular action emerges, adapted to the structure of socio-political relations [FOR 97]. Just like Castells in his trilogy, they demonstrate the radical modifications of the relationships to time and space resulting from reticulation [CAS 98, CAS 99a, CAS 99b], while nuancing the "revolutionary" significance of the network and the action associated with it. Similarly, the reticular rationalities are also examined in Arquilla and Ronfeldt. They propose the concept of *cyberwar*, in the sense of the military use of networks and not specifically in a cyber war [ARQ 93].

Above all, they analyze the more general evolution of the forms of conflict at a societal level, proposing the concept of *netwar* as a form of network-centric mobilization, which it refers to non-violent actions striving to generate an influence or insurrections [ARQ 01]. They argue that societal *netwar* and strategic *cyberwar* are not only subordinate to the emergence of information technologies but more specifically to its social consequences and, in the military domain, the possibility of breaking the lines of enemy communication like tearing the mesh of a net. In the case of *cyberwar* as *netwar*, the disappearance of hierarchies for the benefit of reticulated organizational forms results in, according to the authors, a change in the conduct of war[22]. In particular, the phenomena of mobilization are studied from the perspective of logics of *swarming* allowed by the conjunction of the individualization of the decision and the networking of actors [EDW 00, ARQ 01]. So, we are in a hybridization between individual and collective intelligence. However, in an interesting way, if the authors consider *cyberwar* to be a conceptual break, they struggle to conceptually reconfigure strategy, so that the reformulation of the art of war that they invoke only appears very superficially and constitutes more of an attempt at enemy mapping than anything else.

But we can question the relevance for the conduct of military operations of logics linked to reticular actions. Of course, the authors working on these conceptions quickly state that they qualify as those organizational practices that are in reality much older. It is also interesting to note that the practices of "combined war" – which networks forces with different origins and

---

22 In a much more debatable way, they also argue for a change in its nature.

modes of combat and whose contributions, although definitely differentiated, are mutual – can be observed very early in history [MUR 12]. But these same authors, while they do offer a new perspective on organic or operational strategy, are nonetheless confronted with the impossibility of redefining the principles and the characteristics of the conduct of war itself.

6.2.3. *Principles of war in the age of networks*

In a bout of positivist optimism in the 19th Century, strategic thinking sought to isolate laws that could ensure victory [GAT 91]. Practically, most of the authors who worked on this question preferred to speak of principles: whereas a law has a systematic character at all times and in all places, a principle only applies in a variable manner. The principles can be thought of as ingredients for the recipe of a successful operation, but the art of war is a kitchen where the ingredients vary depending on the dishes prepared. The facts are stubborn: the diversity of conflicts shows that the principles, as essential as they are, are applied in a variable way. Above all, there is a question of their number: only one principle does not help the strategy, but too many principles make reflection more difficult. Foch sought to find the essentials and he settled on three (freedom of action, concentration of efforts, and economy of means). Other authors have come up with more than 30. The principles are an integral part of the grammar of strategy – even the heart of its praxeology – but at what point are they affected by the appearance of networks? Because the maintenance of the fog of war and uncertainty has not totally been lifted, their value remains universally recognized.

If we start from the list of American principles, no principle has been fundamentally discredited, whether it is the objective, the concentration of forces, the economy of efforts, of surprise, of the mass, of the offensive, of the maneuver, of certainty, of simplicity or of unity of command. Rather, the question revolves around the consequences of the RMA/*Transformation* principles. While we will not return to the question of objective – which is a condition more than a principle of war – we can estimate that several of the principles were affected. The principle of the economy of forces indicates that all offensive concentration on an objective must be carried out in relation to the priority accorded to the objective, attempting to rationalize the use of forces as much as possible. While the generalized use of the combination of intelligence/precision munitions favors this, it also relativizes it. In effect, the adoption of dispersed machines capable of generating cross fire at a level that is no longer tactical but operative and strategic – this is one of the consequences of *swarming* – makes the economy of forces no longer a principle that is followed or not, but rather a structural fact of contemporary engagements. More broadly, the use of precision-guided weapons radicalizes the economy of forces with the possibility of carrying out "equational combat" where each target must be destroyed by a single munition [MUR 02, MAN 93]. However, this vision corresponds to a regular logic where the target is actually found. The question of economy is also budgetary in the context of a costly RMA. While it is striking when a tank that costs several million dollars is destroyed by a laser-guided bomb that cost $30,000, the economy of forces is relativized when the same weapon is used against a second-hand pick-up.

The question of the economy of forces merges with that of mass, which is interpreted in different ways depending on the country. Arranging a mass and working according to an economy of forces involves creating reserves which can be used to face an impromptu situation. In Israel, the economy of forces is associated with reserves and the search for depth. As an adjustment factor when faced with uncertainty, mass also produces a concentration of forces at the appropriate moment. It must be noted that mass is the principle that is the most frequently – and the most unanimously – challenged, due to the precision of weapons [LIT 00]. However, this questioning of mass is motivated by specific representations of military efficiency. If mass matters less in the context of regular engagements where technology partially compensates for quantitative reduction, this is decidedly less true in counter-irregular operations. As a direct consequence, in 2015, when the war in Afghanistan gave way to the formation of Afghan security forces, one of the most universal lessons of the war was that there was no substitute for mass and the coalition forces were never in a position to realize their objectives because of clearly insufficient resources.

An informal acknowledgement of the significance of mass occurred in the *Surge* in Iraq in 2007. It consisted of developing a local concentration of forces by increasing the volume of forces engaged in Iraq with massive recruitment, just like the volume of all American forces before that. D. Petraeus used a mass locally, drawing on the reserves. While the mass concentrated the forces, the latter was also challenged as a principle due to technological advances and the combination of networks and precision weapons. Historically, the concentration involved gathering forces before moving them to a point of the enemy disposition. However, the increase in fire sources with variable ranges – from the 4 km range of anti-tank missiles to the 1,500 km range of cruise missiles, including the 30–40 km range of artillery – can be used without assembling at a single point. Consequently, it is more often a question of a "concentration of effects" than a concentration of forces. It is also the case that contemporary operations involve as much "knowing" as "informing", with the generation of effects located equally at the level of perception. In this sense, the geography of the action is deconstructed between the actions completed at the local level by forces located at the regional level, with a global impact.

The fact remains that the concentration of effects also has limitations: targeting from a distance requires the ability to locate a target, which is a particularly arduous task in counter-irregular operations. In that case as well, the debates carried out since the 2000s continually recall the importance of a presence on the ground – and, logically, a concentration of forces. The latter also benefits from the logics of war in a network. *Swarming* involves temporarily concentrating forces coming from different horizons, using a ground route or an air-ground route. Consequently, its application according to the logics integral to the economy of forces requires a resilient and fluid C2 system, which can coordinate forces engaged in the operations as back-up fire [EDW 00]. The presence is temporary and the forces are then called to disengage – the foremost example is the raid. This rationality naturally has an incomplete geography of battle spaces. As the volumes of "transformed" forces are insufficient to fill empty spaces, the maneuvering of forces becomes indispensable: the control involves ubiquity by the movement, which is not itself allowed by technological intermediary, consisting of either mechanization/motorization or the use of helicopters.

Originally, the principle of maneuver focused on the kinematics of military planes, the enemy being placed in an unfavorable position [SCH 98] by the *"combination of fire and movement"*[23]. In this regard, the literature seems to favor the latter with new technologies but it also tends to overestimate their efforts, especially on the question of the quality of intelligence necessary for the conduct of movements [GUM 97]. The value of the "principle of war" of maneuver should be reconsidered as soon as the movement is not a principle of force but a possibility. The movement of forces is not automatic: if, on the tactical level, "staying still kills", then on

---

23 [YAK 09, p. 7].

the strategic plan, a surplus of activity borders on militancy and places forces in a situation of overheating. This type of situation borders on the overestimation of effects of technologies and a strict equivalence between quality and quantity – even though these two terms are not comparable. On the operative plan, maneuver can also prove to be difficult to lead, which is less due to new technologies than to the limitations proper to older technologies. The speed of the conduct of operations in Iraq, in March and April 2003, resulted in tiring the penetration because the logistics infrastructure of a hyper-technological army did not allow it to ever scale back its culminating point[24].

While this is a question of maneuver as a principle and not maneuver in the absolute, it must also be noted that the logics of informationalization increase the possibilities offered to armies. This is the case on the ideal aspect, in the sense that J. Boyd gives it. Movement is not so much an end in itself as a way to disorganize the enemy with the chaos it generates, disturbing its decision cycle and thickening the fog of war. For Boyd, this kind of action involved a unity of command centered on a shared understanding of objectives *of* and *in* war, that he strove to reach using *Auftragstaktik* but that could also be reached by the network. This is the case on the material side, on the other hand. In that case, the informationalization allows very diversified forces to cooperate through the figure of an interoperability that is not a given, historically, even within the same State. During operation *Desert Storm*, the US Navy and US Air Force fighter jets were allotted specific portions of the Iraqi sky, determined in a rigid way, in order to avoid friendly fire when the crews could not communicate amongst themselves. Not only can they do that today, but they can even do it with the planes of other air forces.

Networks considerably fluidify the circulation of information, and accelerate it. In 1991, the *air tasking orders* detailing the individual missions of each plane had to be printed and then transported onboard American aircraft carriers every day. Today, they are transmitted in real time and can be modified at will: the flexibility of the tactical planning is incomparable [HEN 05]. This evolution refers to several other principles of war. The first is the unity of command: while work can be completed in a network, it remains necessary to have only one commander and not several authorities

---

24 Or, according to Clausewitz, the point of effort above which all pursuit becomes counter-productive.

who could compete and create friction. Above all, the resulting flexibility also refers to the principles of the offensive and surprise. The first requires the practitioner to seize and preserve initiative to impose his own operational tempo. The second requires that the commander of a force does not reveal his intentions until the last moment, so that the enemy system cannot adapt in a preventative way. In this way, surprise is correlative to security: intentions that are too clear are vulnerable to enemy attack, which is a substantial concern because "transformed" forces do not necessarily have the mass to bear that.

The relevance of the principles of war is hardly affected by the process of informationalization. On the contrary, if well understood and well used by an inventive and ingenious commander, these principles actually increase in value. At least in theory, this is an optimistic vision of the effects of technology. It enhances the freedom of maneuver. However, this view should also be challenged, because the process of informationalization involves speed as a structural factor of combat: the commander must be more inventive, faster. Without this, the risk of a tactical/operative exhaustion is substantial, because it is dictated by the tempo of operations, not the reasoning of the command. This view should also be challenged because everything that has been written on the military superiority offered by networks assumes that their architectures remain functional and operational – yet, one of the problems of the RMA/*Transformation* is to tend to render military action unilateral, to the detriment of taking into account the enemy and his actions. In other words, relying on only one network for command management involves violating the principle of security.

Many resources exist to avoid such a breach. Several armies work with networks at the same time, while conducting exercises using occasionally deteriorated work arrangements. By doing so, the network becomes a limitation, because it involves a weighing-down of training loads from the section to the highest levels. Yet, the reduction of the formats of armies, due to the positive effects predicted for these technologies, also involves a reduction of the operational availability, or that of the volume of knowledge acquired by the soldiers in a given time. This brings us to simplicity, another principle of war that can counter these harmful effects. Responding to the friction, it is itself offset by the complexity of reticulated systems whose very design implies major vulnerabilities. In the political fiction novel *Ghost fleet*, these weaknesses are also at the heart of the fictive conflict analyzed [SIN 15]. Stemming from information technology systems, these vulnerabilities have been singled out as one of the main threats for Western armed forces since the beginning of the 2000s. Paradoxically, the simplicity of operation plans and procedures, which are a sign of success and which are potentially increased by the fluidity offered by networks, collide with the complexity of the networks.

The first of Foch's principles, freedom of action, is not listed as a principle of war in the United States – no more than others used elsewhere, such as destruction, preparation, or morality[25] [VAU 83]. However, even if "freedom of action" is, in the conduct of operations, the product of the combination of several principles (simplicity, security, mass, maneuver, etc.), it is also a value in itself. In reality, it is not only a result. It is also and above all the first condition of tactical inventiveness and adaptation: it is the great possibility of tactical or operative choices that make it so that an action may surprise an enemy and so that a potential weakness can be transformed into a strength. In this sense, everything that is liable to reduce this freedom of action is problematic. Also, while networks offer significant advantages, their characteristics complicate the work of military managers: if watching the security of their disposition is historically complex, they enter in a situation of dependence forcing them to also ensure the security of their networks. This is not a problem in itself, as soon as the history of the art of war is also that of the construction of a massive work of new functions, notably of support. On the contrary, the risk is located at the level of an over-focalization on technical factors, which are always distancing themselves a bit more from strategic rationalities – the dialectic of opposite will – and politics
(the "why") of war.

For now, no war waged by "transformed" forces seems to have been lost by networks, which have up to now played a role of multiplier of force, fortifying the strategic choices of armed means which saw their force abundantly increased, even though operations led for 20 years have centered on the struggle against insurrections. But, besides the fact that the aforesaid wars were not necessarily won – mainly due to strategic deficits – it must also be noted that at least one state has lost a war by networks. Iraq in 2003 saw, from the first hours of *Iraqi Freedom*, the destruction of all of its nodes of communication and several fiber optic points of passage. Added to this were the now-traditional attacks on radar systems and posts of command

---

25 The latter was considered in the United States as a "principle of operation" [GLE 98].

[DE 07b]. The reduction of the freedom of movement in Baghdad – already weakened by more than 10 years of embargo and the war in 1991 and a series of strikes of varying magnitude – was thus rapidly reduced. It did not crumble definitively, as attested by the maps found after the operations, which clearly show the positioning of American forces, or the conduct of several tactically relevant actions. But the fact remains that Iraqi forces could not immediately lead localized tactical actions; their style of command, very centralized and deprived of communications, did not permit a rearticulation of the disposition. This is no doubt a matter for reflection.

7

Striking in Network-centric Conditions

While the conduct of military operations is certainly affected by networks, these networks only demonstrate the full power of their resources through precision strikes – another key component of the RMA/ *Transformation*. Together, they produce military effects but doing so requires the use of intermediary targeting processes: the "what" to strike. While it is relatively simple tactically speaking – we strike what we see – it is, however, considerably less simple when fighting over great distances and, *a fortiori*, when the engagements are expeditionary. This is where we find the theme of the search to fluidify solid spaces, with all the hazards and limitations of such a logic that we discussed previously. However, it should be noted that this process of fluidification has already been – at least conceptually – at work since the 19th Century, when the art of strategy came of age and the question of the strategic anatomy of the enemy appeared. This led to the issue of the center of gravity raised by Clausewitz becoming central to strategic thought. Representing the "hub of power", the center of gravity is the source of the enemy force – so it can be identified as a critical vulnerability, especially because it is a force. Generally, eliminating it would lead to certain defeat, the enemy having lost all strength.

It is not a coincidence that the center of gravity appears at the heart of reflections on air strategy by Warden and Deptula [FAD 98, WAR 98, MET 99, WAR 95]. As the subject of in-depth theoretical reflections [HIA 99], the concept remains difficult to manipulate from an operational point of view and is still one of the nightmares of students of war who must learn how to isolate it. While a center of gravity can be material, it is more often immaterial – typically, an ideology – and is thus difficult to target[1]. Nevertheless, it maintains the illusion of a fatal blow that would allow for leading a decisive battle and offers the prospect of an "easy war" that naturally resonates with the discourse supported by the RMA/*Transformation*. Networks also play a dual role with regard to the concept. On the one hand, sharing information of all kinds can be used to build a representation of the enemy, which, consequently, involves a more refined capacity for synthesis and analysis on the part of military planners. On the other hand, the rationality of the network aids in understanding the complex interactions that make up the anatomy of the enemy. In this case as well, however, the network requires that the planners acquire a sharper capacity for analysis. Beyond that, the issue of the center of gravity is not without consequences for the way in which operations are conducted.

One of the advantages of the concept is to highlight the non-kinetic factors of strategic actions by mobilizing the diplomatic line of operation, media operations and influence, or even electronic war. In this way, it allows us to return to the fundamentals of strategy and leave behind a view where the strike is the objective in itself, because in reality it is only one intermediary of many when obtaining a politico-military effect. Nevertheless, non-kinetic actions are not necessarily enough – if only because they rely on the possibility of kinetic action – and must most often be used simultaneously. However, the structure of kinetic action has itself changed due to the use of rationalities related to networks. In this chapter, we will first concentrate on the developments linked to precision and the sometimes paradoxical effects it generates. Second, it seems necessary to offer a contrast to this issue by highlighting the fact that it is not uniquely linked to "transformed" forces, because the potential enemy is gradually appropriating it.

7.1. A paradoxical precision

The combination of precision weapons and networks had major effects on the structure of operations, from the tactical level to the strategic level, in the field of air strategy more than anywhere else. Since the 1950s – and notably

---

1 In parallel with identifying a strategic center of gravity, the process consists of determining an operational center of gravity, necessarily material and which can be attacked. Achieving the latter paves the way for achieving the former.

during the Vietnam War – an air strike was carried out, ideally, in one of two ways:

– Missions of *Close Air Support* (CAS), which included pilots communicating with troops on the ground and causing them to intervene "on demand".

– Raids, the results of complex planning (deliberate targeting). They included the grouping of several dozens of planes representing a variety of complementary functions: attack, air superiority, suppression of enemy air defense, in-flight refuelling and eventually, reconnaissance and electronic warfare.

Complex in their planning, raids are part of a pretty rigid framework that networks partly initiated. Beyond the fact that flexibility has allowed us to reduce the number of planes engaged, the logics of information sharing have led to a comparison of the rationalities of CAS and deliberate targeting. While the latter is always used when the necessary intelligence is available, operations in Kosovo and later in Afghanistan showed a shift towards *flex targeting*. In this framework, the planes remain on patrol tracks until being sent "on demand" to objectives, and the munitions, free-falling or equipped with propulsion, can themselves be fired from a holding position. Networks have allowed for an increase in the reaction: during *Desert Storm*, reaction time was several hours, but during operations in Afghanistan, it was less than 10 min – sometimes even less than 5 min. The planes engaged were themselves loaded with a variety of precision munitions with different effects, offering variable fire power and able to adapt to a large number of operations. By reducing the risks of friendly fire, guided weapons are just as effective for strikes conducted in close proximity to friendly forces as those conducted at the heart of enemy territory, including in urban environments where the risk of civilian losses is higher.

7.1.1. *Certainty of striking*

However, while "precision" is measurable in terms of the weapons used – and has become a regime unto itself [MAH 11] – it is not necessarily perceived as such because war is a chaotic environment where errors are always possible. "One death is one death too many": this can often be heard or read when it comes to a question of moral judgements on war and its consequences. If the weaponry and precision strikes change the situation from a tactical point of view, is this also the case from a political point of view – the only one that matters when it comes to war? The answer to this question may seem evident at first: because it leads to a greater tactico-technical efficiency, precision automatically has political effects. However, looking more closely, it is not that simple, especially from a point of view of shaping perceptions and especially in an environment witnessing the generalization of drones, which have the connotation of an automation of war. In the past few years, there have been a large number of published works and articles dedicated to armed drones, most often from a legal-ethical angle. This is a unique and extraordinary phenomenon when we compare the themes approached in works on strategic questions since the 2000s. The combination of MALE drones and their guided weaponry is seen as a particularly deadly weapon regarding civilian populations.

It would be a weapon of the morally weak, and involves a distancing with no possibility of response for populations while being used in crises whose classification as a conflict may not be clear. While these arguments, which can be found summarized in the work of Grégoire Chamayou[2] are largely dismissed [JEA 13a JEA 13b], it must also be said that the concern regarding civilian losses is a social fact in itself. It has been compounded by the use of the term "collateral damage", which emphasizes firing error and its low probability, while euphemizing death and distancing it from the reality. In reality, while the statements of several armies still use this term, which has been reasonably condemned for its inability to reflect the reality, the reference term in these same armies is "civilian losses" or CIVCAS (*Civilian Casualties*). Where does this anxiety towards civilian losses come from, despite being in part deconstructed by an objective analysis of the use of weapons?

Of course, it is a question of targeting: more than just the weapon, it is the enactment of the rules of use and their respect that matters. Beyond this is the question of the weapon as a producer, by its own inherent effectiveness, of vulnerabilities. In other words, there is a "paradox of precision" in which the weaponry, because it is considered to be advanced technology, is perceived as less lethal for populations and, indeed, as "less ineffective". In the wake of this, all CIVCAS are liable to be criticized precisely because our perception of the weapon is skewed. This means that being effective is

---

2 [CHA 13b] Note that the English translation, expected for 2015, was refused by Oxford because the method was not considered scientific.

politically problematic, especially when carrying out "war amongst the people" or within army communication and marketing. To figure out how it came to this, it is helpful to put the very origin of the idea of precision into perspective. Fundamentally, precision is above all a measure of the economy of forces. A bomb or precision missile must produce an "equational combat" or each weapon must destroy an objective, thus streamlining the use of munitions.

Recalling that weaponry precision is central to the idea of the second *offset strategy*, the quality should compensate for quantity [TOM 07]. The logic is to increase the number of hits by available effector – tank, plane, soldier – in a given time; the only intermediary to do this being precision. For tanks, the representation of this approach was the fire control electronic system combined with the canon stabilization that made it possible to fire while moving, because radio networks could ensure the best possible coordination. Military journals in the 1970s and 1980s showed the calculations according to which each NATO tank would be able to destroy five or six tanks of the Warsaw Pact before it gets destroyed itself, to hope for a conventional victory, avoiding the need for recourse to nuclear fire. For aviation, the rationality was similar. Historically, two options were available to pilots. A low altitude strike could be precise but had the potential for friendly losses. On the other hand, the targeting technologies developed for high-altitude strikes were so unreliable that some navigators of the bombers in World War II preferred not to use their sights. Even when the bombers were equipped with the Norden sights, the precision was still very low.

In 1941, the planners of the *Air War Plan Division*, who arranged strikes on Germany, estimated that the probability that a 30 m by 30 m target would be hit by one of the 108 bombs dropped by 54 planes was 75%. Being certain of hitting a target that size involved dropping 135 bombs[3]. It is even doubtful that this relative precision was ever reached. So, by the spring of 1944, only 7% of bombs dropped during the bombing campaign had exploded closer than 304 m to their objective [HAL 95]. Between April and May 1945, only 13% of the bombs dropped on Germany refineries fell within 300 m of the targeted point of impact, with the others landing outside that range [HAY 95]. The technological advances at the level of platforms did not guarantee a better precision during the war. During the summer of 1944, 47 B-29 bombers used their Norden sights to drop 376 bombs on the

---

3 Keep in mind that probability 1 does not exist in mathematics.

Yamata steel mills but only one bomb actually hit the factory [HAL 95]. In the end, results were actually achieved against industrial targets[4] but the image associated with strikes is that of German, British and Japanese villages in flames and massive losses of a population deliberately targeted. Between 400 and 600,000 German civilians and more than 300,000 Japanese civilians were killed by Allied raids. On 9 March 1945, the largest raid of the whole war, on Tokyo, caused between 80 and 100,000 deaths on its own.

Still, World War II saw the appearance of the first guided weapons in the naval domain, though their use was only marginal. The B-24 was used to release acoustically guided torpedoes and Germany successfully used the *Fritz-X* missile. After the war, the Americans worked on ideas for bombs guided by AZON, RAZON and TARZON radio but the weapons, a few of which were used during the Korean war, were not very reliable. The experience of the war led the US Navy to develop the *Bullpup* missile and the *Walleye*, an electro-optically guided bomb. Nevertheless, it was not until 1964 that the first laser-guided weapons were tested. The irregular context of the Vietnam War pushed technological innovation: it consisted of striking roads and bridges, sometimes in urban zones. As of 1968, some of these bombs were tested in combat, but it was not until 1972 and the destruction of the Thanh Hoa bridge that their value was recognized. Between 1965 and 1972, the treatment of the heavily defended bridge took 873 sorties and involved the loss of 11 planes. Despite several hits – though poorly placed – the bridge resisted until an attack carried out on 27 April 1972 by 12 F-4 *Phantom II* of which eight were equipped with laser-guided weapons. Two other attacks on 3 May and 6 October rendered the bridge unusable until its restoration by North Vietnam in 1973.

Laser guiding also became available for deep strike missions as well as for CAS. Four hundred bridges were destroyed or damaged with only 4,000 guided weapons during the Vietnam War. Similarly, 70% of the tanks destroyed during the North Vietnamese Easter offensive in 1972 were destroyed by these weapons. At the end of the war, 28,000 laser-guided weapons had been dropped, representing less than 1% of aviation bombs. Immediately after, the US Air Force concentrated on developing new guided munitions, seeking to reduce the limitation of uses linked to lasers. This mode of guiding was vulnerable to diffraction of the ray when it was raining

4 The German transport capacities by rail were thus reduced by 50%, the production of aviation fuel by 90%, and the production of steel in Ruhr by 80% [MEI 03].

or snowing, during sand storms, or even when the fog was especially thick. These efforts resulted in programs like the AGM-65 *Maverick*, which used several types of guiding (laser, infrared, electro-optical). However, the assimilation of new capacities of precision fire by the military would take some time. Until the beginning of the 1990s, air reference ammunitions were free-fall bombs or rockets, which are, by definition, not guided. In the mid-1970s, aeronautical journalists still classified them as costly gadgets. Nevertheless, precision brought about a true tactical revolution: *Desert Storm* was the first war where a single plane could hit several targets in a single outing[5]. The era of *flight packages* where several planes were assembled for targeting a single target was virtually over.

7.1.2. *Certain to succeed?*

From this point of view, the "social discovery of precision" took place with *Desert Storm*, even if only 7% of the air munitions used during that war were precision weapons. This "social discovery" was only possible because of the wide distribution of images from optronics showing bombs passing by windows or chimneys or cruise missiles "turning around a street corner". These capacities had been available since the 1970s – the first work on the *Tomahawk* missile occurred in the 1960s – and would have been used in the event of a conflict between NATO and the Warsaw Pact in the 1980s. Nevertheless, it was the media focus on the strikes that solidified what was possible with precision in the eyes of the public, political levels included. The impression was further amplified because the power of the Iraqi forces had been overestimated – because they had the "fourth largest army in the world" – and because stealth and anti-missile defense technologies (themselves also relatively old[6]) were also widely broadcast. The operation also encouraged the development of new guided weapons, especially those guided by GPS – about 30 cruise missiles equipped with the first version of this guiding were fired in the greatest secrecy during that war. One of the results was the JDAM (*Joint Direct Attack Munition*), guided by GPS and which, though less precise (15 m of CEP[7]) than a laser-guided weapon, was all-weather.

---

5 The "target" should be distinguished from the "objective", which can be made up of several targets.

6 The F-117, used for the first time in operation in Panama in 1989, flew for the first time at the beginning of the 1980s. The *Patriot* missile entered service in 1984.

7 Circular Error Probability: the radius in which a weapon has a 50% probability of hitting.

Since 1991, the use of guided weapons has only increased, in both transformed forces and others [MAH 11]. A second break, essential for understanding the contemporary model of engagement of forces, came about with operation *Deliberate Force* (1995). From April 1992 to August 1995, Sarajevo was besieged by Serbian forces from Bosnia, resulting in 14,340 civilian deaths[8]. UN forces – including French forces – were also present in the city, but after some of its soldiers were taken hostage and attacks occurred on the city streets NATO decided to intervene with artillery and air strikes on the positions surrounding Sarajevo. Specifically, 3,515 sorties were carried out over 22 days, dropping 1,026 bombs (of which 69% were guided weapons) on 338 targets, of which 80% were seriously hit. French and British artillery, supported by German intelligence, were also engaged [HEN 05]. Not only did the Bosno-Serbian forces retreat from their positions but the operation was one of the main factors that led to the negotiations at Dayton, which put an end to the war in Bosnia. The operation was a military and political success obtained at the price of losses that were considered acceptable: about 20 Serbian civilians and one *Mirage 2000D*. However, although *Deliberate Force* is a model of its kind, its value as an example also biases the perceptions of future war.

The operation around Sarajevo carries the seeds of the myth of "precise war" with "zero deaths" that operation *Allied Force*, on Kosovo and Serbia, abolished in 1999. Out of 23,000 weapons dropped, 35% were precision weapons but the increase in altitude in order to counter the Serbian anti-air threat produced unconvincing results. Besides the fact that Serbian forces were barely hit, primarily because they used jamming systems, the Serbian civilian losses were considerable with more than 500 deaths. Of course, this could be considered an "improvement" with 0.002 civilian deaths per bomb dropped on Kosovo versus 0.019 civilian deaths around Sarajevo 4 years earlier. However, the operation in Kosovo was widely criticized for a series of reasons not connected with the use of precision munitions: the relevance of its launch, counter-productivity, the use of depleted uranium shells, and targeting errors that caused the destruction of both a bridge on which there were civilians and the Chinese embassy in Belgrade. So it is *despite* the relative decrease in civilian casualties that the operations – which did reach the desired goals – were criticized.

---

8 The total loss due to this siege was 18,888 people.

The question was raised again with the engagement of drones in strike operations in Yemen, Pakistan and Afghanistan in a counter-irregular context. They were equipped with sensors/designators that were very powerful but that could not correctly "paint" the target with a laser (so the missile is liable to miss) when the planes are lighter than combat planes and consequently more sensitive to climatic and aerological hazards. Beyond that, being piloted – the drone not being "without a pilot" and therefore less of a "killer robot" – from a distance and from the ground allowed the operators to be joined by specialists on intelligence or rights of armed conflicts. Evidently, these practices cannot be adopted by combat pilots or by the commander of a submarine launching cruise missiles, which renders the debate about the use of drones that tends to inappropriately simplify the technology even more surprising[9]. The precision of shots fired by drones depends whether they are 227 kg laser-guided weapons (of which about half have explosive loads) or AGM-114 *Hellfire* missiles, also laser guided, but with an explosive load around 8–9 kg, depending on the version.

When conditions are ideal, precision reduces lethality, and the same can be observed about weapons equipped with DIME (*Dense Inert Metal Explosive*) loads, optimized for engagements in urban zones, which reduce the lethal radius of the weapon's explosion. This type of load was used in the Gaza strip by the Israelis. However, in these different cases, where the precision munitions are consistently used, the strikes are also contested. The problem is not necessarily the weaponry and the sights, but the intelligence and the decision process that leads up the firing. The weaponry can be criticized, however, because DIME munitions use an alloy of toxic tungsten, which is carcinogenic for whomever it touches. In fact, the topographical and tactical situation has changed: contemporary engagements occur in an urban or constructed environment, against an enemy who is "immersed" in the population and can only be distinguished by observing behavior and/or who can operate from civilian infrastructure. In the law of armed conflicts, they become legitimate targets but in an environment of high human and media density, the legitimacy of a strike stems less from a respect of procedures or a correct work of targeting than from how it is perceived. The Israeli case is especially illuminating in this regard: the strikes carried out in Gaza are in one of the densest urban environments in the world.

---

9 From this point of view, the use of drones revives the previous practices involving the traditional combat of air or naval forces.

Almost automatically, this leads to increased losses: 1,463 civilians killed during Operation "Protective Edge" in 2014 (UN High Commissioner for Refugees); 105 during Operation "Pillars of Defense" in 2012 (Palestinian Center for Human Rights); 926 during Operation "Cast Lead" in 2009 (Palestinian Center for Human Rights) [LAM 12, KUR 14]. While the absence of data about the number of munitions fired means that we cannot establish a ratio of civilian deaths per weapon fired, it should be noted that the interference between civilians and combatants would remain problematic despite the quality of the Israeli systems used (targeting pods, weapons). As a matter of fact, the issue with sensors has hardly evolved since the Vietnam War. While they have certainly improved in terms of technical performance – their resolution, multispectral ability and a greater precision at night – the main difficulty is not in the observation, but in the interpretation. It is possible to see better, but the character of contemporary conflicts means that we understand less. The logics inherent to networks of the reconnaissance-strike – to use the Soviet term – collide with logics related to the perception and its models, including networks.

7.1.3. *Wars lost by precision?*

Precision is equally liable to be deconstructed, here as elsewhere. Social networks can transmit every error, with supporting images, on a massive scale, but they can also construct artificial losses for political ends. There are several cases of photos of people affected by other conflicts being used in this way. Similarly, the format of these networks – like Twitter's famous 140 characters – do not allow for any contextualization or reframing: the civilian killed draws more attention than the legitimacy of the objective in which they found themselves at the wrong moment. The very fact that anyone can publish on these networks opens the door to the potential for manipulation. One illustrative example in the matter is the Saudi strike on a Yemeni munitions depot in May 2015, filmed close-up and showing the rapid ascension of a ball of fire and a mushroom formation. Commentators concluded that an Israeli F-16 camouflaged in Saudi colors carried out a strike with a neutron bomb [DUF 15], a technically and politically absurd scenario.

These issues of mass manipulation are not new. During the Six Days' War, the Egyptian press reported that the Israelis were using nuclear weapons against the Cairo forces, when they were really using napalm.

Nevertheless, large-scale manipulation is much easier today, at least once a war is the subject of media attention. While it is not a question of minimizing the extent of civilian losses in media-intensive wars, it must be noted that the media covered is distinguished according to the case. The Sri Lankan operations in 2009 that put an end to the secessionist tendencies of the Tamil Tigers revealed an accumulation of war crimes. An estimated 20,000 civilians were killed, mostly by an indiscriminate use of artillery [PHI 09]. As it happens, Colombo banned all media coverage, literally cutting off the rest of the world [MOO 14]. Several of the "dirty wars" were, paradoxically, the subject of less criticism than wars where precision weapons are used and where the civilian losses resulted from errors and were not deliberate. Added to this, as concerns traditional media, is the classic but underestimated problem of the "journalistic fog" in the treatment of conflicts.

This kind of fog results from a convergence of problems: cross-checking information, obtaining non-manipulated information, giving politico-strategic context, obtaining a general view (and not the situation of a specific given zone), and understanding the supporters and accomplishments of strategic issues. Yet, the training of journalists rarely takes into account politico-military issues, especially in continental Europe [MIE 16b]. Paradoxically, what represents a substantial part of the subjects treated on a daily basis in newspapers or radio and television news is thus liable to be insufficiently explained, even involuntarily left open to manipulation. The ultimate paradox is that journalists specialized on questions of defense in the general media only rarely speak about the analysis of conflicts, making recourse to consultants whose quality is not always assured[10]. Actually, the technical precision of weapons is diluted by media imprecision and a fog of war that also affects the editing.

The fact is that in the process of legitimizing the use of guided bombs, the ethical imperative only occurred later (in fact, with the expeditionary operations in the 2000s) compared to the search for the economy of forces. Since then, ethics has been exploited rather than thought out on the political level: the "fair strike", especially by precision, has become a factor of legitimacy in the context of military operations where the national interest –

---

10 *De facto*, it is rare for media outlets to offer compensation to contributors, several of whom end up becoming weary of repeated presentations, with little value on their academic qualifications. So, the withdrawal of competent researchers opens the door to less qualified researchers.

perceived as "dirty", especially by the supporters of the idealist trend in international relations – was discredited in relation to the moral interest. This is the main paradox of precision: the technical subject has become an ethical guarantee of a "good war", but as soon as the technique is no longer strategically effective by itself, the moral quality of war collapses with the first civilian death. We can justify a war if it is conducted "properly" – if this is technically possible – but ethics cannot be a substitute for policy and the definition of a clear discourse around the objectives in and around war… which are too often absent. As it happens, the very improbable possibility of the certainty of a "good" war does not eliminate the role of the national interest, just like it opens the door to a political non-responsibility for the one who is waging war.

This paradox also opens the door to another one, also linked to the notion of national interest. When national interest seems the most fragile, the tolerance of civilian and friendly losses decreases and is not compensated for by the precision of the weaponry or a greater attention paid to intelligence and targeting processes. Then, the greater the importance of the perceived precision of weapons, the greater the expectation that strikes are conducted with integrity. The notion of the "perception of precision" matters here because it is not necessarily linked to real precision, which remains dependent on a certain number of factors: weather condition, overlapping of combatants and non-combatants, and quality of laser "painting". The paradox resides in the increasingly harsh criticisms while the weaponry becomes increasingly precise, which is not without consequences for the design of a new array of systems. The next generation of guided weapons, like the GBU-38 SDB II, the SPEAR or the *Spice 250*, are fired at greater and greater distances and use multimodal guiding that includes *fire and forget* modes with automatic target detection. Of course, this is a generalization of the break initially integrated with the *Brimstone* missile or the AGM-84H/K SLAM-ER, the first weapons with an automatic attack capability (ATA – *Automatic Target Acquisition*). The latter were only used in very particular circumstances, in order to define a *kill-box*, where the new generation of weapons are virtually weapons of general use adapted to urban environments.

This generalization of multimodal guiding can raise erroneous accusations about the use of the ATA mode, the drones giving way to their missiles as "killer robots" in the debates. In this regard, whatever the progress registered in the technology of the weaponry or that of the conduct of operations, nothing can replace their political legitimation in due form. Legitimacy does not and cannot come from a technology, no matter how sophisticated; the tool does not make the craftsman, it is the good craftsman who knows how to choose the right tools. This is the end of the rationality supported by networks, whether it consists of the technological artifacts or practices that they create. This rationality can mask the political fact beneath technical effectiveness, a fact that goes back to (or should go back to) the practitioner at the highest sections of the art of war. The promise of quick wars without unjust deaths that are technically perfect – efficient and effective – are certainly attractive, especially for Western societies motivated by technological innovation and steeped in a managerial view of social relations. Nevertheless, the nature of war endures, and with it, the profoundly political nature of these social relations.

7.2. The retaliation against the Transformation: techno-guerillas and hybrid war

Reading the previous pages may lead one to believe that the RMA/*Transformation* is liable to cause considerable problems for Western forces and that networks are partly at the source. This would be a double error. On the one hand, the technological artefacts are only problematic once they have been mythologized, or once war is only considered in relation to them in what is no longer an increasing technicization – the use of more advanced technologies – but a technologization. This means that all strategic acts are only considered through the filter of technology [HEN 13b]. On the other hand, the technological artefacts of the RMA/*Transformation* have undergone a process of global scale distribution as well as change, which affects states as much as sub-state combatant groups. The consequences of this process are still not very clearly defined but have already been demonstrated in military operations for years. It is produced by rearticulating the modes of regular and irregular war, combining their comparative advantages through the intervention of judicious choices carried out with resource strategy [HEN 14b]. These evolutions result in a return to the solidification of spaces that the RMA/*Transformation* attempted to fluidify. These new mixed orders herald "guerillas on steroids", super-empowered [OLL 16] and distinctly more powerful because they have significant fire power and have appropriated logics linked to networks.

7.2.1. *The state incubator*

States, from this point of view, have played the role of technostrategic incubators. On the one hand, this is because they allowed the development of weaponry that is relevant for these techno-guerrillas, as they are both portable and easy to train users on. This is the case of MANPADS (*Man Portable Air Defense System*) and MANPATS (*Man Portable Anti-Tank System*) missiles, whose original design goes back – once again – to the 1960s and 1970s, in preparation to equip armies expanded by conscription. It was also the case for other light weaponry (mines) as well as a series of heavier systems (anti-ship missiles, surface-to-surface rockets, heavy anti-aircraft munitions) that states could provide for groups to which they were allied. This is typically the case of Iran with regard to Hezbollah, or Russia with regard to the eastern Ukrainian separatists or even, unintentionally, when combatants of the Islamic State take possession of the stocks of Iraqi or Syrian forces. Similarly, the groups armed with this equipment also seize media and communication technologies, developed by the private sector, as well as social networking platforms, which allow them to develop a declaratory strategy and refined influence.

States have also played an incubation role from a conceptual point of view. The origins of the concepts of the techno-guerrilla and hybrid wars goes back to the works of French commander Guy Brossolet in the 1970s [BRO 79]. It consisted of optimizing the strategy of French forces faced with a possible invasion of the Warsaw Pact. As the ratio of forces was not in France's favor in terms of numbers, how could they be more effective with the available means? The officer's answer was simple but brilliant: by avoiding a mythologized decisive battle, avoiding giving large targets to Soviet tactical nuclear fire, and putting in place a "scientific guerrilla warfare"[11]. The author combined a network of 2,500 mobile "presence units" assigned to a zone of about 20 km^2, abundantly equipped with anti-tank weapons, 200 units equipped with three combat helicopters, and 20 "heavy units", the tank regiments of the time, to deal the knockout blow. All together, it functioned as a self-adapting network due to the use of communication systems as well as a command style centered on *Auftragstaktik* that allowed the survivors of a badly affected unit to automatically join the closest units to reinforce them.

---

11 [BRO 79, p. 107].

In his view, it consisted of wearing down the enemy forces, first stuck in a dense territorial networking (the "pinpricks"), which made it possible to determine the lines of enemy penetration. Covering all of the French front from Pas-de-Calais to Italy – and at a depth of 120 km – this networking allowed them to avoid tactical or operative surprises. Once the enemy attrition occurred and the assailants realized their penetration of 120 km, the surviving forces could then be handled with the classic armoured forces (the "punches"), with a ratio of force distinctly more favorable for French forces. The whole thing, a deterrent in itself, was completed by nuclear deterrence and forces destined for foreign operations. This view was very popular: all of the debate in the 1980s about alternative strategies hinged on similar ideas, whether in Germany or Sweden. The view was also practiced without being necessarily qualified according to the terms of the debate on alternative strategy. This was the case in Austria, Switzerland, Yugoslavia and Albania [HEN 14b]. With the end of the Cold War, attention turned towards expeditionary operations more than territorial defense, and these ideas seemed to become obsolete.

While this was actually the case for some states, in particular those engaged in the process of the *Transformation*, the idea has been integrated/assimilated by a certain number of sub-state groups assimilating ideas and practices. Their strategic rationality is fundamentally identical to the one designed in the 1980s in Europe: faced with enemy superiority, heavy equipment is powerful, but can be easily destroyed. So, it consists of working by dispersion, maintaining the coherence of a whole, and taking advantage of assets provided by modern technologies. The prime example, amply commented on and analysed, is the Lebanese Hezbollah [JOH 11, HAR 08]. In the summer of 2006, the organization provoked a war with Israel in which the latter found itself in a bad position, not only due to the defensive barrier that it came up against (one tank was hit with 14 missiles) and the unpreparedness of its forces, but also because the Hezbollah had a stock of long-range rockets that allowed them to lead an offensive deep in Israeli territory as well as a real media infrastructure. The organization had the four pillars of all military strategy – declaratory, operational, resources and organic strategies – and had deliberately selected options that made it less vulnerable.

The example of the Hezbollah is not unique, even if the forms of techno-guerrillas have naturally diversified as the context changes. The Tamil Tigers, the POLISARIO Front (in the 1970s and 1980s), some Mexican cartels and some Palestinian organizations have bit by bit adopted innovative force structures, combining the most militarily interesting aspects of the modes of regular and irregular war. They also immediately excluded everything that could weaken their strategy, especially logistical issues that "weigh down" forces. At the same time, these forces can be extremely innovative, developing their own weapon systems. The Tamil Tigers built their own navy, supported by a chain of mobile coastal radar systems and equipped themselves with small tourist planes outfitted with bomb launchers. Their logistics depots were based at high sea, with small cargo ships maintaining contact with the northern Sri Lanka [EUD 10]. It did not only consist of operating on the ground – the environment focused on by authors in the 1980s – but of investing in particular strategies and thus fluid spaces. It was most often concerned with counter-strategies, seeking to prohibit an enemy's access to a given area and whose effectiveness could be challenged[12]. However, sometimes, it consisted of air and naval strategies in due form, which of course do not equal those of states, but can undermine them on occasion and can support ground operations.

When necessary, other aspects can be invested in: this is evidently the case for influence strategy, and it is also true for a professionalization of intelligence, the use of spatial technologies and improvised chemical weapons. Again, it is not as much about developing the capacities of a State as it is about having reasonably effective systems – which, in the case of chemical or biological agents, means creating panic more than killing on a mass scale. As we saw above, the resource strategy is central to this view because it regulates what is strategically desirable and technologically feasible, which is increasingly important. Advanced technologies have been democratized. The distribution of systems and their utility for these groups is the product of falling prices, a greater ease of use, and a greater interoperability with different tactical functions. A photo of enemy troops taken with the smartphone of a non-combatant member of an organization can be uploaded onto social networks to inform about an attack, while being transmitted to combat echelons and echelons charged with intelligence and capacity analysis.

---

12 An aerial counter-strategy can revolve around the use of MANPADS and ground attacks on air bases. However, not all of the bases can be attacked at once, just like the limit of engagement of missiles fired from the shoulder is usually 6,000 m.

Even so, this view was known as a defensive type – just like the ideas developed in the 1980s – because the agility of the dispositions did not allow for a projection of offensive forces. Yet, precisely because the technologies and knowledge evolved, the situation is in the midst of changing. With the Islamic State organization, there is a change in polarity. The group has been in a position to conduct operations of territorial conquest against regular armies with certain degree of success, although still in very specific conditions – territorial control of states in a situation of civil war or bankruptcy. The Islamic State is liable to become the prototype of the hybrid enemy, relying on an original military strategy that balances quality and quantity, just as it seeks the balance point between performances and restrictions (logistical or otherwise) induced by this performance. We know that the Islamic State has armoured vehicles and crews that can use them – and the necessary support capacities. However, their non-systematic use stems from a pertinent tactical calculation. On the one hand, the armoured vehicles are easily identifiable – meaning they are vulnerable – by air surveillance assets. On the other hand, their use involves a string of logistics and support that is detrimental to tactical and organizational agility.

The Islamic State has also set up a government system that takes advantage politically of tactical military victories. The projection of political governance addresses the shortfalls of states that the organization is fighting against, legitimizing it in the eyes of the population. This is a "total" strategic project, because it is not limited to only military aspects [LUI 15]. Since 2013, it has defeated several states in the region and is the source of a war with a configuration that is strangely similar to that of the Thirty Years War in Europe between 1618 and 1648. The Thirty Years War saw a large number of powers involved in a war whose motivations were officially religious, but actually political, and lead to a political remodelling that definitively put an end to feudalism in Europe [HEN 15a]. While only the future will tell if the analogy is pertinent and if the combination of logics will actually lead to a political victory of the Daesh and the establishment of a state properly speaking, it is probable that the model of strategic development used will be reproduced elsewhere, if only the initial political conditions are present.

7.2.2. *The true RMA and the future of war?*

From this perspective, how can we interpret the appearance of techno-guerrillas inserting themselves into the schemas of hybrid warfare? It should be noted that these military organizations challenge the notion of technostrategic innovation, recalling that military superiority, like technological superiority, is not necessary found with the sophistication of weaponry. The latter is frequently interpreted from a perspective of better performance than the previous generation: greater range, precision, speed, an ever-larger range of use, more controlled effects, etc. In doing so, we forget that the idea of performance results from a social construction in which the role of strategic cultures and technologies most often proves the determining factor [HEN 12b]. Similarly, the objectification of real strategic needs can quickly take a backseat so that resource strategy ends up dictating military strategy, while a healthy situation involves the inverse of this. Consequently, there is no determinism for the strategic actors who understand themselves – and are aware of their biases – and seek to understand their strategic environment. Similarly, relatively young organizations like these irregular groups preserve, *a priori*, a plasticity that is less beholden to their culture (strategically and technologically) and an organizational flexibility that allows them to adapt more quickly than the states.

Beyond this, innovation as an essential component of the process of adapting to conflicts may be material, but it is certainly not limited to this [FAR 02, MUR 11, ROS 91]. In fact, technical innovation is nothing without an appropriate use, which is necessarily of the conceptual domain, technology being the combination *têkhné* and *logos*. Better yet, the idea of innovation itself is most often linked to a combination of pre-existing elements that have been rearranged; so it is more often ideal rather than material. The prime example is the *blitzkrieg*. As applied in 1940, it was based on the synergy and integration of tactical and operational plans for planes (whose first use in combat goes back to 1911), tanks (1917), artillery (16th Century) and, above all, their coordination – in fact, their networking – via the radio (1905). It made it possible for components to communicate at all times, whereas up to that point, interactions had been limited. At this stage, the debates about whether the *blitzkrieg* was the result of an ideological notion formalized before the war, or the result of a practice forged during operations, are not important: the fact is that its achievement represented a major innovation with clear strategic and political consequences. In some regard, it is the same for the process of the RMA/*Transformation*, which incorporated technologies and practices from much before the 1990s; networking played a catalyzing role here as well.

In the years from 2000 to 2010 – and certainly beyond that – we can assume that it is the same for the techno-guerrillas. It is not so much the pre-existing technologies on which they rely that matter, than the way in which they rely on them, redefining their uses in light of the naturally fluid and adaptive mode of combat that is guerrilla warfare – or its extension in the domain of insurrection. Yet, guerrilla warfare entails logics of command and control (or, to use the more precise terms of J. Boyd, influence and monitoring) ontologically involving reticular logics by the very use of *Auftragstaktik*. The establishment of a system through a mode of hybrid warfare involves a networking that is initially a-technological before it can be reinforced – and in some ways, accelerated – by communication technologies. It is in itself a force, because the rationality which is retained results in a systematic resilience, implying that organizations of this type are naturally adapted to work in deteriorated conditions. What is interpreted as technological superiority by Western forces struggles to get a grip on the enemy system when the antagonism no longer translates in terms of technically normalized "measures/counter-measures" but instead imposes a return to the fundamentals of strategy.

The struggle between regular organizations has a tendency to be thought of in terms of linear logics. As a result of the shadow that still looms from the Cold War, each weapon system is thought of as a response to another, with equivalent functions – what François Géré called "*guerre homogène*" (homogenous war) [GER 97]. The accumulated superiority of these systems faced with those of the enemy ought to make it possible to win. However, this logic, reified by the processes of the RMA/*Transformation*, is fundamentally biased: once again, it is not systems of systems that are fighting, but political entities using a certain number of tools that are more or less adapted to the circumstances at a given moment. Yet, the ideological flexibility and mobilization of organizations using techno-guerrilla warfare is the perfect reflection of a strategic – that is, political – view of war, and not only of its techno-tactical view. Also, the "establishment of a resilient system" of techno-guerrillas is not the only issue raised by this type of organization for "transformed" forces. Even if a means to paralyze the networks – technical or not – of techno-guerrillas can be found, one side "wages war" while the other "carries out operations". There is an asymmetry in the opposed wills, already well-documented by authors working on conflicts led by "transformed" forces in the last 20 years and which is fundamental for understanding the evolution of conflicts. It continues to be the case that "*technique never gives a solution to problems that politics cannot solve*"[13].

So, from the perspective of strategic theory, the superiority immediately goes to hybrid organizations. While it is incredibly difficult, we must accept, as much with the awareness of the policy-maker as that of the strategist, that the idea of military superiority stems from practices and not from idealized representations that we may have about our forces and their technical qualities. It is not these representations, which are toxic because they are implicated even as far as the decisions to enter into war, that matter, but the Clausewitzian "tribunal of force", in which we can only survive as victors by adapting. We are in a paradoxical situation where superiority does not lean in favor of well-organized, normalized organizations that are perceived as "advanced" because they use advanced technologies. This does not mean that techno-guerrillas and users of hybrid warfare are organized chaotically. On the contrary, their power comes from an "ordering" of forces that borders on professionalization and sometimes even the beginnings of bureaucratization. However, again, the perceptions shared by the members, whether they are political or military, play a powerful role: fighting is primarily an act of armed militancy. So, this militancy translates into narrations that the *zeitgeist* of the moment tends to convert into power through networks that play roles of mobilization, recruitment and propaganda [HEN 14b].

The second consideration on the superiority of hybrid combat organizations is that they have the advantage of the fact that the battle for legitimacy is currently unfolding in a relativist environment with regard to ideas, where all perspectives are equal to one another, whether they are more sophisticated or based on a demonstration. This phenomenon of the "equalizing of political causes" always refers back to the fundamentals of war communication, but it is now greatly increased by social networks. Social networks are an unedited platform in an age of the individualization of information [HEC 09]. This development is paired with the crumbling of technical barriers that existed a few years ago in matters of setting up media systems: founding magazines, radios and even television channels – although they must pass through the internet – is no longer reserved for the

---

13 [GER 97, p. 242].

most powerful irregular groups. Following the example of what was observed in the domain of "kinetic weaponry", the distribution and use of "moral weaponry" was considerably easier. Similarly, the energy used to search for resources and technical expertise could be assigned to editorial knowledge, making political use of these new technologies. There too, "transformed" armies found themselves in an uncomfortable situation. In the context of the individualization of information and relativism, these armies appeared to be immediately caught up with – and surpassed – by their enemies. Of course, this depends on the fact that the uses of information in democracies are judiciously framed and that a state cannot do anything it wants in terms of propaganda, at the risk of losing the battle of legitimacy. However, the fact remains that the combination of the ontology of irregularity – the act of defining rules that are exclusively subject to a political goal – and new accessible technologies generates power.

The diagnostics chart of the potential enemy has changed considerably since the 1990s and the debates about the RMA, which leads to a third consideration about the military superiority of hybrid enemies. The technologization of strategic debates means that the asymmetrical enemy is considered to be more of a nuisance because it is not of the same technical level as a real threat for expeditionary forces. However, beyond the fact that the Afghan and Iraqi operations demonstrated the difficulty for "transformed" forces to clear "simple" insurrections, a very serious warning much closer to contemporary hybrid threats was given in 2002, in the form of the huge *Millennium Challenge* exercise that took place over 13 days and cost an estimated $250 million. Supposed to validate the principles of the *Transformation*, it featured a "blue" team with air, sea and amphibious forces issuing a 24-h surrender ultimatum to a "red" team, commanded by the director of the Marine Corps University, General Paul Van Riper. To avoid electro-magnetic pulses, he relied on communications by courier or light signals and used swarms of small boats to determine the position of the blue force. Immediately following the detection, on the second day of the exercise, the simulated firing of anti-ship missiles resulted in the destruction of one aircraft carrier, 10 destroyers and five of six amphibious ships – or the theoretical loss of 20,000 men. A second wave, involving small suicide-boats that were hard to detect, led to more blue losses.

Unsettling for the new direction of American defense, this phase was simply wiped from the exercise and the red team was ordered to turn on their radar systems without the possibility of trying to hit the blue combat planes.

Unsurprisingly, in such conditions, the blues were victorious in the end [ARQ 10]. The *Millennium Challenge* exercise sums up the technostrategic hubris of the RMA/*Transformation*, because the demonstration of a major problem of strategic thinking did not entail a formal reassessment, while a healthy strategy would have. Yet, the conditions in which the initial phase of the exercise had been conducted can be expected to be more or less reproduced. Considering only the technological point of view on the affair, the proliferation of weapon systems that are evolved and easily usable by the greatest number was proven, whether voluntary or not for the states involved. The question of "use by the greatest number" of these weapons is essential, because it determines the appearance of a powerfully armed mass, a true hybrid infantry of the new generation. From this perspective, this evolution could be comparable to that observed in "the" military revolution from the 15th to the 17th Centuries. One of the premises was making the infantry accessible to the masses, because it was easier to understand how to manipulate firearms than the throwing weapons used previously, even though the firearms were not yet very reliable. As a consequence, the structure of forces was shaken: firearms allowed for increased mass, while the war built up the state, which used fiscal resources to pay for new weapons. In the 18th Century, a cycle was secured with a nation of weapons that could always count on easily learning firearms; this was the end of the armies of the old regime [FOR 09].

The knight on his mount, the archer, the crossbowman – archetypes of the "soldier-technician" mobilizing their most advanced equipment of their time – also disappeared through the weight of mass, just like cannons forced the evolution of the fortress. Will the "soldier-technician" of the "new armies of the old regime", a resource which has become rare and costly, disappear in turn as a result of new masses equipped not with the first firearms of the 14th Century, but the nocturnal combat capacities and anti-tank missiles of the 20th Century? Surely it is too early to say, but it is difficult not to see it as both a "retaliation" against and a result of the RMA, so it seems relevant to consider it as a serious possibility. The political consequences of these "new masses" are potentially significant. By combining quality, quantity and motivation, these techno-guerrillas are liable to challenge regional political orders. In effect, they are equipped with a true deterring power towards States who want to cause the political project they support to fail. States would no longer intervene except when their supreme interests are at play, the expeditionary model being definitively beaten. Of course, as elsewhere, there is no determinism, but we can question the ability of "transformed" forces like states to face this.

7.2.3. *Adaptation by networks?*

If "transformed" forces have partly drawn technical lessons from the Millennium Challenge exercise as well as Afghan and Iraqi operations, notably by increasing adapted sensors and weapons, how should they act on a strategic level when faced with the challenges posed by techno-guerrillas? Attempting to answer this question requires straying from traditional schemas in which only "transformed" forces intervene, and imagining that forces that developed differently could be implemented in a coordinated way by the states themselves. In effect, it must be noted here that several states have historically resorted to – and continue to resort to – forms that are more or less related to hybrid war. In China, from the revolution in 1949 until the 1980s, the choice was made – as much for ideological reasons as for necessity – to steer towards a mass army that combined the characteristics of regular forces and an inclination towards the conduct of guerrilla warfare with the features of the idea of a "People's war" and then the "People's war in modern conditions" and finally a "People's war in the 21st Century". The development of armored/mechanized units, perceived as "technical weapons", was restricted by Mao. Compensating for a lack of power in relation to his potential enemies[14], he connected the territory with units founded on a huge mass of conscripts and former military personnel, utilizing old images of peasants placing explosives under enemy tanks. Equipped with light weapons, mines, rocket-launchers even anti-aircraft cannons, these units could fight in a decentralized way.

However, the counterpart to this strong decentralization was a social control that was enforced by local bodies of the Communist party. Reforms were launched in the 1980s by Deng Xiaoping, followed by more in the 1990s, and the transformation/professionalization of the People's Liberation Army seem to indicate a reassessment of this view. However, for all that, reserves and militia were not abandoned and the system was reformed in 1998. In addition to support missions for regular units, some militia, police and reserves were assigned missions in the war of information, while other militia units were created to restore critical infrastructures that might be

---

14 This did not deter China from carrying out one-off actions, like in India in 1962 or in Vietnam in 1979.

attacked. The role of these units is considered central for when military operations are required to last more than a few days. At the same time, despite a modernization of conventional forces, the reform in 1998 allowed for the densification of territorial cover by reserve forces and the creation of units in the provinces (the main referent for reserve forces) that were not equipped[15]. As it happens, the reservists were usually the previously active soldiers, and each unit seemed to benefit from a small core of active soldiers playing the role of coordination and mobilization. Civil sector specialists (chemical industry, telecommunications) were assigned to units in relation to their skills, so that these units would not be systematically considered as second rank but as prime actors of force. In the end, for Dennis Blasko, the reserves and paramilitary forces injected between 450,000 to 600,000 supplementary people into the operations [BLA 07].

The Chinese example has been more or less reproduced elsewhere. In the United States, the different national guards are veritable armies which are well-equipped and can be engaged in operations. In Great Britain, different reforms conducted since the 2000s have resulted in an increasingly significant reliance on reserve forces – it was really envisioned as relief for the reduction of active units. In France, a "cyber citizen reserve" aims to incorporate cybersecurity specialists and be able to count on them in case of problems. Elsewhere in Europe, some states that have suspended conscription are reflecting on its reintroduction, in a voluntary or obligatory form – but for the most part, these measures were taken following the invasion of part of Ukraine by Russia [MIE 16a]. While these solutions are interesting, the fact remains that they do not really break with the logics of the "new armies of the old regime", because they only constitute marginal evolutions. Yet, just like the *Transformation*, these evolutions do not respond to issues raised by the political substrate in which techno-guerrillas develop, of which one of the characteristics is to "glocalize" by being able to act and be supported in a transnational manner, whether from the point of view of the conduct of attacks, political communication, or support for diasporas.

Other options could be highlighted, notably in the already very specific Swiss case (where the army is not "national" but a "militia") where B. Wicht

---

15 So, that year, the units numbered 43 divisions and two regiments. In 2003, the structure of the forces increased to 40 divisions, six regiments and 10 brigades, each province now having a division or a brigade of infantry in reserves.

proposed the model of the "Swissbolah" [WIC 13]. He defined this as corresponding to *"a prospective approach seeking a possible way of restoring the City and strategic action. For the citizen, such a recovery necessarily requires a reformulation of freedom and the combination of it with a structure, an organization other than the nation-State. Therefore, the concept aims to reposition the citizen, emphasizing its right to self-defense, noting that "without his gun is not a taxpayer" by developing a discourse - the autonomy and Rebel opposing the tyranny (…) This contraction between Swiss and Hezbollah strives to illustrate possible combination of local autonomy of the Ancient Confederates with new forms of military-political organization that dominate today's battlefield (…)"*[16]. Nevertheless, this view enacts the end of the nation-state as a relevant body of war conduct and is not necessarily reproducible. For the time being, the nation-state remains the main political and strategic frame of reference, not only conserving the monopoly on legitimate violence, but also constituting the primary framework to which several irregular organizations aspire.

Consequently, three options, non-exclusive from one another, are available to state military organizations. The simplest, conceptually, comes back to extending the logics of the *Transformation* by proceeding to a costly increase in power centered on a large "transformed mass". The second option consists of playing the card of the "security-defense" *continuum*, which takes into account the glocalization of the potential enemy. Specifically, it consists of coming back to a view centered on a strategy of national security that revolves around Poirier's integral strategy and really synergizes all of the actors in national security, from the police to the military. However, this option is difficult to manipulate when the occupation and specifications of one are not those of the other and the principles of security inside borders are not those governing the art of war – which applies to law the same as it does to operational practices. We must beware of viewing the police as potential military personnel, or the opposite, and understand that their specific features are complementary.

The third option is the historical melting pot of hybrid war[17] and rests on a reticular view of the use of different forces: *compound warfare*. It consists of *"simultaneous use of a regular or main force and an irregular or*

16 [WIC 15, p. 42].
17 By its use, without restricting the examples, by the Romans, in North America with the integration of Native Americans into French and British troops, in Spain during the Napoleonic Wars and even during the Vietnam War.

guerrilla force against an enemy[18]. In so doing, it creates a hybrid that *"increases his military leverage by applying both conventional and unconventional force at the same time"*[19]. Conventional forces engage their comparative advantages – in matters of aviation or intelligence – but benefit from the mass brought by "unconventional" or "guerrilla" forces. In the view of T. M. Huber, they are most often home-grown and therefore know the terrain as well as the sociopolitical subtleties of the zone in which they operate. So, a "compound war" is only an *ad-hoc* gathering of forces, put in place as a function of the necessities of the time and which is based on pre-existing forces or the setting up of a specific organization. This type of integration is close to the "Afghan model" of S. Biddle, when special forces led Massoud's Northern Alliance at the end of 2001, benefitting from diversified air support [BID 05]. The same organizational scheme was also proposed during the planning of what would become operation *Iraqi Freedom* before being rejected for a more classic kind of intervention [HEN 07a]. However, the American forces would come back to this idea: it consists of re-establishing – after dismantling – the armed forces and the police while setting up allied militia like the *Sons of Iraq*.

In some way, we can also question the value of the compound operation of the *Allied Force* (Kosovo, 1999), in which NATO air forces were responsible for driving out Serbian forces from Kosovo, where the Kosovo Liberation Army (KLA) also operated. While the interaction between the forces present was stretched thin, it did, actually work. We can also question the value of operation *Harmattan* (Libya, 2011) as a compound operation, in which NATO air forces and special forces intervened in support of insurgent forces of the National Transitional Council, bringing about the fall of Gaddafi. While the operation was never officially presented as such, it also consisted of and used coalition air power against identifiable elements of Libyan forces, with the insurgent forces progressing on the ground and making it possible to actually conquer the terrain – not, incidentally, without a high degree of coordination being required between the forces. Very often, the NATO forces only knew the rebel positions with the aid of their sensors and not due to liaison elements – at the risk, as on 7 April 2011, of killing the rebels who had seized armoured vehicles. As it happens, this form of combat is not unique to armies with a strong technological capacity.

---

18 [HUB 02, p. 1].
19 *Ibidem.*

Compound combat was also observed in Somalia, where the regular Ethiopian forces fought, as of 2007, with more or less regular local forces.

It is doubtless in the context of counter-insurrection and the struggle against hybrid enemies that compound combat can bring about the maximum of military effects. Practically, they are naturally distributed operations, which we estimate to be the most capable for fighting against hybrid enemies. This allows for the networking of a given zone by a mass of control/domination while simultaneously benefitting from nodes created by a mass of technically developed maneuvres, the latter of which acts in the framework of support or spontaneous operations. The affair is evidently more complex to realize than it is to imagine, because it depends on the degree of cohesion/synergy at work between the actors and imposes the implementation of appropriate command processes as well as identical political objectives. It also depends on the qualities of the forces used for the networking, their training quickly appearing as essential. If only the set can be coordinated to sufficient degree, the tactical advantages offered by both can enter into synergy. Better yet, the mass of maneuvres, technically more developed, can implement operative actions more naturally, being supported as required (logistics, intelligence) by the forces of the network. So, we return to the logic that Brossollet defended by reintroducing a rationality of fluid spaces into solid spaces, and all this in a logic that is decidedly less techno-centric.

Conclusion

The RMA/*Transformation* is an eminently paradoxical phenomenon, in several respects. It is above all based on a social discovery of the effects of technology, of which one of the major trials was the Vietnam War and its consequences, which included the second *offset strategy*, about the planning of American defence. However, even the Vietnam experience is paradoxical in itself, as an attempt to apply rationalities proper to fluid spaces in one of the most solid spaces there is – a country with a geography profoundly marked by jungles, rice fields, swamps and mountains. In this sense, the military practices were directed towards a verticalization of the battle spaces [ADE 13], in a perspective seeking to simultaneously get away from the reality of the war and attempting to seize what was relevant. However, the fact remains that reality is stubborn and the art of war is based on its own rationality. From Khe Sanh to Kandahar or Kerbala, advanced technologies do not compensate for a strategy that is fundamentally flawed any more today than it did yesterday. The search for a "perfect war" has hardly even resulted (again) in a confrontation of its fundamentals. It is in solid environments that politics transpires, so we cannot avoid them [HEN 13a].

Certainly and evidently, the process of informationalization of war through the development of the combination of the "hunter/killer" and logics of reticulation – the "reconnaissance-strike complex" of Soviet military theory in the 1980s – is not without utility. In addition to constituting a technological fact, its distribution in military institutions transformed it into a social fact, which actually produced a comparative advantage. The logics of informationalization, from this point of view, represent a non-negotiable advancement and even a break in due form, which we can reasonably qualify as "a revolution in military affairs", albeit taking a certain number of precautions. But the true question is that of its status in relation to strategic theory: does it change the way war is conducted, and beyond that, war itself? We can, with hardly any risk, immediately answer negatively to the second part of the question. War remains "a confrontation between opposite wills using force" and is not modified at all by the appropriation of new technologies – even the "nuclear revolution" did not (totally) come to pass[1]. The answer to the first part, however, has certain nuances.

So, while the strategic practices partly evolved, the theory of this practice, or the grammar of strategy, was only marginally affected by the RMA/*Transformation*. Besides the fact that this proves the "conceptual solidity" of the theory of strategy and also its relevance, there is also a powerful warning as regards their "revolutionary" value of technological combinatorics. On a tactical/operative level, however, the effects – positive and negative – are very real and confirm the view of those who consider the RMA/*Transformation* to be above all a new operational art. The fact remains that they exert a powerful effect of attraction: if the debate on the RMA was born in the United States, it has since been exported to Europe through NATO before spreading elsewhere. The *Transformation* has become a global norm allowing the standardization of military regimes. There again, though, the upheaval was not total. On the one hand, strategic cultures are naturally resilient: established over hundreds of years, they can change in merely two decades. Consequently, the appropriation of the *Transformation* occurred more by cultural integration than by assimilation. On the other hand, the use of tools, from networks to precision technologies, are distinguished.

Paradoxically in effect, by striving for technical perfection in the conduct of military operations, the RMA/*Transformation* resulted in a radical interpretation of its propositions. The confrontation between the fundamentals of strategy and the new technologies of the *Transformation* led to techno-guerrillas refusing, as it were, the military order supported by the RMA. We could see a reinterpretation there, but in reality it consists of more than that. Taking into account the fact that political effectiveness matters much more to war than techno-tactical effectiveness, that refusal may well be the actual RMA. While the gains in freedom of maneuver of

---

1 While it changes the object of war – surviving by deterrence more than fighting at the risk of extinction – its practice shows that nuclear strategy does not operate independently from other strategies.

"transformed" armies are increasingly limited by the constraints imposed by new technologies, hybrid armies are increasing their freedom to maneuver with a correct interpretation of what strategy is. At the same time, the distribution of these technologies also benefits potentially enemy States that adopt a defensive position or a projection of their forces to their border, like Russia. Since about 2010, it has increased the number of surprise exercises that sometimes included the deployment of tens of thousands of men in 48 h. The "transformed" forces of NATO hope to increase from the ability to deploy 600 men in 48–72 h to 30,000 in a week.

So, the entire expeditionary model of regular "transformed" forces, founded on the agility of dispositions and their technological superiority, could be up for review. Nevertheless, the combination of the bureaucratic tendencies of armies and new technologies is highly addictive: the "perfect war" promoted by the RMA requires normalized "perfect institutions" and hardly tolerates organizational adaptations or distinguished levels of preparation/equipment. The RMA entails a managerial view of the art of war, which tends to discredit its theoretical foundations and which carries the risk of a negation, or at least, a consideration of the adversary/enemy though the abolition of the dialectical nature of war. From this negation results a non-exhaustive list of problems which the hybrid adversary/enemy does not face: socio-political ignorance of the battle zones, reduction of war to a succession of tactical actions ("tacticization"), reproduction of confirmation biases in the understanding of technology, overestimating the effects of that understanding, confusion between the ends and the means of war, etc.

All of the issues surrounding autonomous robotics, drones, super/ hypersonic missiles, or cyber war make up a large portion of the body of recent publications on the "war of the future" and, by overlooking strategy, tend to simplify it beyond what is reasonable. The fascination with technologies is certainly very understandable. However, the new "aesthetics of power", to use the expression by Martin Van Creveld, is measured less in kilotons or the mass of a useful load or in terms of designs giving off a sense of power, than in terms of terabytes, bandwidth and processing speed. We may be tempted to see a future that is reassuring and intellectually comfortable because it is configured and controllable by civil engineers, whose help that is even more welcome because the volume of armies has been reduced. However, because aesthetics is not power, it certainly seems more likely that this future will be decidedly less glorious, much more baroque, and doubtless much more lethal, because the enemy will not have confused the tool and the mission. To use the expression of L. Henninger one last time, rather than seeking to fluidize the solid like we have done since World War II, the enemy will seek to solidify the fluid, which involves fewer weapon systems and information technology systems than a view that carefully combines material and conceptual aspects – strategy.

Glossary

A2/AD:	Anti-Access/Area Denial
ACT:	Allied Command Transformation
AESA:	Active Electronically Scanned Array
ARGUS-IS:	Autonomous Real-time Ground Ubiquitous Surveillance Imaging System
ATA:	Automatic Target Acquisition
ATACMS:	Army Tactical Missile System
AWACS:	Airborne Warning and Control System
BADGE:	Base Air Defense Ground Environment
BMEWS:	Ballistic Missile Early Warning System
BVRAAM:	Beyond Visual Range Air-to-Air Missile
C3:	Command, Control, Communications
C3I:	Command, Control, Communications, Intelligence
C4ISR:	Command, Control, Communications, Computers, Intelligence, Surveillance, Reconnaissance
CAS:	Close Air Support
CHAMP:	Counter-electronics High-powered Advanced Missile Project
CIVCAS:	Civilian Casualties

CO:	Central Operations
COTS:	Cost Off the Shelf Technologies
DARPA:	Defense Advanced Research Project Agency
DIME:	Dense Inert Metal Explosive
DSP:	Defense Support Program
EMP:	Electromagnetic Pulse
ESM:	Electronic Support Measures
FCS:	Future Combat System
FEBA:	Forward Edge of the Battle Area
FLIR:	Forward Looking Infra Red
GCA:	Ground Controlled Approach
GCCS:	Global Command and Control System
GCI:	Ground Controlled Interception
GPS:	Global Positioning System
HUMRRO:	Human Resources Research Office
IADS:	Integrated Air Defense System
IED:	Improvised Explosive Device
IRST:	Infra-Red Search and Track
ISC:	Infiltration Surveillance Center
ISR:	Intelligence, Surveillance, Reconnaissance
JDAM:	Joint Direct Attack Munition
JSF:	Joint Strike Fighter
JSTARS:	Joint Surveillance Target Attack Radar System
MALE:	Medium Altitude, Long Endurance
MANPADS:	Man Portable Air Defense System
MANPATS:	Man Portable Anti-Tank System

MiDAS:	Missile Defense Alarm System
MIT:	Massachusetts Institute of Technology
MLRS:	Multiple Launch Rocket System
MRAP:	Mine Resistant, Ambush Protected
MRASM:	Medium Range Air-Surface Missile
NADGE:	NATO Air Defense Ground Environment
NCW:	Network-Centric Warfare
NORAD:	North American Air Defense Command
OFT:	Office of Force Transformation
OODA:	Observation, Orientation, Decision, Action
PACCS:	Post Attack Command and Control System
QDR:	Quadrennial Defense Review
R&D:	Research and Development
RBA:	Revolution in Business Affairs
RDO:	Rapid Decisive Operations
RMA:	Revolution in Military Affairs
ROVER:	Remotely Operated Video Enhanced Receiver
RPMA:	Revolution in Political and Military Affairs
SAC:	Strategic Air Command
SACCS:	SAC Control System
SADARM:	Sense and Destroy Armor
SAGE:	Semi-Automatic Ground Environment
SAM:	Surface-to-Air Missiles
SBIRS:	Space-Based Infra-Red System
SDI:	Strategic Defense Initiative
SFW:	Sensor-Fused Weapon

SIC:	System Information and Command (Information System and Command)
SMArt 155:	*Suchzünder Munition für die Artillerie 155* (Submunition for Artillery)
STSS:	Space Tracking and Surveillance System
TGSM:	Terminally Guided Sub-Munition
TISEO:	Target Identification System Electro-Optical
UCK:	Kosovo Liberation Army
USAF:	United States Air Force
WWMCCS:	World-Wide Military Command and Control System

Bibliography

[ADA 08] ADAMSKY D., "Through the looking glass: the Soviet military-technical revolution and the American revolution in military affairs", *The Journal of Strategic Studies*, vol. 31, no. 2, pp. 257–294, April 2008.

[ADA 10] ADAMSKY D., *The Culture of Military Innovation: The Impact of Cultural Factors on the Revolution in Military Affairs in Russia, the US, and Israel*, Stanford University Press, Stanford, 2010.

[ADE 13] ADEY P., WHITEHEAD M., WILLIAMS A.J., *From Above. War, Violence and Verticality*, Hurst, London, 2013.

[ALL 87] ALLEN T., *War Games: The Secret World of the Creators, Players, and Policy Makers Rehearsing World War III Today*, McGraw-Hill, New York, 1987.

[AND 98] ANDREWS T.D., Revolution and Evolution. Understanding Dynamism in Military Affairs, National Defence University, Washington DC, 1998.

[ARQ 93] ARQUILLA J., RONFELDT D., "Cyberwar is coming!", *Comparative Strategy*, vol. 12, no. 2, pp. 141–165, 1993.

[ARQ 97] ARQUILLA J., RONFELDT D., "A New Epoch – and Spectrum – of Conflict", in ARQUILLA J., RONFELDT D. (eds), *In Athena's Camp: Preparing for Conflict in the Information Age*, RAND Corp., Santa Monica, 1997.

[ARQ 01] ARQUILLA J., RONFELDT D., *Networks and Netwars. The Future of Terror, Crime and Militancy*, RAND Corp., Santa Monica, 2001.

[ARQ 10] ARQUILLA J., "The new rules of war", *Foreign Policy*, available at: http://foreignpolicy.com/2010/02/11/the-new-rules-of-war/, March/April 2010.

[BAC 96] BACEVICH A.J., "Just War II: morality and high technology", *The National Interest*, no. 45, pp. 37–47, Fall 1996.

[BAL 03] BALZACQ T., ""Bienvenue" dans la guerre high-tech", in BALZACQ T., DE NEVE A. (eds), *La Révolution dans les Affaires Militaires*, Economica/ISC, Paris, 2003.

[BAR 08] BARDIES L., MOTTE M., *De la guerre? Clausewitz et la pensée stratégique contemporaine*, ISC/Economica, Paris, 2008.

[BAT 03] BATTISTELLA D., *Théories des relations internationales*, Presses de Sciences Po, Paris, 2003.

[BAU 97] BAUMANN R.F., "Historical perspective on future war", *Military Review*, pp. 40–48, March–April 1997.

[BAU 09] BAULON J.-P., *L'Amérique vulnérable? (1946–1976)*, Economica/ISC, Paris, 2009.

[BEA 72] BEAUFRE A., *Stratégie pour demain. Les problèmes militaires de la guerre moderne*, Plon, Paris, 1972.

[BEA 85] BEAUFRE A., *Introduction à la stratégie*, IFRI/Economica, Paris, 1985.

[BEL 73] BELL D., *The Coming of the Post-Industrial Society: A Venture in Social Forecasting*, Basic Books, New York, 1973.

[BEN 07] BENKLER R., "Les rôles que peuvent jouer les drones sur le "champ de bataille vide", *Technologie & Armement*, no. 7, pp. 56–63, August–September 2007.

[BER 16] BERNARD S., "Prenez garde à la révolution dans les affaires militaires", in GARON R. (ed.), *Penser la guerre au futur*, Presses de l'Université Laval, Québec, 2016.

[BET 06] BETZ D.J., "The more you know, the less you understand: the problem with information warfare", *The Journal of Strategic Studies*, vol. 29, no. 3, pp. 505–533, June 2006.

[BEY 92] BEYERCHEN A.D., "Clausewitz, nonlinearity and the unpredictability in war", *International Security*, vol. XVII, no. 3, pp. 59–90, Winter 1992.

[BID 05] BIDDLE S.D., "Allies, airpower and modern warfare: the Aghan model", *International Security*, vol. 30, no. 3, pp. 161–176, Winter 2005.

[BIH 12] BIHAN B., "Les temps de la décision", *Défense & Sécurité Internationale*, no. 87, pp. 32–35, December 2012.

[BIH 14a] BIHAN B., "Doctrines importées", *Défense & Sécurité Internationale*, no. 102, pp. 36–39, April 2014.

[BIH 14b] BIHAN B., "Le commandement, reflet de la conception de la guerre", *Défense & Sécurité Internationale*, no. 106, pp. 34–37, September 2014.

[BIH 14c] BIHAN B., "Les opérations militaires futures. Approche prospective", *Histoire & Stratégie*, no. 18, May-July 2014.

[BIH 15] BIHAN B., "Les niveaux de la guerre. Une *"Kriegsanschauung"* américaine", in TAILLAT S., HENROTIN J., SCHMITT O. (eds), *Guerre et stratégie. Approches, Concepts*, PUF, Paris, 2015.

[BLA 91a] BLACK J., *A Military Revolution? Military Change and European Society, 1550–1800*, Palgrave Macmillan, Basingstoke, London, 1991.

[BLA 91b] BLACKWELL J., MAZARR M.J., SNIDER D.N., *The Gulf War: Military Lessons Learned*, CSIS, Washington DC, 1991.

[BLA 97a] BLAKER J.R., "Understanding the revolution in military affairs", *The Officer*, pp. 23–34, May 1997.

[BLA 97b] BLANK S.J., "Preparing for the next war: reflections on the revolution in military affairs", in ARQUILLA J., RONFELDT D. (eds), *In Athena's Camp: Preparing for Conflict in the Information Age*, RAND Corp., Santa Monica, CA, 1997.

[BLA 07] BLASKO D.J., "People's war in the 21st Century: the militia and the reserve", in FINKELSTEIN D.M., GUNNES K. (eds), *Civil-Military Relations in Today's China. Swimming in New Seas*, CNA Corporation, Armonk, NY, 2007.

[BOL 04] BOLIA R.S., "Overreliance on technology in warfare: the Yom Kippur war as a case studies", *Parameters*, pp. 46–56, Summer 2004.

[BON 14] BONNEMAISON, A, DOSSE S., *Attention: Cyber! Vers le combat cyber-électronique*, Economica, Paris, 2014.

[BRA 73] BRAUDEL F., *Civilisation matérielle, économie et capitalisme (Tome 3: les temps du monde)*, Armand Colin, Paris, 1973.

[BRA 93] BRACKEN B., "The military after next", *The Washington Quarterly*, vol. 16, no. 4, pp. 157–174, 1993.

[BRA 02] BRAILLARD P., MASPOLI G., "La "révolution dans les affaires militaires": paradigmes stratégiques, limites et illusions", *Annuaire français de relations internationales*, vol. III, Bruylant, Brussels, 2002.

[BRA 05] BRACKEN P., "Sidewise technologies: national security and global power implications", *Military Review*, pp. 64–67, September–October 2005.

[BRO 73] BRODIE B., BRODIE F., *From Crossbow to H-Bomb*, Indiana University Press, Bloomington, 1973.

[BRO 79] BROSSOLLET G., *Essai sur la non bataille*, Belin, Paris, 1979.

[BRU 99] BRU J., S.V., "Guerre et technique – L'intervention de la technique dans la guerre", in CHALIAND G., BLIN A. (eds), *Dictionnaire de stratégie militaire*, Perrin, Paris, 1999.

[BRU 05] BRUSTLEIN C., "Innovation, émulation et adaptation face à la puissance militaire occidentale", in PASCALLON P. (ed.), *Quelles menaces, demain, sur la sécurité de la France?*, L'Harmattan, Paris, 2005.

[BRZ 70] BRZEZINSKI Z., *Between Two Ages: America's Role in the Technetronic Era*, Viking Press, New York, 1970.

[BUN 94] BUNKER R.J., "The transition to fourth epoch war", *Marine Corps Gazette*, no. 78, pp. 20–32, September 1994.

[BUN 96] BUNKER R.J., "Generations, waves and epochs. Modes of war and the RPMA", *Airpower Journal*, pp. 23–25, Spring 1996.

[BUN 97] BUNKER R.J., "Epochal change: war over social and political organizations", *Parameters*, pp. 15–25, Summer 1997.

[BUR 94] BURK J., *The Military in New Times: Adapting Armed Forces to a Turbulent New World*, Westview Press, Boulder, 1994.

[CAP 99] CAPLOW T., VENNESSON P., *Sociologie militaire*, Armand Colin, Paris, 1999.

[CAS 98] CASTELLS M., *La société en réseaux. 1. L'ère de l'information*, Fayard, Paris, 1998.

[CAS 99a] CASTELLS M., *La société en réseaux. 2. Le pouvoir et l'identité*, Fayard, Paris, 1999.

[CAS 99b] CASTELLS M., *La société en réseaux. 3. Fin de millénaire*, Fayard, Paris, 1999.

[CEB 98] CEBROWSKI A.K., GARSTKA J.J., "Network-centric warfare: its origin and future", *US Naval Institute Proceedings*, pp. 28–38, January 1998.

[CER 83] CERUZZI P., *Reckoners: The Prehistory of the Digital Computer, From Relays to the Stored Program Concept, 1939, 1945*, Greenwood Press, Westport, 1983.

[CHA 13a] CHALMIN S. (ed.), *Gagner une guerre aujourd'hui?*, Economica, Paris, 2013.

[CHA 13b] CHAMAYOU G., *Théorie du drone*, Editions La Fabrique, Paris, 2013.

[COC 95] COCHET F., HENRY G.M., *Les révolutions industrielles. Processus historiques, développements économiques*, Armand Colin, Paris, 1995.

[COH 97] COHEN E.A., "American views of the revolution in military affairs", *Mideast Security and Policy Studies*, no. 28, pp. 1–11, 1997.

[COK 01] COKER C., *Humane Warfare*, Routledge, London, 2001.

[COK 13] COKER C., *Warrior Geeks. How 21st Century Technology is Changing the Way We Fight and Think About War*, Hurst, London, 2013.

[COL 92] COLSON B., "Histoire et stratégie dans la pensée navale américaine", in COUTAU-BEGARIE H. (ed.), *L'évolution de la pensée navale*, vol. II, FEDN/Economica, Paris, 1992.

[COL 93] COLSON B., *La culture stratégique américaine. L'influence de Jomini*, Economica, Paris, 1993.

[COL 15] COLLINS J., FUTTER A. (eds), *Reassessing the Revolution in Military Affairs: Transformation, Evolution and Lessons Learnt*, Palgrave Mcmillan, London, 2015.

[CON 72] CONTAMINE P., *Guerre, État et société à la fin du Moyen Age*, Mouton/EHESS, Paris, 1972.

[COO 97] COOPER J.R., "Another view of the revolution in military affairs", in ARQUILLA J., RONFELDT D. (eds), *In Athena's Camp: Preparing for Conflict in the Information Age*, RAND Corp., Santa Monica, 1997.

[COU 97] COUTAU-BEGARIE H., "Révolution ou rupture? Sur la mutation stratégique en cours", *Stratégique*, no. 65, pp. 4–18, 1997/1.

[COU 01] COUTAU-BEGARIE H., *Les structures de la recherche stratégique en France*, ISC/CFHM, Paris, 2001.

[COU 05] COUTAU-BEGARIE H. *et al.*, *Géostratégie du Pacifique*, ISC/DAS, Paris, 2005.

[COU 11] COUTAU-BEGARIE H., *Traité de stratégie*, 8th ed., Economica/ISC, Paris, 2011.

[CUS 15] CUSSET P.-Y., "Améliorer les capacités humaines. Actualité d'un vieux rêve", *Défense & Sécurité Internationale*, Special issue no. 45, pp. 8–11, December 2015–January 2016.

[DAV 87] DAVIES O., "Robotic warriors clash in cyberwars", *Omni*, pp. 76–88, January 1987.

[DAV 96] DAVIS N., "An information based revolution in military affairs", *Strategic Review*, pp. 43–53, Winter 1996.

[DE 92] DE BENOIST A., "La leçon des armes. Entretien avec le général Pierre M. Gallois", *Krisis*, nos. 10–11, pp. 145–153, April 1992.

[DE 97] DE GUILI J.-M., FAUCON F., "Les champs d'engagement futurs", *Stratégique*, no. 68, pp. 85–96, 1997/4.

[DE 01a] DE DURAND E., "Le "nouveau paradigme stratégique" républicain", *Revue Française d'Etudes Américaines*, no. 90, pp. 95–114, 2001/4.

[DE 01b] DE ROSNAY J., "Biologie et informatique. Promesses et menaces pour le XXIème siècle", in FERENCZI T. (ed.), *Les défis de la technoscience*, Complexe, Brussels, 2001.

[DE 04] DE NEVE A., HENROTIN J., WASINSKI C., "Quelles conséquences stratégiques?", in HENROTIN J. (ed.), *Au risque du chaos. Leçons politiques et stratégiques de la guerre d'Irak*, Armand Colin, Paris, 2004.

[DE 05] DE NEVE A., MATHIEU R., *Les armées d'Europe face aux défis capacitaires et technologiques*, Bruylant, Brussels, 2005.

[DE 06] DE NEVE A., HENROTIN J., "La guerre réseaucentrique: de son développement à Iraqi Freedom", *Stratégique*, nos. 86/87, pp. 53–76, 2006.

[DE 07a] DE NEVE A., "*Iraqi Freedom*: un modèle de guerre technologique?", in RMES (eds), *Iraqi Freedom, Analyse politique, stratégique et économique de la troisième guerre du Golfe*, L'Harmattan, Paris, 2007.

[DE 07b] DE NEVE A., "La guerre réseaucentrique et son implémentation dans les opérations militaires coalisées en Irak: une révolution dans le commandement et le contrôle?", in RMES (eds), *Iraqi Freedom, Analyse politique, stratégique et économique de la troisième guerre du Golfe*, L'Harmattan, Paris, 2007.

[DE 10] DE SAINT VICTOR F., "Guerre des chiffres et chiffres de guerre", *Défense & Sécurité Internationale*, no. 62, pp. 52–55, September 2010.

[DE 11] DE LESPINOIS J., *La bataille d'Angleterre, juin-octobre 1940*, Tallandier, Paris, 2011.

[DE 14] DE DURAND E., BRUSTLEIN C., TENENBAUM E., *La suprématie aérienne en péril. Menaces et contre-stratégies à l'horizon 2030*, La Documentation française, Paris, 2014.

[DE 15] DE DURAND E., "Planification de défense: la belle Arlésienne?", in TAILLAT S., HENROTIN J., SCHMITT O. (eds), *Guerre et stratégie. Approches, concepts*, PUF, Paris, 2015.

[DEL 98] DELPECH T., *La guerre parfaite*, Flammarion, Paris, 1998.

[DEP 92] DEPARTMENT OF DEFENSE, Conduct of the Persian Gulf War. Final Report to Congress, US Government Printing Office, Washington, DC, April 1992.

[DER 01] DER DERIAN J., *Virtuous War*, Westview Press, Boulder, 2001.

[DES 01] DESPORTES V., *Comprendre la guerre*, Economica, Paris, 2001.

[DES 02] DESPORTES V., *L'Amérique en armes. Anatomie d'une puissance militaire*, Economica, Paris, 2002.

[DES 06] DESPORTES V., "La Transformation en difficulté. Vers l'adaptation, nouveau paradigme?", *Défense & Sécurité Internationale*, no. 20, pp. 34–39, November 2006.

[DIC 76] DICKSON P., *The Electronic Battlefield*, Indiana University Press, Bloomington, 1976.

[DIX 89] DIXON H.L., *Low Intensity Conflict: Overview, Definitions, and Policy Concerns*, Army-Air Force Center for Low Intensity Conflict, Langley AFB, 1989.

[DOW 92] DOWNING B.M., *The Military Revolution and Political Change. Origins of Democracy and Autocracy in Early Modern Europe*, Princeton University Press, Princeton, 1992.

[DUF 15] DUFF G., SMITH G., "Nuclear War has Begun in Yemen", available at: http://www.veteranstoday.com/2015/05/28/nuclear-war-has-begun-in-yemen/, 2015.

[DUN 93] DUNNIGAN J.F., MACEDONIA R.M., *Getting it Right. American Military Reforms After Vietnam to the Persian Gulf and Beyond*, William Morrow and Company, New York, 1993.

[DUP 84] DUPUY T.N., *The Evolution of Weapons and Warfare*, Da Capo, New York, 1984.

[ECH 92] ECHEVARRIA A.J., SHAW M., "The new military revolution: post-industrial change", *Parameters*, pp. 70–77, Winter 1992–93.

[ECH 04] ECHEVARRIA A.J., *Toward an American Way of War*, Strategic Studies Institute, Carlisle Barracks, 2004.

[EDW 95] EDWARDS P.N., "Cyberpunks in cyberspace: the politics of subjectivity in the computer age", in STAR S.L. (ed.), *Cultures of Computing*, Keele, 1995.

[EDW 97] EDWARDS P.N., *The Closed World. Computers and the Politics of Discourse in Cold War America*, The MIT Press, Cambridge, 1997.

[EDW 00] EDWARDS S., *Swarming on the Battlefield: Past, Present and Future*, RAND Corp., Santa Monica, 2000.

[EHR 95] EHRENBERG A., *L'individu incertain*, Hachette, Paris, 1995.

[EK 00] EK R., "A revolution in military geopolitics?", *Political Geography*, vol. 19, no. 7, pp. 841–874, 2000.

[ENT 14] ENTRAYGUES O., *Le stratège oublié. J.F.C. Fuller, 1913–1933*, Brèches Editions, Paris, 2014.

[EUD 03] EUDES Y., "Soldats du futur", *Le Monde*, p. 56, 6 March 2003.

[EUD 10] EUDELINE H., "Guérilla et terrorisme maritimes. Sri Lanka contre Tigres tamouls", in COUTAU-BÉGARIE H. (ed.), *Stratégies irrégulières*, Economica, Paris, 2010.

[EVA 03] EVANS M., "From Kadesh to Kandahar. Military theory and the future of war", *Naval War College Review*, vol. LVI, no. 3, pp. 132–150, Summer 2003.

[FAD 98] FADOK D.S., *La paralysie stratégique par la puissance aérienne. John Boyd et John Warden*, Economica/ISC, Paris, 1998.

[FAI 88] FAIVRE M., *Les nations armées. De la guerre des peuples à la guerre des étoiles*, Economica/Fondation pour les Etudes de Défense Nationale, 1988.

[FAR 02] FARRELL T., TERRIFF T. (eds), *The Sources of Military Change. Culture, Politics and Technology*, Boulder, Lynne Rienner, 2002.

[FIN 75] FINER S.E., "State and nation building in Europe: the role of the military", in TILLY C. (ed.), *The Formation of National States in Western Europe*, Princeton University Press, 1975.

[FIT 87] FITZGERALD M.C., *Marshal Ogarkov & the New Revolution in Soviet Military Affairs*, Center for Naval Analyses, Alexandria, 1987.

[FIT 91] FITZGERALD M.C., "The Soviet image of future war: through the prism of the Gulf War", *Comparative Strategy*, vol. 10, no. 4, pp. 393–435, 1991.

[FOR 97] FORGET P., POLYCARPE G., *Le réseau et l'infini. Essai d'anthropologie philosophique et stratégique*, Economica/ISC, Paris, 1997.

[FOR 09] FORTMANN M., *Les cycles de Mars. Révolutions militaires et édification étatique de la Renaissance à nos jours*, Economica, Paris, 2009.

[FRA 97] FRANCART L., "L'évolution des niveaux stratégique, opératifs et tactiques", *Stratégique*, no. 68, pp. 19–27, 1997/4.

[FRE 98] FREEDMAN L., *The Revolution in Strategic Affairs*, Adelphi Paper 318, The International Institute for Strategic Studies, Oxford University Press, Oxford, 1998.

[FRE 02] FREEDMAN D.H., "Killed at their Keyboards", *Business 2.0 Magazine*, p. 38, 31 January 2002.

[FRE 03] FREEDMAN L., *The Evolution of Nuclear Strategy*, 3rd ed., Palgrave Mcmillan, New York, 2003.

[FRE 13] FREEDMAN L., *Strategy. A History*, Oxford University Press, 2013.

[GAD 93] GADDIS J.L., "International relations theory and the end of the Cold War", *International Security*, no. 17, pp. 5–58, Winter 1993.

[GAL 95] GALDI T.W., *Revolution in Military Affairs? Competing Concepts, Organizational Responses, Outstanding Issues*, Foreign Affairs and National Defence Division, Washington, DC, December 1995.

[GAR 95] GARDINER S., FOX D.B. *et al.*, *Understanding RMAs*, RAND Corp., Santa Monica, April 1995.

[GAT 91] GAT A., *The Origins of Military Thought, From the Enlightenment to Clausewitz*, Oxford University Press, 1991.

[GÉR 97] GÉRÉ F., *Demain, la guerre*, Calmann-Lévy, Paris, 1997.

[GÉR 00] GÉRÉ F., "RMA or new operational art? A view from France", in GONGORA T., VON RIEKHOFF H. (eds), *Toward a Revolution in Military Affairs? Defense and Security at the Dawn of the Twenty-First Century*, Greenwood Press, Westport/London, 2000.

[GIA 14] GIACOMETTI N., "B61-12: un programme en débat", *Défense & Sécurité Internationale*, no. 106, pp. 78–83, September 2014.

[GID 90] GIDDENS A., *The Consequences of Modernity*, Polity Press and Stanford University Press, Cambridge and Stanford, 1990.

[GLE 98] GLENN R.W., "No more principles of war", *Parameters*, pp. 48–66, Spring 1998.

[GOL 05] GOLDMAN E., *Information and Revolutions in Military Affairs*, Routledge, London, 2005.

[GOM 98] GOMBOA J., "The cost of revolution", *Proceedings*, pp. 58–61, December 1998.

[GON 98] GONGORA T., "The revolution in military affairs: what should the CF do about it?", *The Defence Associations National Networks News*, vol. 5, no. 2, pp. 6–8, Summer 1998.

[GON 99] GONGORA T., "The shape of things to come: sizing-up the revolution in military affairs", in HAGLUND D., MACFARLANE S.N. (eds), *Security, Strategy and the Global Economics of Defense Production*, McGill-Queen University, Kingston, 1999.

[GON 00] GONGORA T., VON RIEKHOFF H., "Introduction: sizing up the revolution in military affairs", in GONGORA T., VON RIEKHOFF H. (eds), *Toward a Revolution in Military Affairs? Defense and Security at the Dawn of the Twenty-First Century*, Greenwood Press, Westport/London, 2000.

[GOU 97] GOURÉ D., SZARA C.M. (eds), *Air and Space Power in the New Millenium*, CSIS, Washington, DC, 1997.

[GRA 93] GRAY C.S., *Weapons Don't Make War*, University Press of Kansas, Lawrence, 1993.

[GRA 95] GRAY C.H., MENTOR S., FIGUEROA-SARRIERA H.J. (eds), *The Cyborg Handbook*, Routledge, New York, 1995.

[GRA 97] GRAY C.H., *Postmodern War. The New Politics of Conflict*, Routledge, London, 1997.

[GRA 99a] GRAY C.S., "Clausewitz rules OK?", *Review of International Studies*, vol. 25 pp. 161–182, (Special Issue), 1999.

[GRA 99b] GRAY C.S., SLOAN G. (eds), *Geopolitics. Geography and Strategy*, Frank Cass, London, 1999.

[GRA 02] GRAY C.S., *Strategy for Chaos. Revolutions in Military Affairs and the Evidence of History*, Frank Cass, London, 2002.

[GRA 05] GRAY C.S., "How has war changed since the end of the Cold War?", *Parameters*, pp. 14–26, Spring 2005.

[GRI 15] GRISSOM A., "Innovation et adaptation", in TAILLAT S., HENROTIN J., SCHMITT O. (eds), *Guerre et stratégie. Approches, Concepts*, PUF, Paris, 2015.

[GRO 97] GROPMAN A., *The Big L. American Logistics in WW II*, NDU, Washington, DC, 1997.

[GUM 97] GUMAHAD A.T., "The profession of arms in the information age", *Joint Force Quarterly*, pp. 14–20, Spring 1997.

[HAL 95] HALLION R.P., *Precision-Guided Munitions and the New Era of Warfare*, Air Power Studies Centre Paper no. 53, Royal Australian Air Force, Fairbairn, 1995.

[HAL 97] HALL B.S., *Weapons and Warfare in Renaissance Europe*, John Hopkins University Press, Baltimore and London, 1997.

[HAN 90] HANSON V.D., *Le modèle occidental de la guerre*, Les Belles Lettres, Paris, 1990.

[HAR 92] HARAWAY D., "The promises of monsters: a regenerative politics for inappropriate/d others", in GROSSBERG L., NELSON C., TREICHLER P. (eds), *Cultural Studies*, Routledge, New York, 1992.

[HAR 97] HARLEY J.A., "Information, technology, and center of gravity", *Naval War College Review*, vol. L, no. 1, pp. 65–80, Winter 1997.

[HAR 08] HAREL A., ISSACHAROFF A., *34 Days: Israel, Hezbollah, and the War in Lebanon*, Palgrave Macmillan, New York, 2008.

[HAS 03] HASSEL J., "A mixed bag of setbacks and successes", *Newhouse News Service*, available at: http://www.globalsecurity.org/org/news/2003/030329-mixed-bag01.htm, 29 March 2003.

[HAY 95] HAYS PARKS W., "'Precision' and 'area' bombing: who did which, and when?", *Journal of Strategic Studies,* vol. 18, no. 1, pp. 145–174, March 1995.

[HEC 09] HECKER M., RID T., *War 2.0. Irregular Warfare in the Information Age*, Praeger Security International, Westport, 2009.

[HEI 60] HEILBRONER R.L., *The Future as History*, Harper & Row, New York, 1960.

[HEI 87] HEINLEIN R.A., *Starship Trooper*, Ace Books, New York, 1987.

[HEN 98] HENRY R., PEARTREE E., "Military theory and information warfare", *Parameters*, pp. 121–135, Autumn 1998.

[HEN 03] HENROTIN J., "Le retour au chevalier: une vision critique de l'évolution bionique du combattant", *Hermès Revue Critique*, available at: https://charro 1010.wordpress.com/2009/11/29/le-retour-au-chevalier-%C2%AB-une-vision-critique-de-levolution-bionique-du-combattant-%C2%BB-joseph-henrotin/, no. 9, Winter 2003.

[HEN 04] HENROTIN J. (ed.), *Au risque du chaos. Leçons politiques et stratégiques de la guerre d'Irak*, Armand Colin, Paris, 2004.

[HEN 05] HENROTIN J., *L'Airpower au XXIème siècle. Enjeux et perspectives de la stratégie aérienne*, Bruylant, Brussels, 2005.

[HEN 07a] HENROTIN J., "No plan survives the start line. L'interaction des plans et de la doctrine durant Iraqi Freedom", in RMES (eds), *Iraqi Freedom, Analyse politique, stratégique et économique de la troisième guerre du Golfe*, L'Harmattan, Paris, 2007.

[HEN 07b] HENROTIN J., "Une opération paradoxale. *Iraqi Freedom* entre classicisme stratégique et chronostratégie", in RMES (eds), *Iraqi Freedom, Analyse politique, stratégique et économique de la troisième guerre du Golfe*, L'Harmattan, Paris, 2007.

[HEN 12a] HENNINGER L., "Espaces fluides et espaces solides: nouvelle réalité stratégique?", *Revue Défense Nationale*, no. 753, pp. 1–3, October 2012.

[HEN 12b] HENROTIN J., "Mars et Vulcain. Technologie et art de la guerre", *Histoire & Stratégie*, no. 12, October–December 2012.

[HEN 13a] HENNINGER L., "Le fluide et le solide", *Défense & Sécurité Internationale*, no. 89, pp. 43–47, February 2013.

[HEN 13b] HENROTIN J., *La technologie militaire en question. Le cas américain et ses conséquences en Europe*, 2nd ed., Economica, Paris, 2013.

[HEN 13c] HENROTIN J., "Conséquences tactiques du hacking radar", *Défense & Sécurité Internationale*, no. 89, pp. 98–103, February 2013.

[HEN 14a] HENROTIN J., "AirSea Battle: à la recherche de la contre-guerre littorale", *Défense & Sécurité Internationale*, Special issue no. 38, pp. 68–77, October–November, 2014.

[HEN 14b] HENROTIN J., *Techno-guérilla et guerre hybride. Le pire des deux mondes*, Nuvis, Paris, 2014.

[HEN 14c] HENROTIN J., LANGLOIT P., "F-35 Lightning II: les déboires d'un rêve aéronautique", *Défense & Sécurité Internationale*, no. 108, pp. 92–103, November 2014.

[HEN 15a] HENROTIN J., "L'Etat islamique, catalyseur d'une nouvelle guerre de trente ans?", *Défense & Sécurité Internationale*, Special issue no. 40, pp. 8–13, February–March 2015.

[HEN 15b] HENROTIN J., "De l'identité fluide des opérations aériennes", *Défense & Sécurité Internationale*, no. 113, pp. 56–61, April 2015.

[HEN 15c] HENROTIN J., "L'hybridité à l'épreuve des conflits contemporains. Le cas russe", *Défense & Sécurité Internationale*, no. 116, pp. 62–67, July–August 2015.

[HEW 82] HEWISH M., "Le programme Assault Breaker – une technologie d'avant-garde pour les armes à longue portée", *Revue Internationale de Défense*, no. 9, pp. 56–67, 1982.

[HIA 99] HIANG LEE S., *Center of Gravity or Center of Confusion. Understanding the Mystique*, The Wright Flyer Paper, no. 10, Maxwell AFB, December 1999.

[HOF 65] HOFSTADTER R., *The Paranoid Style in American Politics and Other Essays*, Random House, New York, 1965.

[HOL 86] HOLMES R., *Acts of War – The Behavior of Men in Battles*, The Free Press, New York, 1986.

[HUB 02] HUBER T.M. (ed.), Compound Warfare: That Fatal Knot, Combat Studies Institute, Command and General Staff College, Fort Leavenworth, September 2002.

[HUB 09] HUBIN G., *Perspectives Tactiques*, 3rd ed., Economica, Paris, 2009.

[HUG 15] HUGHES M.P., "Lockheed Martin and the controversial F-35", *Journal of Business Case Studies*, vol. 11, no. 1, pp. 1–14, 2015.

[HUN 99] HUNDLEY R.O., *Past Revolutions, Future Transformations: What Can the History of Revolutions in Military Affairs Tell Us About Transforming the US Military*, Santa Monica, RAND, 1999.

[IRO 04] IRONDELLE B., JOANA J., "Etat de l'art sur la sociologie des politiques d'armement. Les approches ango-saxonnes", in GENIEYS W. (ed.), *Le choix des armes. Théories, acteurs et politiques*, CNRS Editions, Paris, 2004.

[JAB 94a] JABLONSKY D., *The Owl of Minerva Flies at Twilight: Doctrinal Change and Continuity and the Revolution in Military Affairs*, Strategic Studies Institute, Carlisle Barracks, May 1994.

[JAB 94b] JABLONSKY D., "US military doctrine and the Revolution in Military Affairs", *Parameters*, pp. 18–36, Autumn 1994.

[JAN 71] JANOWITZ M., *The Professional Soldier: A Social and Political Portrait*, The Free Press, New York, 1971.

[JEA 13a] JEANGÈNE-VILMER J.B., "Idéologie du drone", available at: http://www.laviedesidees.fr/IMG/pdf/20131204_jbjv_-_ideologie_du_drone-2.pdf, 4 December 2013.

[JEA 13b] JEANGENE-VILMER J. B., "Légalité et légitimité des drones armés", Politique étrangère, no. 3, pp. 119–132, Autonomous 2013.

[JOH 96] JOHNSON S.E., LIBICKI M.C., *Dominant Battlespace Knowledge*, National Defense University Press, Washington, DC, 1996.

[JOH 11] JOHNSON D.E., *Hard Fighting. Israel in Lebanon and Gaza*, RAND Corp., Santa Monica, 2011.

[JOS 99] JOSHI A., "A holistic view of the revolution in military affairs", *Strategic Analysis*, vol. XXII, no. 11, pp. 1743–1759, February 1999.

[KAL 81] KALDOR M., *Baroque Arsenal*, Hill and Wang, New York, 1981.

[KAL 05] KALDOR M., "Iraq: the wrong war", *openDemocracy*, available at: https://www.opendemocracy.net/conflict-iraq/wrong_war_2591.jsp, 9 June 2005.

[KAN 71] KANE F.X., "Space age geopolitics", *Orbis*, vol. 14, no. 4, pp. 911–933, Winter 1971.

[KAP 83] KAPLAN F., *Wizards of Armageddon*, Touchstone Books, New York, 1983.

[KAP 05] KAPLAN R.D., "Imperial grunts – with the army special forces in the Philippines and Afghanistan – laboratories of counterinsurgency", *The Atlantic Monthly*, pp. 84–93, October 2005.

[KEA 93] KEANEY T.A., COHEN E.A., *Gulf War Air Power Survey Summary Report*, US Government Printing Office, Washington, DC, 1993.

[KEE 94] KEEGAN J., *A History of Warfare*, Alfred A. Knopf, New York, 1994.

[KEE 03] KEEGAN J., *Intelligence in War. Knowledge of the Ennemy from Napoleon to Al Qaeda*, Alfred Knopf, New York, 2003.

[KIA 03] KIAN HUAT R., "Balancing change and continuity – some toughts on the transformation of the SAF", *Pointer*, vol. 29, no. 2, pp. 28–35, April–June 2003.

[KIP 01] KIPP J.W., GRAU L.W., "The fog and friction of technology", *Military Review*, pp. 1–14, September–October 2001.

[KIS 79] KISSINGER H., *A la Maison-Blanche. 1968–1973, Tome 1*, Fayard, Paris, 1979.

[KNO 01] KNOX M.K., MURRAY W. (eds), *The Dynamics of Military Revolutions – 1300–2050*, Cambridge University Press, Cambridge, 2001.

[KOK 98] KOKOSHIN A.A., *Soviet Strategic Thought, 1917–1991*, MIT Press, Cambridge, 1998.

[KRE 94] KREPINEVITCH A.F., "From cavalry to computers. The pattern of military revolutions", *The National Interest*, vol. 37, pp. 30–42, Fall 1994.

[KRE 15] KREPINEVICH A.F., WATTS B.D., *The Last Warrior. Andrew Marshall and the Shaping of Modern American Defense Strategy*, Basic Books, New York, 2015.

[KRI 13] KRISHNAN A., *War as Business. Technological Change and Military Service Contracting*, Ashagate, Farnham, 2013.

[KRU 99] KRULAK C.C., "The strategic corporal: leadership in the three block war", *Marines Magazine*, Marine Corps Gazette, vol. 83, no. 1, p. 18–23, January 1999.

[KUH 72] KUHN T.S., *La structure des Révolutions Scientifiques*, Flammarion, Paris, 1972.

[KUR 14] KURZ A., BROM S. (eds), *The Lessons of Operation Protective Edge*, INSS, Ramat Aviv, 2014.

[LAF 04] LAFONTAINE C., *L'empire cybernétique. De la machine à penser à la pensée-machine*, Seuil, Paris, 2004.

[LAÏ 00] LAÏDI Z., *Le sacre du présent*, Flammarion, Paris, 2000.

[LAM 97] LAMBETH B.S., "The technology revolution in air warfare", *Survival*, no. 39, pp. 65–83, Spring 1997.

[LAM 03] LAMBAKIS S.J., "Reconsidering asymmetric warfare", *Joint Forces Quarterly*, no. 36, pp. 102–108, Autmun 2003.

[LAM 12] LAMBETH B.S., "Israel's war in Gaza: a paradigm of effective military learning and adaptation", *International Security*, vol. 37, no. 2, pp. 81–118, Fall 2012.

[LAN 99] LANHAM A., "Re-imagining warfare: the revolution in military affairs", in SNYDER C.A. (ed.), *Contemporary Security and Strategy*, Macmillan, London, 1999.

[LAN 15] LANGLOIT P., "Robotique terrestre: le grand désenchantement?", *Défense & Sécurité Internationale*, no. 111, pp. 88–91, February 2015.

[LAS 90] LASH S., *Sociology of Postmodernism*, London, Routledge, 1990.

[LAT 02] LATHAM A., "Warfare transformed: a Braudelian perspective on the "revolution in military affairs"", *European Journal of International Relations*, vol. 8, no. 2, pp. 231–266, 2002.

[LAW 14] LAWSON S. T., *Nonlinear Science and Warfare. Chaos, Complexity and the US Military in the Information Age*, Routledge, London, 2014.

[LEP 87] LEPINGWELL J., "The laws of Combat?", *International Security*, vol. 12, no. 1, pp. 89–134, Summer 1987.

[LIB 94] LIBICKI M., HAZLETT J., "The revolution in military affairs", *Strategic Forum*, no. 11, pp. 1–4, 1994.

[LIB 97] LIBICKI M., The Intersystems, or the RMA Reified, National Defense University, Washington DC, 1997.

[LIB 00] LIBICKI M.C., "What is information warfare", in GONGORA T., VON RIEKHOFF H. (eds), *Toward a Revolution in Military Affairs? Defense and Security at the Dawn of the Twenty-First Century*, Greenwood Press, Westport/London, 2000.

[LIF 57] LIFE, "Pushbutton defense for air war", *Life*, vol. 6, no. 42, pp. 62–67, 1957.

[LIN 89] LIND W.S., SCHMITT J.F., WILSON G.I., "Faces of war into the fourth generation", *Military Review*, vol. LXIX, no. 10, pp. 2–11, October 1989.

[LIN 94] LIND W.S., SCHMITT J.F., WILSON G.I., "Fourth generation warfare: another look", *Marine Corps Gazette*, pp. 34–37, December 1994.

[LIN 04] LIND W.S., "Understanding the fourth generation war", *Military Review*, pp. 12–16, September–October 2004.

[LIT 00] LITTON L.L., "The information-based RMA and the principles of war", *Air & Space Power Chronicles*, pp. 1–12, September 2000.

[LON 99] LONSDALE D.J., "Information power: strategy, geopolitics and the fifth dimension", in GRAY C.S., SLOAN G. (eds), *Geopolitics. Geography and Strategy*, Frank Cass, London, 1999.

[LON 04] LONSDALE D.J., *The Nature of War in the Information Age. Clausewitzian Future*, Frank Cass, London/New York, 2004.

[LOO 08] LOO B. (ed.), *Military Transformation and Strategy: Revolutions in Military Affairs and Small States*, Routledge, London, 2008.

[LUI 15] LUIZARD J-P., *Le piège Daech. L'Etat islamique ou le retour de l'histoire*, La Découverte, Paris, 2015.

[LUT 84] LUTTWAK E.N., *The Pentagon and the Art of War*, Simon & Schuster, New York, 1984.

[LUT 89] LUTTWAK E.N., *Le Paradoxe de la Stratégie*, Odile Jacob, Paris, 1989.

[LUT 95] LUTTWAK E.N., "Toward post-heroic warfare", *Foreign Affairs,* vol. 74, no. 3, pp. 109–122, May/June 1995.

[LUV 95] LUVAAS J., "Military history: is it still practicable?", *Parameters*, vol. 25, no. 2, pp. 82–97, Summer 1995.

[LYO 79] LYOTARD J-F., *La condition postmoderne. Rapport sur le savoir*, Éditions de Minuit, Paris, 1979.

[MAC 92] MACGREGOR D.A., "Future battle: the merging levels of war", *Parameters*, vol. 29, no. 2, pp. 165–184, Winter 1992.

[MAC 97] MACGREGOR D., *Breaking the Phalanx. A New Design for Landpower in the 21st Century*, Praeger, Westport, 1997.

[MAC 99] MACFARLANE S.N., "International security and the RMA", in HAGLUND D., MACFARLANE S.N. (eds), *Security, Strategy and the Global Economics of Defense Production*, McGill-Queen University, Kingston, 1999.

[MAH 97] MAHNKEN T.G., WATTS B.D., "What the Gulf War can (and cannot) tell us about the future of warfare", *International Security*, vol. 22, no. 2, pp. 151–162, Fall 1997.

[MAH 08] MAHNKEN T.G., *Technology and the American Way of War since 1945*, Columbia University Press, New York, 2008.

[MAH 11] MAHNKEN T.G., "Weapons: the growth and spread of the precision strike regime", *Daedalus*, vol. 140, no. 3, pp. 45–57, Summer 2011.

[MAN 93] MANN E., "One target, one bomb. Is the principle of mass dead?", *Airpower Journal*, pp. 35–43, Spring 1993.

[MAR 99] MARTINOT-LEROY R., "La question du machinisme dans l'armée française à partir des écrits du Lieutenant-Colonel Gallois (1947–1959)", *Les Champs de Mars*, no. 6, pp. 131–148, 2nd half 1999.

[MAR 01] MARSH H., "The revolution in military affairs (RMA) revisited", *The Defence Associations National Networks News*, vol. 8, no. 2, pp. 1–7, Summer 2001.

[MAS 99] MASTNY V., "Did NATO win the Cold War? Looking over the wall", *Foreign Affairs*, vol. 78, no. 3, pp. 176–189, May–June 1999.

[MAZ 93] MAZARR M., JEFFREY S., BENJAMIN E. *et al.*, *The Military Technical Revolution. A Structural Framework*, CSIS, Washington, DC, March 1993.

[MAZ 94] MAZARR M., *The Revolution in Military Affairs. A Framework for Defense Planning*, Strategic Studies Institute, US Army War College, Carlisle Barracks, April 1994.

[MCF 15] MCFATE S., *The Modern Mercenary: Private Armies and What they mean for World Order*, Oxford University Press, 2015.

[MCR 84] MCRAE R., *Mind Wars. The True Story of Secret Government Research into the Military Potential of Psychic Weapons*, St Martin's Press, New York, 1984.

[MEI 03] MEILINGER P.S., *Airpower Myths and Facts*, Air University Press, Maxwell AFB, 2003.

[MET 99] METS D.R., *The Air Campaign. John Warden and the Classical Air Theorists*, Air University Press, Maxwell AFB, 1999.

[MET 94a] METZ S., "A wake for Clausewitz: toward a Philosophy of 21st-Century warfare", *Parameters*, vol. 24, pp. 126–132, Winter 1994–95.

[MET 94b] METZ S., KIEVIT J., The Revolution in Military Affairs and Conflict Short of War, Strategic Studies Institute, USAWC, July 1994.

[MET 95] METZ S., KIEVIT J., Strategy and the Revolution in Military Affairs. From Theory to Policy, USAWC, Carlisle Barracks, June 1995.

[MET 00] METZ S., Armed Conflicts in the 21st Century: The Information Revolution and Post-Modern Warfare, Strategic Studies Institute, Carlisle Barracks, 2000.

[MET 01] METZ S., JOHNSON D.V., Asymmetry and US Military Strategy: Definition, Background, and Strategic Concepts, Strategic Studies Institute, US Army War College, Carlisle Barracks, January 2001.

[MIE 16a] MIELCAREK R., "Conscription et milices. Le retour des peuples en armes en Europe", *Défense & Sécurité Internationale*, no. 122, pp. 36–41, March–April 2016.

[MIE 16b] MIELCAREK R., "Médias généralistes: quelle place pour les spécialistes de la défense?", *Défense & Sécurité Internationale*, no. 122, pp. 76–81, March–April 2016.

[MIK 48] MIKSCHE F-O., "Europe occidentale atout maître de la guerre", *Forces Aériennes Françaises*, pp. 156–168, December 1948.

[MIK 49] MIKSCHE F-O., "Défense aéroterrestre moderne", *Forces Aériennes Françaises*, no. 26, pp. 112–135, December 1949.

[MOL 02] MOLLER B., The revolution in military affairs: myth or reality?, COPRI working paper, no. 15, 2002.

[MOM 03] MOMYER W.W., *Airpower in Three Wars*, Air University Press, Maxwell, 2003.

[MOO 14] MOORCRAFT P., *Total Destruction of the Tamil Tigers. The Rare Victory of Sri Lanka's Long War*, Pen & Sword, London, 2014.

[MOS 94] MOSKOS C.C., BURK J., "The postmodern military", in BURK J. (ed.), *The Military in New Times: Adapting Armed Forces to a Turbulent New World*, Westview Press, Boulder, 1994.

[MOS 02] MOSKOS C., "Our will to fight depends on who is willing to die", *Wall Street Journal*, p. 22, 20 March 2002.

[MUN 16] MUNGER S., "Du soldat antique au supersoldat de l'âge géopolitique post-héroïque, le modèle occidental de la guerre entre Achille et Iron Man", in GARON R. (ed.), *Penser la guerre au futur*, Presses de l'Université Laval, Québec, 2016.

[MUR 95] MURRAY W., WATTS B.D., Military innovation in peacetime, Report prepared for OSD Net Assessment, available at: http://indianstrategicknowledge online.com/web/MIilInnovPeace.pdf, accessed on 15 February 2016, 20 January 1995.

[MUR 98a] MURAWIEC L., *Innovation, Element of Power*, Geopol/CSBA, Washington DC, 1998.

[MUR 98b] MURRAY W., "Preparing to loose the next war", *Strategic Review*, vol. 26, no. 2, pp. 51–62, Spring 1998.

[MUR 99] MURRAY W., "Does military culture matter?", *Orbis*, vol. 7, no. 2, pp. 27–42, January 1999.

[MUR 00] MURAWIEC L., *La guerre au XXIème siècle*, Editions Odile Jacob, Paris, 2000.

[MUR 01a] MURRAY W., "Thinking about innovation", *Naval War College Review*, vol. LIV, no. 2, p. 120, Spring 2001.

[MUR 01b] MURRAY W., MCGREGOR K., "Thinking about revolutions in warfare", in MCGREGOR K., MURRAY W. (eds), *The Dynamics of Military Revolutions – 1300–2050*, Cambridge University Press, 2001.

[MUR 02] MURDOCK P., "Principles of war on the network-centric battlefield: mass and economy of force", *Parameters*, vol. 32, no. 1, pp. 86–95, 2002.

[MUR 11] MURRAY W., *Military Adaptation in War. With Fear of Change*, Cambridge University Press, 2011.

[MUR 12] MURRAY W., MANSOOR P.R. (eds), *Hybrid Warfare. Fighting Complex Opponents from the Ancient World to the Present*, Cambridge University Press, 2012.

[NAI 91] NAIR, *War in the Gulf. Lessons for the Third World*, Lancer International, Atlanta, 1991.

[NEW 10] NEWMAYER J., "The revolution in military affairs with Chinese characteristics", *The Journal of Strategic Studies*, vol. 33, no. 4, pp. 483–504, August 2010.

[OCO 94] O'CONNELL E.P., DILLAPLAIN J.T., "Nonlethal concepts implications for air force intelligence", *Aerospace Power Journal*, vol. 7, no. 4, pp. 26–33, Winter 1994.

[ODO 93] ODOM W.E., *America's Military Revolution: Strategy and Structure after the Cold War*, American University Press, Washington DC, 1993.

[OHA 98] O'HANLON M., Beware of RMA'nia!, paper presented at the National Defense University, 9 September 1998.

[OHA 00] O'HANLON M., *Technological Change and the Future of Warfare*, Brookings Institution Press, Washington DC, 2000.

[OLL 16] OLLIVANT D.A., "The rise of the hybrid warriors: from Ukraine to the Middle East", *War on the Rocks*, available at: http://warontherocks.com/ 2016/03/the-rise-of-the-hybrid-warriors-from-ukraine-to-the-middle-east/, accessed 13 March 2016.

[OSI 06] OSINGA F., *Science, Strategy and War: The Strategic Theory of John Boyd*, Routledge, Londres, 2006.

[OWE 95] OWENS W.A., "The emerging system of systems", *US Naval Institute Proceedings*, pp. 36–39, May 1995.

[OWE 00] OWENS W.A., *Lifting the Fog of War*, Farrar Straus Giroux, New York, 2000.

[PAL 05] PALMER M., *Command at Sea: Naval Command and Control Since the Sixteenth Century*, Harvard University Press, Cambridge, 2005.

[PAR 76] PARKER G., "The "military revolution", 1550–1660 – A myth?", *Journal of Modern History*, no. 48, pp. 195–214, 1976.

[PAR 88] PARKER G., *The Military Revolution. Military Innovation and the Rise of the West of the West. 1500–1800*, Cambridge University Press, Cambridge, 1988.

[PAR 95] PARIS H., *Stratégie soviétique et chute du Pacte de Varsovie. La clé de l'avenir*, Publications de la Sorbonne, Paris, 1995.

[PAT 94] PATRICK J.J., Reflections on the revolution in military affairs, Project on Defense Alternatives, available at: http://www.comw.org/rma/fulltext/reflect. html, 17 October 1994.

[PER 95] PERRY C.M., PFALTZGRAFF R.F., CONWAY J.C., Long-Range Bombers and the Role of Airpower in the New Century, Institute for Foreign Policy Analysis, Cambridge, 1995.

[PET 95] PETERS R., "After the revolution", *Parameters*, vol. 25, pp. 7–14, Summer 1995.

[PHI 09] PHILIPS C., "The hidden massacre: Sri Lanka's final offensive against Tamil Tigers", *The Times*, 29 May 2009.

[PIE 00] PIEROT J-P., "Paul Virilio: une guerre peut en cacher une autre", *L'Humanité*, 18 January 2000.

[PI 01] PI SHEN S., "The revolution in military affairs (RMA): challenge to existing military paradigms and its impacts on the Singapore armed forces (SAF)", *Pointer*, vol. 27, no. 2, pp. 15–19, April–June 2001.

[PLE 00] PLEHN M.T., *Control Warfare: Inside the OODA Loop*, SAAS, Maxwell AFB, 2000.

[POI 88] POIRIER L., *Des stratégies nucléaires*, Complexe, Brussels, 1988.

[POS 97] POSSONY S.T., POURNELLE J.E., KANE F.X., *The Strategy of Technology*, Electronic Edition, available at: http://www.webwrights.com, 1997.

[PRA 97] PRAZUCK C., "L'attente et le rythme. Modeste essai de chronostratégie", *Stratégique*, no. 68, no. 4 pp. 112–128, 1997/4.

[PRE 01] PRESS D.G., "The myth of air power and the future of warfare", *International Security*, vol. 26, no. 2, pp. 5–44, Fall 2001.

[PRI 01] PRICE A., *War in the Fourth Dimension. US Electronic Warfare, from the Vietnam War to the Present*, Greenhill Books, London, 2001.

[RAT 01] RATTRAY G., *Strategic Warfare in Cyberspace*, The MIT Press, Cambridge/London, 2001.

[REI 14] REICH S., LEBOW R.N., *Goodbye Hegemony. Power and Influence in the Global System*, Princeton University Press, 2014.

[RID 13] RID T., *Cyberwar Will Not Take Place*, Oxford University Press, 2013.

[ROB 56] ROBERTS M., The Military Revolution, 1560–1660, Belfast, 1956.

[ROB 67] ROBERTS M., "The military revolution, 1560–1660", in ROBERTS M. (ed.), *Essays in Swedish History*, Weidenfeld and Nicholson, London, 1967.

[ROG 93] ROGERS C.J., "The military revolutions of the hundred years war", *The Journal of Military History*, vol. 57, no. 2, pp. 258–275, 1993.

[ROG 00] ROGERS C.J., ""Military revolutions" and "Revolutions in military affairs": an historian perspective", in GONGORA T., VON RIEKHOFF H. (eds), *Toward a Revolution in Military Affairs? Defense and Security at the Dawn of the Twenty-First Century*, Greenwood Press, Westport/London, 2000.

[RON 76] RONA T., Weapons System and Information at War, Boeing Aerospace Co., July 1976.

[RON 96] RONA T., "From scorched earth to information warfare", in CAMPEN D.H., DEARTH D.H., GOODEN R.T. (eds), *Cyberwar: Security, Strategy and Conflict in the Information Age*, AFCEA International Press, Halifax, 1996.

[ROS 91] ROSEN S.P., *Winning the Next war. Innovation and the Modern Military*, Cornell University Press, Ithaca, 1991.

[ROS 10] ROSEN S.P., "The impact of the office of net assessment on the American military in the matter of the revolution in military affairs", *The Journal of Strategic Studies*, vol. 33, no. 4, pp. 469–482, August 2010.

[SAR 06] SARTINI V., "La guerre numérisée – La 6ème BLB en exercice", *Défense & Sécurité Internationale*, no. 16, pp. 64–69, June 2006.

[SAR 08] SARTINI V., "La guerre des mines "Made in USA" bientôt chez nous?", *Défense & Sécurité Internationale-Technologies*, no. 14, pp. 58–63, November–December 2008.

[SCH 97] SCHMITT G., "Memo to opinion leaders. Defense reorganization and the office of net assessment", available at: http://www.newamericancentury.org/defnov1097.htm, 10 November 1997.

[SCH 98] SCHNEIDER B.R., "Principles of war for the battlefields of the future", in GRINTER L., SCHNEIDER B.R. (eds), *Battlefield of the Future. 21st Century Warfare Issues*, Air University Press, Maxwell AFB, 1998.

[SIM 78] SIMON, H-A., "Rationality as a process and as a product of thought", *American Economic Review*, vol. 68, no. 2, pp. 1–16, 1978.

[SIM 12] SIMPSON E., *War From The Ground-Up: Twenty-First Century Combat As Politics*, Hurst, London, 2012.

[SIN 96] SINGH A., "Time. The new dimension in war", *Joint Forces Quarterly*, no. 10, pp. 56–61, Winter 1995–1996.

[SIN 03] SINGER P.W., *Corporate Warriors: The Rise of the Privatized Military Industry*, Cornell University Press, Ithaca, 2003.

[SIN 09] SINGER P.W., *Wired for War. The Robotics Revolution and Conflict in the 21st Century*, The Penguin Press, New York, 2009.

[SIN 15] SINGER P.W., COLE A., *Ghost Fleet*, Houghton Mifflin Harcourt Publishing, New York, 2015.

[SLA 13] SLAYTON, R, *Arguments that Counts. Physics, Computing and Missile Defense 1949–2012*, MIT Press, Cambridge, 2013.

[SLO 02] SLOAN E.C., *The Revolution in Military Affairs*, McGill-Queen's University Press, Montreal/Kingston, 2002.

[SMI 85] SMITH M.R., WHITELAM J. (eds), *Military Enterprise and Technological Change: Perspectives on the American Experience*, MIT Press, Cambridge, 1985.

[SMI 07] SMITH R., *L'utilité de la force. L'art de la guerre aujourd'hui*, Economica, Paris, 2007.

[SMI 15] SMITH M.L.R., MARTIN JONES D., *The Political Impossibility of Modern. Counterinsurgency*, Columbia University Press, New York, 2015.

[SPA 02] Sparks M., Nothing Learned from Black Hawk Down, available at: http://www.g2mil.com/BlackhawkDown.htm, 2002.

[STE 99] Sterner E.R., "You say you want a revolution (in military affairs)?", *Comparative Strategy*, no. 18, pp. 293–308, 1999.

[STE 09] Steed B., *Piercing the Fog of War. Recognizing Change on the Battlefield*, Zenith, Minneapolis, 2009.

[STI 15a] Stiennon R., *There Will be Cybewar. How the Move to Network-Centric War Fighting Has Set the Stage for Cyberwar*, IT-Harvest, Birmingham, 2015.

[STI 15b] Stillion J., Trends in Air-to-Air Combat. Implications for Future Air Superiority, CSBA, Washington, DC, 2015.

[STR 03] Struye de Swielande T., *La politique étrangère américaine et les défis asymétriques*, PUL, Louvain-la-Neuve, 2003.

[STR 13] Strachan H., *The Direction of War. Contemporary Strategy in Historical Perspective*, Cambridge University Press, Cambridge, 2013.

[SUL 93] Sullivan G.R., Dubik J., "Land warfare in the 21st Century", *Military Review*, pp. 13–32, September 1993.

[SUM 82] Summers H.G., *On Strategy. A Critical Analysis of the Vietnam War*, Presidio Press, New York, 1982.

[SUS 05] Sussan R., *Les utopies posthumaines. Contre-culture, cyberculture, culture du chaos*, Omniscience, Paris, 2005.

[TAP 93] Tapscott D., Caston A., *Paradigm Shift: The New Promise of Information Technology*, McGraw-Hill, New York, 1993.

[TEL 00] Tellis A.J., Bially J., Layne C. *et al.*, *Measuring National Power in the Postindustrial Age*, RAND Corp., Santa Monica, 2000.

[TEN 15] Tenenbaum E., *Le piège de la guerre hybride*, Focus stratégique no. 63, IFRI, October 2015.

[TER 98] Tertrais B., "Faut-il croire à la "révolution dans les affaires militaires?"", *Politique Etrangère*, no. 3, pp. 611–629, Autumn 1998.

[THE 89] Theweleit K., *Male Fantasies. Vol. 2: Psychoanalysing the White Terror*, University of Minnesota Press, Minneapolis, 1989.

[THI 99] Thieblemont A. (ed.), *Cultures et logiques militaires*, PUF, Paris, 1999.

[TOF 94] Toffler A., Toffler H., *Guerre et contre-guerre*, Fayard, Paris, 1994.

[TOM 07] Tomes R.R., *US Defense Strategy from Vietnam to Operation Iraqi Freedom. Military Innovation and the New American Way of War, 1973–2003*, Routledge, London, 2007.

[TUA 98] Tuathail G.Ó., Dalby S., *Rethinking Geopolitics*, Routledge, London, 1998.

[TUR 90] Turner B.S. (ed.), *Theories of Modernity and Postmodernity*, Sage, Newbury Park, 1990.

[VAN 85] Van Creveld M., *Command in War*, Harvard University Press, Cambridge, 1985.

[VAN 98] Van Creveld M., *Les transformations de la guerre*, Editions du Rocher, Paris, 1998.

[VAU 83] Vaughn T.B., "Morale: the 10th principle of war", *Military Review*, pp. 23–39, May 1983.

[VIC 95] Vick I., *Snakes in the Eagle's Nest: A History of Ground Attacks on Air Bases*, RAND Corp., Santa Monica, 1995.

[VIR 77] Virilio P., *Vitesse et politique: essai de dromologie*, Editions Galilée, Paris, 1977.

[VIV 11] Vivenot E., "Combat asymétrique: quelle place pour les MRAP?", *Défense & Sécurité Internationale*, no. 74, pp. 92–97, October 2011.

[VIV 14] Vivenot E., "MRAP: l'avenir d'un concept", *Défense & Sécurité Internationale*, hors-série no. 36, pp. 80–85, June–July 2014.

[WAR 95] Warden J.F., "L'ennemi en tant que système", *Stratégique*, no. 59, pp. 116–146, 1995/3.

[WAR 98] Warden J.F., *La campagne aérienne. Planification en vue du combat*, Economica/ISC, Paris, 1998.

[WAS 04] Wasinski C., *Clausewitz et le discours stratégique américain*, ISC, Paris, 2004.

[WAS 10] Wasinski C., *Rendre la guerre possible. La construction du sens commun stratégique*, PIE Peter Lang, Brussels, 2010.

[WAT 84] Watts B.D., *The Foundations of US Air Doctrine: The Problem of Friction in War*, Air University Press, Maxwell AFB, 1984.

[WAT 95] Watts B.D., *What is the Revolution in Military Affairs?*, Northrop Grumman, Analysis Center, 1995.

[WAT 96] Watts B.D., *Clausewitzian Friction and Future War*, Institute of National Strategic Studies, National Defense University, Washington DC, 1996.

[WAV 46] WAVELL A., *Speaking Generally*, MacMillan, London, 1946.

[WIC 13] WICHT B., *Europe Mad Max demain? Retour à la défense citoyenne*, Favre, Lausanne, 2013.

[WIC 15] WICHT B., "Vers le citoyen-soldat 2.0?", *Défense & Sécurité Internationale*, no. 120, pp. 60–65, December 2015.

[WIE 00] WIENER N., *God & Golem Inc.: Sur quelques points de collision entre cybernétique et religion*, L'Eclat, Nîmes, 2000.

[WIL 03] WILLIS S., "The immutable nature of war", interview by Paul Von Riper, *Nova*, available at: http://www.pbs.org/wgbh/nova/military/immutable-nature-war.html, 17 December 2003.

[WIN 99] WINK J., "Secret Weapon", *The Washingtonian*, April 1999.

[WIT 15] WITTES B., BLUM G., *The Future of Violence. Robots and Germs, Hackers and Drones. Confronting a New Age of Threat*, Basic Books, New York, 2015.

[WOH 95] WOHLFORTH W.C., "Realism and the end of the cold war", *International Security*, no. 19, pp. 91–129, Winter 1995.

[WRI 05] WRISTON W.B., "Bits, bytes and diplomacy", *Foreign Affairs*, vol. 76, no. 5, pp. 172–182, September/October 2005.

[WYL 14] WYLIE J.C., *Military Strategy. A General Theory of Power Control*, Naval Institute Press, Annapolis, 2014.

[YAK 06] YAKOVLEFF M., *Tactique théorique*, Economica, Paris, 2006.

[YAK 09] YAKOVLEFF M., "Le concept de manœuvre", in MALIS C. (ed.), *Guerre et manœuvre*, Economica, Paris, 2009.

[ZAJ 15] ZAJEC O., "Recension. L'hybridation, une tendance stratégique universelle?", *Stratégique*, no. 108, pp. 241–257, 2015/1.

[ZUB 12] ZUBELDIA O., *Histoire des drones*, Perrin, Paris, 2012.

Index

Other titles from

in

Information Systems, Web and Pervasive Computing

MONINO Jean-Louis, SEDKAOUI Soraya
Big Data, Open Data and Data Development

SALGUES Bruno
Health Industrialization

VENTRE Daniel
Information Warfare – 2ⁿᵈ edition

2015

ARDUIN Pierre-Emmanuel, GRUNDSTEIN Michel,
ROSENTHAL-SABROUX Camille
Information and Knowledge System
(Advances in Information Systems Set – Volume 2)

BÉRANGER Jérôme
Medical Information Systems Ethics

BRONNER Gérald
Belief and Misbelief Asymmetry on the Internet

IAFRATE Fernando
From Big Data to Smart Data
(Advances in Information Systems Set – Volume 1)

KRICHEN Saoussen, BEN JOUIDA Sihem
Supply Chain Management and its Applications in Computer Science

NEGRE Elsa
Information and Recommender Systems
(Advances in Information Systems Set – Volume 4)

POMEROL Jean-Charles, EPELBOIN Yves, THOURY Claire
MOOCs

SALLES Maryse
Decision-Making and the Information System (Advances in Information Systems Set – Volume 3)

SAMARA Tarek
ERP and Information Systems: Integration or Disintegration (Advances in Information Systems Set – Volume 5)

2014

DINET Jérôme
Information Retrieval in Digital Environments

HÉNO Raphaële, CHANDELIER Laure
3D Modeling of Buildings: Outstanding Sites

KEMBELLEC Gérald, CHARTRON Ghislaine, SALEH Imad
Recommender Systems

MATHIAN Hélène, SANDERS Lena
Spatio-temporal Approaches: Geographic Objects and Change Process

PLANTIN Jean-Christophe
Participatory Mapping

VENTRE Daniel
Chinese Cybersecurity and Defense

2013

BERNIK Igor
Cybercrime and Cyberwarfare

CAPET Philippe, DELAVALLADE Thomas
Information Evaluation

LEBRATY Jean-Fabrice, LOBRE-LEBRATY Katia
Crowdsourcing: One Step Beyond

SALLABERRY Christian
Geographical Information Retrieval in Textual Corpora

2012

BUCHER Bénédicte, LE BER Florence
Innovative Software Development in GIS

GAUSSIER Eric, YVON François
Textual Information Access

STOCKINGER Peter
Audiovisual Archives: Digital Text and Discourse Analysis

VENTRE Daniel
Cyber Conflict

2011

BANOS Arnaud, THÉVENIN Thomas
Geographical Information and Urban Transport Systems

DAUPHINÉ André
Fractal Geography

LEMBERGER Pirmin, MOREL Mederic
Managing Complexity of Information Systems

STOCKINGER Peter
Introduction to Audiovisual Archives

STOCKINGER Peter
Digital Audiovisual Archives

VENTRE Daniel
Cyberwar and Information Warfare

2010

BONNET Pierre
Enterprise Data Governance

BRUNET Roger
Sustainable Geography